PROGRAMMING A MICROCOMPUTER: 6502

CAXTON C. FOSTER
University of Massachusetts, Amherst

ADDISON-WESLEY PUBLISHING COMPANY
Reading, Massachusetts • Menlo Park, California
London • Amsterdam • Don Mills, Ontario • Sydney

This book is in
ADDISON-WESLEY'S JOY OF COMPUTING SERIES

Second printing, July 1978

This book was reproduced by Addison-Wesley from camera-ready copy approved by the author.

Library of Congress Catalog Card No. 77-90174.

ISBN 0-201-01995-7
BCDEFGHIJK-AL-79

To
Bobbie and Dick

CONTENTS

1
BASIC IDEAS

INTRODUCTION

In this book we are going to study a small computer and learn how it functions. In addition to this book, you will need a "system" manual or "hardware" manual for the machine you have chosen to work with.

Most of what we have to say will apply equally well to any of the microcomputers available today. Occasionally, in order to be specific, we will have to pick a particular machine and talk about its structure. The machine we have selected is the KIM-1 produced by M.O.S. Technology. It is an 8-bit machine quite similar to the other popular machines. It is more typical of most mini- and microcomputers than, say, the 8080, and is somewhat advanced over the 6800. Most important, it comes all assembled in a standard package, so that we can be very specific about what hardware you are assumed to have. This has the great advantage of lending concreteness to what otherwise might be a vague concept.

If you have a computer different from the KIM-1 you will have to look up certain specifications in your hardware manuals. However, most of what we have to say will have obvious parallels, and translation should be fairly straightforward.

THE FUNDAMENTAL ANALOGY

In order to introduce the basic ideas of this book, we are going to present what has been called the "homuncular (little man) theory of computers." Imagine, if you will, a clerk sitting at a large desk. On the desk there is a sheet of paper marked off into square cells. This collection of cells is called the "memory," since it is where information is *remembered*. Each cell has a *label* or *name*, this is called the *address* of the cell. For convenience we will imagine that these labels are numbers beginning with zero, one, two, etc., each cell having a unique name or number associated with it. In each cell there is space for the clerk to write down a small amount of information; just one word in each cell. In addition to these cells, he has two scratch-pads called the "accumulator" and the "instruction register," where he can keep temporary information.

At one side of the desk there are a few baskets, some with *in* signs on them and some with *out* signs. These baskets have addresses just like memory cells. If the regular memory cells are labeled 0-997, then the in basket might be labeled 998 and the out basket 999. Within convenient reach of the clerk there is a mechanical counter -- the kind used to tally the number of people going through a gate or to indicate who is next to be served at a meat market or stamp-redemption store. Each time the clerk pushes the button on the top of the counter, the number displayed by the counter is increased by one. There are also knobs on the front of the counter, so that he can set a completely new number into the counter if he so desires. This counter is called the "program counter" (pc) and is used by the clerk to find out what he should do next. Finally, on the desk there is a telephone, which rings occasionally. When it rings the clerk drops what he is doing and answers the phone. This is called an interruption or "interrupt" for short.

On the wall, where the clerk can see it every time he raises his eyes, there is a framed motto by which he guides his every action. It says:

1. FETCH NEXT INSTRUCTION

2. INCREMENT PROGRAM COUNTER

3. CARRY OUT INSTRUCTION

4. GO BACK TO STEP 1.

This is what the clerk does all day long, every day. He looks at the number in the program counter. Suppose it is "123". He "fetches" (reads) the word written in cell 123 and copies it into the instruction register scratch-pad. This word tells him what instruction to carry out. Instructions are usually very simple: add one to the number in the accumulator scratch pad, erase the number in the accumulator, and replace it with a copy of the number in cell 456 (for example). We will shortly look at the repertoire of instructions the clerk can "execute."

After fetching the next instruction, and before executing it, the clerk pushes the button on the program counter, thus adding one to the number shown there. If the number was 123, it is now 124. He does this incrementation at this time so that he does not forget to do it. Therefore, when he comes back to step one of his motto, he will get a different instruction -- the one stored in cell 124 in our example.

Now, after fetching the instruction and putting it into the instruction register and then incrementing the program counter, he is ready to perform (execute, carry out) the instruction. He does. Then he goes back to step 1 of his motto and repeats the whole cycle. Again, and again, and again. This is the basic cycle of every computer. It is called the "fetch--execute cycle."

TYPES OF INSTRUCTIONS

Continuing with our analogy of the clerk, let us see what types of instructions he can execute, and then "write" a couple of short programs (lay down a sequence of instructions, which if carried out in order, will achieve the desired results).

MOVE DATA

The first general type of instruction that the clerk can carry out is the data move type. There are two varieties of this type, called "loads" and "stores." For our simple-minded clerk, who has only one scratch-pad or "register" that he can work with (the instruction register is always busy holding the current instruction, so he cannot use that one for data), there are only two instructions of this type: load accumulator (LDA), and store accumulator (STA). Each of these instructions consists of two parts (as do many other instructions). These parts are the operation to be performed (the op code) and the name of the cell to which the operation should be applied (the address). Thus the load accumulator instruction says "read the contents of cell named in the address part of this instruction and then copy those contents into the accumulator." So "LDA 123," where cell 123 holds the number 737, will cause the number 737 to appear in the accumulator. The old contents of the accumulator (the number that used to be there) are lost. The cell named in the address field is not changed in any way. Given the execution of LDA 123, we have the following situation:

	Before	After
Accumulator:	Some number	737
Cell 123:	737	737

Using some shorthand symbols, we can simplify the explanation. Parentheses around a number (or a name) mean "the contents of this cell," so (123) = 737. A left arrow (⟵) means that the value on the right of the arrow "goes into" or replaces the contents of the cell named on the left. We can then write:

LDA 123 means Acc ⟵ (123)

where Acc is an abbreviation for "accumulator."

The other instruction of this type (STA) works just the opposite. The contents of the accumulator are copied into the cell named in the address field.

STA 123 means 123 ⟵ (acc)

and

	Before	After
Acc:	562	562
Cell 123	some number	562

In many machines, the "clerk" has more than one scratch-pad or register to work with. When this is the case, there is usually (but not always) a load and store instruction for each of his registers. Thus, if one of his registers is called the "index" register, we will find an LDX and a STX instruction in the repertoire, to enable him to move data in and out of the index register.

ARITHMETIC AND LOGICAL INSTRUCTIONS

Some of the instructions the clerk gets tell him to perform arithmetic. He always uses his accumulator scratch-pad to do this. A typical arithmetic instruction is ADD 123. This tells the clerk to add a number to the number already in the accumulator and put the sum into the accumulator. At first glance, you might think that he was supposed to add the number 123 to the accumulator, but you would be wrong. He is supposed to add the number stored in cell 123 to the accumulator. Thus:

ADD 123 means $Acc \longleftarrow (Acc) + (123)$.

and

	Before	After
Acc.	10	15
Cell 123	5	5

Perhaps the world would have been a nicer place to live in if, 20 years ago, the early computer pioneers had written ADD C123, where the C was to remind you that the number following was a cell address, or even if they had written ADD(123), where the parentheses take their conventional meaning of "the contents of." But they didn't, and we are now stuck with ADD 123. Life will be a little better later on, when we begin referring to addresses by symbolic names.

For example, we may say ADD SMITH, where SMITH is the name of a variable that is stored in some cell or other of the memory. But we might just as well face it now: sometimes we do mean to add the number given in the address field and not the contents of the cell with that number as its name. This is called immediate addressing, and to distinguish these two cases we write:

ADD # 123 which means $Acc \longleftarrow (Acc) + 123$

where the # stands for immediate, and:

	Before	After
Acc:	10	133
Cell 123:	5	5

In addition to the ADD instruction, most small computers have a subtract instruction, abbreviated SUB, and we write:

SUB 123 which means $Acc \longleftarrow (Acc) - (123)$

where:

	Before	After
Acc	15	10
Cell 123	5	5

We can also have immediate subtracts SUB # and immediate loads: LDA# 1 puts the number "1" in the accumulator.

Question: Describe the action of SUB # and LDA #.

Question: We never find a STA # (store accumulator _immediate_). What would that mean, if anything?

Several other instructions are included in this arithmetic group. In large computers, we often have _multiply_ and _divide_ instructions, but they are almost never found in micros and seldom in minis. Another group of instructions (AND, XOR, IOR, and NOT) are lumped in here and are called _logical_ instructions. We will discuss these in detail later, after we have talked about the representation of data.

JUMP

The next instructions we are going to consider are the ones that change the number in the program counter. This means that they change the place from which the next instruction is going to be taken. They are called _jump_, or _transfer_, instructions and they come in two sorts: "conditional jumps" and "unconditional jumps." Consider first an _unconditional jump_ instruction:

JMP 123 which means $PC \longleftarrow 123$

Here we have an exception to the usual addressing rules. For jump instructions, it is _not_ the contents of the addressed cell but the _address of the cell_ that is put into the program counter. Suppose the above instruction is stored in memory cell 1000 and the program counter currently contains 1000 -- that is, we are just about to execute the instruction in cell 1000. The following sequence of events takes place:

1. We fetch the contents of the cell pointed at by the program counter and place them in the instruction register. Since (PC) = 1000 and (1000) = JMP 123, we put JMP 123 in the IR.

2. We increment the program counter. It then contains 1001. It turns out that this will be wasted effort, but we do it out of habit.

3. We execute the instructions in the instruction register. This says "put 123 into the PC," so, after execution, (PC) = 123.

4. We have now completed a fetch/execute cycle so we fetch again. This time the program counter points to cell 123, so we take our next instruction (whatever it may be) from there.

A conditional jump is very much like an unconditional jump. The difference is that we don't always make the jump -- only under certain conditions. For example,

```
        JMA     123
```

is a "jump on minus accumulator." It says "if the accumulator is less than zero (minus), put 123 in the program counter. If the accumulator is greater than or equal to zero (positive), do nothing." Then if we have the number -3 in the accumulator, a JMA is just like a JMP, but if we have +3 in the accumulator, the JMA instruction does nothing and the next instruction is taken from the cell following the cell holding the JMA instruction.

PROGRAM 1

Now we are ready to try a first program for our microcomputer. This one will be just a pencil-and-paper exercise because we don't know enough to get our machine running yet, but it will serve to explain some of the ideas we have just been over.

> STATEMENT OF THE PROBLEM: Suppose we have a switch and a light. We wish to hook them up to a microcomputer in such a way that when the switch is "on," the light is "on," and when the switch is "off," so is the light.

As you will no doubt observe, we scarcely need a computer to manage this, but we are going to use one anyway. We have purposely chosen a simple-minded task to perform, so that we can concentrate on the computer part of the problem.

DISCUSSION

As our first step, let us concentrate on the switch part of the problem. The computer must be able to discover somehow what position the switch is in; that is, whether the switch is on or off. The only way a microcomputer can tell what is going on around it is through its input ports (in baskets). A typical input port consists of eight wires. These wires are what the computer "reads" when the input port is looked at by a program. For the sake of this discussion, we will pretend that there is only one wire at the input port: namely wire I_0. If this wire is connected to a +5-volt power supply, the computer will see the number 1 when it reads the input port. If this wire is connected to 0 volts, the computer will see the number 0 when it reads the port. If the wire is left dangling in the air, connected to neither 0 V nor +5 V, some computers will see a 0 and some will see a 1. It depends on the computer, so we will be sure to connect to one or the other voltage so that there is no ambiguity.

We will take a single-pole double-throw (spdt) switch. This type of switch has three contacts on the back, arranged in a line:

0
0
0

When the switch handle is "up," the middle contact is connected to the top contact:

When the switch handle is "down," the middle contact is connected to the bottom contact:

The usual method of drawing such a switch is:

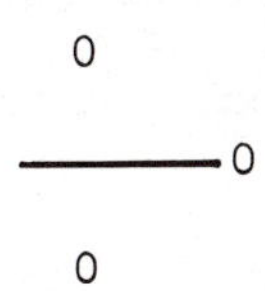

where the line represents both the switch handle that you move and the metal part that makes the connection between the middle contact and one of the two outside contacts.

Now we are ready to hook up the switch and the computer (Figure 1.1)

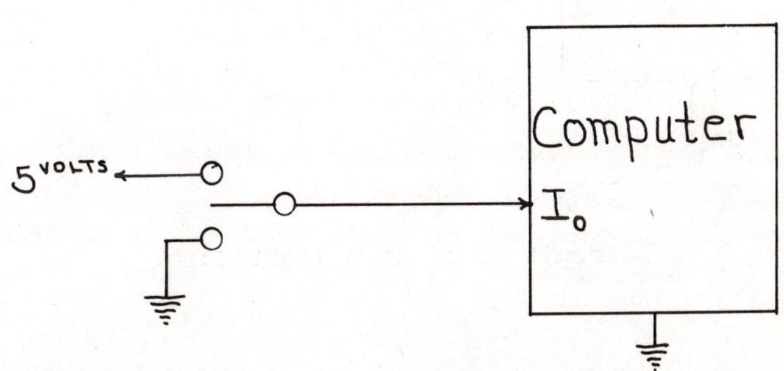

The reader should note the symbol ⏚ which is always used for 0 V. In electrical parlance, it is called "ground potential" or simply "ground." Note particularly that the computer is also "grounded." All ground connections are tied together, and this symbol is used to reduce the number of lines on diagrams.

If we assume that the input port has an address of 998 and we execute the instruction

```
LDA 998      copy input port to accumulator
```

then, if the switch is down, the number we get in the accumulator is *zero*. If the switch is up, we get a *one*.

Now let's look at the output side. The output port of a microcomputer usually has eight wires just like the input port. They are labeled O_7 through O_0. Concentrating for now on just O_0, we find that, if the output holds a *zero*, then O_0 has zero volts on it, while if the output port holds a one, then O_0 has 5 volts on it. That is the theory, at any rate. Actually, the voltages you would measure with a voltmeter would be closer to 1/2 a volt (0.5V) and 4.5V. Moreover, the output wires don't have very much "oomph" behind them (after all, it's only a *little* computer and it can't push very hard).

If you were to connect a 5-volt flashlight bulb across from O_0 to ground, it would never light because the microcomputer can't put out enough current to heat up the bulb; so we need a power amplifier to increase the power output of the output port. There are a number of ways of amplifying power and we are going to choose the simplest. It is a one-transistor DC amplifier. Almost any medium power NPN transistor will do nicely (the 2N2222 and the 2N1890 are fine, as is any NPN that can take 200-300 milliamps of collector current). In addition to the transistor, you need a resistor. A value somewhere around 2200 ohms is ideal, but it is not critical. Figure 1.2 gives the output circuit.

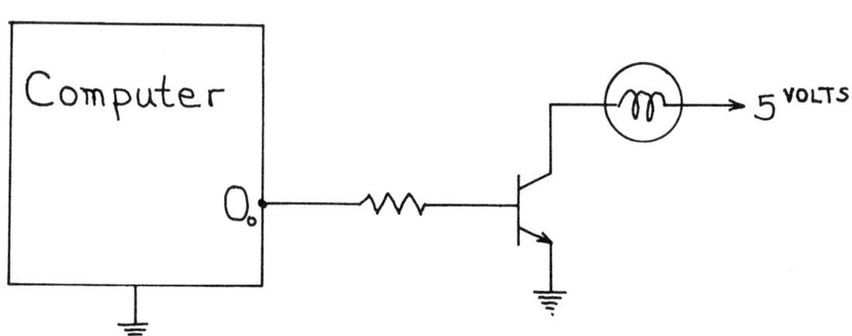

Figure 1.2

Circuit to light a light bulb.

Now we are ready to look at the computer part of the problem. There are three steps to perform:

1. Find out what position the switch is in.

2. Turn on or off the light bulb.

3. Go back to step 1 and repeat the process.

Steps 1 and 2 are pretty obvious from the original statement of the problem, but step 3 isn't necessarily obvious until you think about what happens if you turn the switch on and then turn it off again. It seems to me that we want the light to follow the switch on or off as long as the computer is running -- not just the first time we turn it on. Adding step 3, we make the computer go back and look at the switch again (and again and again -- in fact, forever). Figure 1.3 shows the steps listed above in diagramatic form.

Note that step 3 seems to have gone away. It is replaced by the arrow out of the bottom box leading back to the top box.

This flow diagram is so simple that we can write the program at once. Let us choose to put the program in cells 100-102. It looks like this:

Cell	Instruction	Meaning
100	LDA 998	Get the input (0 if switch down, 1 if switch up)
101	STA 999	Store the accumulator in cell 999 (the output port, so that the output will agree with the input)
102	JMP 100	Put 100 in the program counter so that the next instruction will be taken from cell 100
998	?	The input port
999	?	The output port

We will now go through this program in excruciating detail, so we are sure of what is going on.

1. By magic means, the program counter has been made to contain the number 100 and we are at the beginning of a fetch cycle. The clerk copies the instruction stored in cell 100 into the instruction register. (IR) = LDA 998.

2. The clerk increments the program counter. PC $\longleftarrow$ 101

3. The clerk executes the instruction in the instruction register. This says to copy the information in cell 998 (the input port) into the accumulator: Acc $\longleftarrow$ (998).

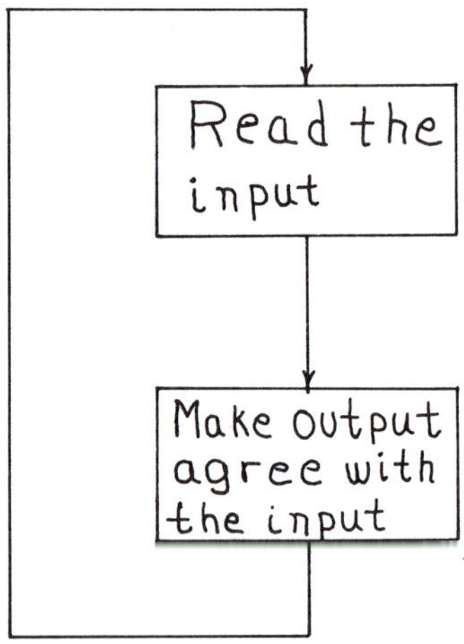

Figure 1.3

A simple flow diagram to light a light when a switch is closed

4. The instruction in the instruction register now having been executed, we fetch a new instruction from cell 101 at which the PC is pointing: (PC) = 101, IR⟵STA 999.

5. The program counter is incremented: PC⟵102.

6. The instruction in the instruction register is executed. This time it says to store the number in the accumulator into cell 999, which is the output port. Cell 999⟵(acc). This will turn the light on or off appropriately.

7. A new instruction is fetched from cell 102 at which the PC is pointing: IR⟵JMP 100.

8. The program counter is incremented. PC⟵103 (It is going to turn out that this was wasted effort, but we can't possibly know that until it is too late -- that is, after we begin to execute the instruction.)

9. The instruction in the IR is executed. This causes the number 100 to be placed in the program counter: PC⟵100.

10. By magic means, the program counter has been made to contain the number 100 and we are at the beginning of a fetch cycle -- but this sounds familiar -- we are back to step 1 again.

And on we go, round and round in an endless loop. If somebody changes the position of the switch, the next time around the loop, we will update the light appropriately.

We are not quite ready to write a program to compute your income tax or to control the moon-lander, but we have passed the first and highest hurdle. We know what a computer does (in anthropomorphic terms, to be sure, but that isn't really a sin) and have watched, in our mind's eye, while it carried out a trivial program. In the next section we are going to introduce the use of the conditional jump instruction. After that it is just a matter of elaboration and the learning of a few standard techniques. I realize you will find it difficult to believe at this point, but if you really did understand steps 1-10 above, you have mastered the hardest part of computer programming. Think back, when you get to the end of the book and see if that is not the case.

Question: Rewrite program 1 to occupy cells 17, 18, and 19. What did you change? Rewrite steps 1-10 above for this new program.

PROGRAM 2

For this problem we want to use the same equipment as in Problem 1, but this time we want the up position of the switch to turn the light off and the down position to turn the light on. Simple, you say, just turn the switch over. But we refuse. We want to change only the program, not the hardware. In the real world, of course, we would be insane not to take the easy way out. Just re-label the switch, and we are done. Remember this when you come to design your own computer control systems. Sometimes a rethinking of a problem can simplify it enormously. But here we want to learn how to use the conditional jump instruction, not turn a light on or off.

STATEMENT OF THE PROBLEM

When the input port contains a one, we want to turn off a light. When it contains a zero, we want the light on.

DISCUSSION

What we have to do is look at the input after we get it and decide whether it is zero or one and then set the output accordingly. Figure 1.4 shows a flow diagram of the general line of attack.

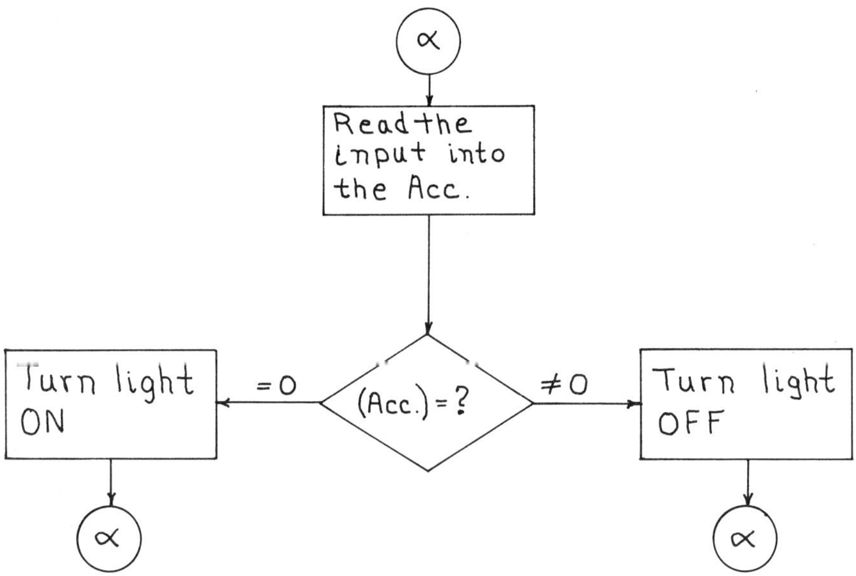

Figure 1.4

Flow diagram for Program 2. Note use of connector symbols and diamond-shaped decision box.

The first thing to note about this diagram is the use of the diamond-shaped decision box. There is one path in and two paths out. Inside the box we ask a question: What are the contents of the accumulator equal to? The outbound paths are labeled (=0 and ≠0, in this case) and which path we take depends on the answer to the question. If the contents of the accumulator are equal to <u>zero</u>, we take the lefthand path. If they are <u>one</u> (that is, not equal to <u>zero</u>), we take the righthand path.

<u>Question</u>: We could relabel these paths with the following label pairs: (=0,=1), (≥0, <0). Do so.

We are going to use the conditional jump instruction to carry out this comparison, but so far we have seen only the JMA -- jump on minus accumulator -- instruction, and neither 0 nor 1 is negative. We could introduce the instruction JZA -- "jump if <u>zero</u> in accumulator" -- which exists on many computers, but let us postpone that for a while. Suppose we subtract <u>one</u> from the number in the accumulator. Then 0 - 1= -1 and is negative, while 1 - 1=0 is considered to be a positive number. Where do we get the <u>one</u> to subtract? We will store it somewhere inside the computer. Let us arbitrarily say we have stored a <u>one</u> in cell 356 and a <u>zero</u> in cell 357 (we will need that in just a moment).

This gives us the following cells with known contents or special uses:

(356) =1
(357) =0
(998) = Input
(999) = Output

When we have decided what the input is, we need to get either a <u>zero</u> or a <u>one</u> into the accumulator to store in the output port. How about finding what we need in either cell 356 or 357? We will begin this program in cell 200 just for variety. Before reading further, see if you can write a program to solve this problem.

Here is my try at the program; compare it with yours. There can be substantial differences between them, which don't change the behavior at all, so look for the actions performed, not the details of the code.

Cell	Instruction or value	Meaning
200	LDA 998	Copy input to accumulator
201	SUB 356	Subtract the number (<u>one</u>) stored in cell 356 from the number in the accumulator and put the difference back in the accumulator.
202	JMA 300	We are going to jump to some location (we chose 300 just for fun) if the accumulator is now minus; that is, if the input was <u>zero</u>. Otherwise we will "fall through" to the instruction in cell 204 (don't jump) if the accumulator is positive -- the input was 1.
203	LDA 357	We come here if input was <u>one</u> so we get a <u>zero</u> from cell 357
204	STA 999	And store it in the output port
205	JMP 200	Then we jump to cell 200 to do it over
300	LDA 356	We come here if the input was <u>zero</u> so we get a <u>one</u> from cell 356 and
301	STA 999	Store it in the output port
302	JMP 200	Then we jump back to cell 200
356	1	Number <u>one</u>
357	0	Number <u>zero</u>
998	?	Input port
999	?	Output port

DISCUSSION OF THE CODE

The major new concept here is the JMA instruction. Let us follow this through under the assumption that the input is zero:

1. The program counter points to cell 200 and we begin a fetch cycle, loading the instruction LDA 998 into the instruction register. IR ⟵ LDA 998.

2. Increment the program counter: PC ⟵ 201.

3. Execute the instruction in the IR, loading (by assumption) a zero into the accumulator: Acc ⟵ input(=0).

4. Fetch next instruction from 201: IR ⟵ SUB 356.

5. Increment PC: PC ⟵ 202.

6. Execute the instruction. Cell 356 has a one in it, so when we subtract (356) from the accumulator we subtract one from zero, getting minus one in the accumulator.

7. Fetch the next instruction from 202: IR ⟵ JMA 300.

8. Increment the PC: PC ⟵ 203. This step is wasted, as it turns out.

9. Execute the instruction. The accumulator is minus, so we do jump. That is, we put the 300 from the instruction register into the program counter: PC ⟵ 300.

10. The next fetch is from location 300: IR ⟵ LDA 356.

11. Increment the PC: PC ⟵ 301.

12. Execute the instruction. We load the accumulator from cell 356: AC ⟵ 1.

13. Fetch next instruction from 301: IR ⟵ STA 999.

14. Increment the PC: PC ⟵ 302.

15. Execute the instruction. We store the 1 in the accumulator in cell 999, which is the output port. This turns on the light: cell 999 ⟵ 1.

16. Fetch next instruction from 302: IR ⟵ JMP 200.

17. Increment the PC: PC ⟵ 303. This step is wasted.

18. Execute the instruction. The instruction is JMP 200, so we put 200 into the PC: PC ⟵ 200.

19. We are back to step 1 and repeat the whole process over again.

As long as the switch is in the "off" position, the computer keeps cycling through these 18 steps time after time. Now suppose that somebody moves the switch to "on." The next time we perform the instruction in cell 200 (LDA 998) -- get a copy of the number in the input port -- we get a 1 in the accumulator. Now, in step 6, when we subtract <u>one</u> from the accumulator, we get <u>zero</u> instead of <u>minus one</u>. Steps 7 and 8 remain the same except that as we will see, step 8 is <u>not</u> wasted in this case. Now, beginning with step 9, we have:

9' Execute the instruction. The accumulator is not minus. <u>Zero</u> is considered to be positive. So this instruction does nothing. In particular, it does <u>not</u> change the PC.

10' Fetch the next instruction. The PC is pointing at cell 203, so we load the IR from there: IR ⟵ LDA 357. Note that it is a good thing that we incremented the PC in step 8.

11' Increment the PC: PC ⟵ 204.

12' Execute the instruction. We load the accumulator from cell 357. Cell 357 has a <u>zero</u> in it, so we get a <u>zero</u> in the accumulator: Acc ⟵ 0.

13' Fetch the next instruction from cell 204: IR ⟵ STA 999.

14' Increment the PC: PC ⟵ 205.

15' Execute the instruction. Store the <u>zero</u> in the accumulator in the output port, thus turning off the light: cell 999 ⟵ 0.

16' Fetch the next instruction from cell 205: IR ⟵ JMP 200.

17' Increment the PC: PC ⟵ 206. This step is wasted.

18' Execute the instruction. Jump unconditionally to location 200. PC ⟵ 200.

19' We are back to step 1 again.

<u>SUMMARY</u>

So far we have learned about loads and stores, input and output, and conditional and unconditional jump instructions. We have also looked at the basic structure of a computer and seen how the fetch/execute cycle is carried out.

In the next chapter we will look at the console controls of a simple microcomputer to see how we can get it to load and execute programs such as those we have discussed above.

Readers not familiar with binary or hexadecimal numbers should read Appendix A before going on to Chapter Two.

2
CONSOLE CONTROLS

This chapter is the one most closely tied to a particular microcomputer. If you do not have a KIM-1 microcomputer, please keep faith. This will become more relevant soon. We will use the KIM-1 as an example of a typical 8-bit microcomputer.

The KIM-1 has a number of programs permanently stored inside it. These programs are stored in a special memory and are used to control the console keyboard and lights and to talk to a teletype (if you have one) and an audio cassette (if you have one of those). As far as the *computer* is concerned, these *resident* programs are just like the ones you will write. When the program counter points to the beginning of one of these programs, the program is executed step by step. As far as *we* are concerned, these resident programs make the machine much easier to use than a bare micro just off the assembly line. In particular they make the console switches and buttons and lights behave in a reasonable fashion, so that we can make the machine do what we want with much less effort.

Consider the KIM-1 console. It has six seven-segment displays arranged in a row. It has 23 push buttons and one slide switch. Turn on the power supply of your KIM and put the slide switch, which controls free-running or single-step mode in the free-running position. Now press the RS or *reset* switch. Note that the six display digits light up. The reset switch is the most important switch on the machine. No matter what the time of day or phase of the moon or what the computer may be doing, when you push that switch the computer drops everything and goes to the beginning of its console control program. In this program the computer watches the 23 buttons to see whether you have pushed any and displays certain information on the display digits. The four lefthand digits of the display are an address from 0000 to FFFF. Of course, your machine may not have that many storage cells (65,536). As it comes from the factory, the KIM-1 has 1024_d cells ($03FF_h$), but the console control program is designed for the largest possible machine you could buy. The right most two digits tell you the contents of that 8-bit memory cell (in two hexadecimal digits).

The top two rows of buttons are commands to the console control program, and the bottom four rows represent the hex charactors 0-F. Press the AD button. There is no visible change, but the console control program now expects you to tell it an address. Push some of the hex character keys (0-F) and watch the address display. Each character you enter appears as the least significant character of the address, and the old characters are shifted to the left one place. The leftmost one disappears. Type 1234 and see the display of "1234". Now type 5 and see the display of "2345". Note that when you change the address, the "data" register will also change -- not every time, but sometimes. This is because the bit pattern stored in that cell is different from the last cell you were looking at.

Enter the address 1800. You are now looking at the console control program itself, but this form of navel contemplation doesn't bother the computer.

Press the + button. This causes the console control program to add one to the address pointer; the address display should now say 1801. Press + again: 1802. Enter a new address: 0000. Press + and get 0001. Pressing + does not change the mode. If you are in the address entry mode, you stay there. Pressing + simply adds one to the address pointer any time you press it.

Return the address pointer to 0000 and then press the DA key. This tells the console control program that you are going to enter data. Now press one of the hex character keys. Observe that the address display does not change but the data display does. Type 12. See 12 on the data display. This eight-bit pattern (0001 0010) is also stored in cell 0000 (assuming the address pointer is still pointing at that cell). Now type a 3. The data display now shows 23. The 1 got shifted off, the 2 moved over, and the 3 came in on the right.

Pick some pattern that you would like to store in cell 0000. Enter the hex characters. Make a note of what you stored there. Now press +. The address display shows 0001 and the data display shows some pair of characters.

Enter a new character pair of your choice. Press + one more time (Address pointer = 0003) and enter yet another character pair.

Now let us go back to see whether those characters really were stored in the cells we thought they were. Press AD to get into address-entry mode and enter 0000. You should see the first pair of characters you entered displayed in the data display. Pressing + will advance the address pointer and you can check that the data you entered in cell 0001 was stored correctly.

This is the way we are going to get programs into our KIM-1. We will set the address pointer to the cell that is to hold the first instruction. Go over to data-entry mode and enter the program word by word, following each character pair by a + to advance to the next cell of storage. When the program is completely entered and verified, we go into address-entry mode, insert the starting address of the program into the address pointer, cross our fingers and press the GO button. We will come back to this point again.

To gain practice in flow diagrams and perhaps to make the operation of the console control program a little clearer, we will now go through a rough functional outline of that program. (See Fig. 2.1)

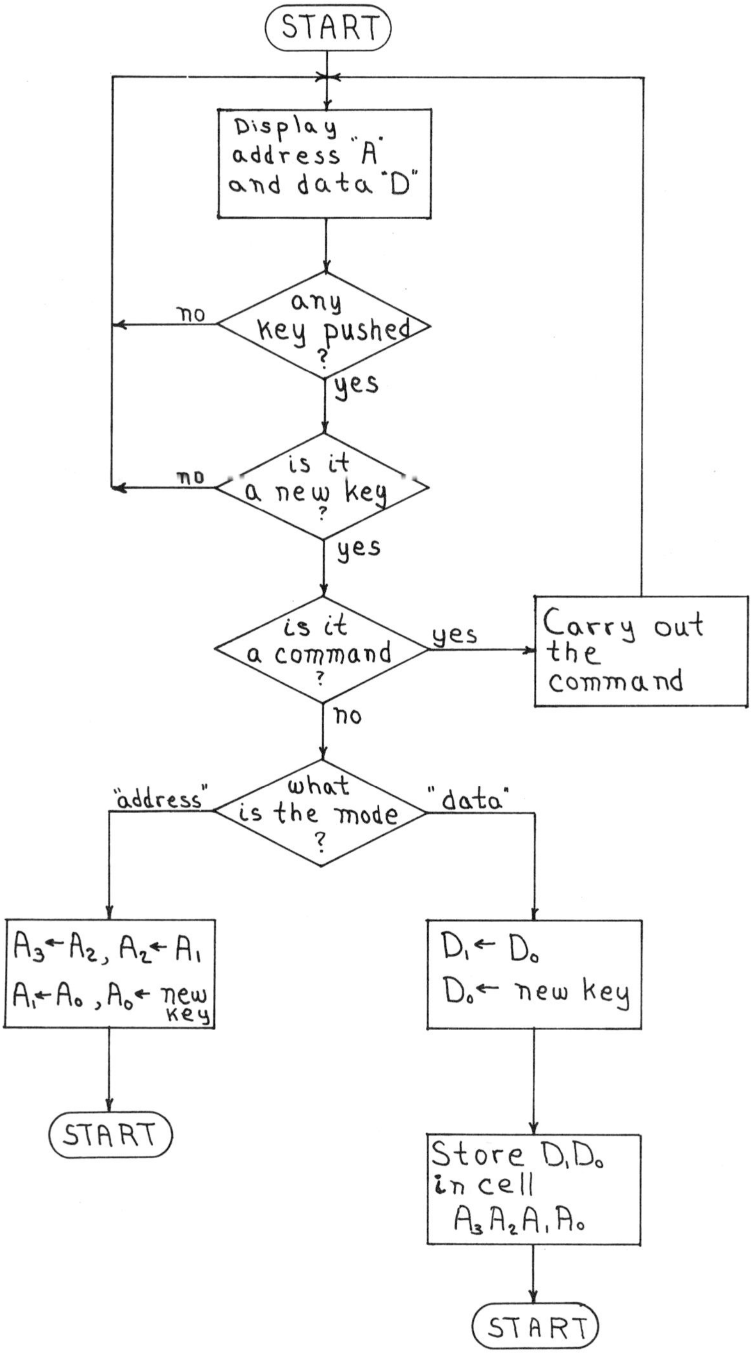

Figure 2.1 Functional diagram of console control program.

When the RS button is pushed, control is transferred to the beginning of the program. The program first outputs the four characters of the address pointer ($A_3A_2A_1A_0$). It then converts these characters to a storage address and retrieves the contents of that cell. The upper four bits from that cell are put out as D_1 and the lower four as D_0. Next the program asks whether any key has been depressed. (We will look into how to accomplish this in a later experiment.) If no key was pushed, it goes back to START. If a key is found depressed, we need to make certain that it is a new key -- not just an old key we have already taken care of. Remember the computer is very much faster than a human and a 1/10-second key depression will be detected many times by the machine. So if it's an old key, we ignore it. If it is a command key, we carry out the command. If it's a hex character, we check to see whether the program is in data- or address-entry mode. If data entry, we move D_0 to D_1, put the new character into D_0, and store a copy of D,D_0 in the cell the address pointer is pointing at.

If we are in address-entry mode, we shift the old characters left one place and put the new character in on the right.

COMMANDS

There are eight keyboard command buttons in the KIM-1. We summarize their uses here.

AD Address-entry mode. Places the console control program in address-entry mode, ready to receive characters to specify an address to go in the address pointer.

DA Data-entry mode. Places the console control program in data-entry mode, ready to receive characters to store in the cell pointed at by the address pointer.

RS Reset. Causes the computer to abandon whatever it is now doing and begin to execute the console control program.

ST Stop. Causes the computer to stop doing what it is currently doing and transfer control (jump) to the program beginning in the cell whose name is in cells 17FA and 17FB. If you store the address 0100 in 17FA and 17FB, then the stop button can be used to cause your program to jump to a special "user interrupt" routine of your choice, beginning in cell 0100. It is much more usual to insert the words "00" and "1C" in 17FA and 17FB, respectively. Then, when the ST button is pressed, control goes to a certain part of the console control program that stores something called the "machine context" in cells 00EF to 00FF for you, and then transfers to the beginning of the console control program. This "machine context" is vital if you want to go back to your program after stopping it. If you stop it with the ST key, you can go back. If you stop it with the RS key you can't. Among other things, the machine context includes the contents of the accumulator (and all the other machine registers you haven't heard of yet) and the program counter where your program was interrupted. The contents of the program counter are also copied into the address pointer so that you can see where you were when you stopped yourself.

GO Begin executing the program at the location pointed to by the address pointer. Before doing this, restore the machine context (except for the program counter, which gets loaded from the address pointer) that was saved when last you pushed the stop button. Suppose you started your program running and after a while wondered what had happened to it. You push ST and your program stops and the address display tells you the name of the cell at which your program counter was pointing when you pushed the stop button. After a moment's thought you realize that everything is operating properly and you want to continue. Push the GO button and you are off and running. The console control program had to save your machine context because it needed to use the machine registers in order to do the display and test for button pushes.

PC Program counter. Causes the address pointer to be loaded from the value of the program counter saved in the most recent exercise of the stop button. Suppose that, in the example given under the GO button description, you had decided that you needed to look in some storage locations to see whether your program was running satisfactorily. So you push stop and then AD and enter the address of the cell you want to look at. After a certain amount of fooling around and perhaps changing some cells, you want to go back and continue your program from where you interrupted it. Pressing PC saves your having to remember where you stopped and having to reload that address in the address pointer.

SST Single step. When in the OFF position the computer runs free, as described above. In the ON or SST position, your user program is interrupted at the completion of each instruction. It is as if you were fast enough to press the ST button before the machine could execute more than one instruction. In single-step mode, each depression of the GO button will cause one user instruction and then come back to the console control program.

In order to exercise all this knowledge about the control console we need a simple program to enter and execute and perhaps single-step through. Let this be a program to add one to the contents of a location and then go back and do it again in endless loop fashion.

We should begin by setting a zero in the location, so we know where we are starting.

Before proceeding further, see if you can work out a flow diagram that will assist in writing a program for adding to the contents of a location. Do not turn this page yet.

It is hard when you start programming to draw flow diagrams with the right amount of detail. The example on the left of Figure 2.2 leaves perhaps a bit too much to the imagination, where as, the one on the right bogs you down in too much detail. Each different individual will find a different level of detail comforable. There is no one right answer. Only what you like.

Now see if you can generate the code needed to carry out the flow diagram in Fig. 2.2(b). Begin your program in cell 0000.

I decided to put the constant zero in cell 21 and the constant one in cell 22. Figure 2.3 is one version of the code.

Location		Instruction	Comments
0000:		LDA 0021	get zero
		STA 0020	Clear counter
	LOOP:	LDA 0020	Increment the counter in
		ADD 0022	Cell 20 by one.
		STA 0020	
		JMP LOOP	Go back to "loop" and do it again.
20:		COUNTER	
21:		00	
22		01	

Figure 2.3

Everything is fine except that you probably assumed that each instruction occupied one cell and where I wrote the word "loop" you wrote "0002". Given what we have said up to now, that is a very reasonable assumption, but, unfortunately, not valid. In the KIM-1 and in most microcomputers, instructions take anywhere from 1 to 3 cells, depending on the instruction. With malice aforethought these instructions have all been selected to take up 3 cells each. That means the LDA 0011 goes in cells 0, 1, and 2. The STA goes in cells 3, 4, 5; and the LDA at LOOP begins in cell 6.

Further, I have to tell you that the use of these 3 cells is not the way a rational person would have expected. The microcomputers almost universally store a 3-word instruction as:

Operation code
Lower half of the address - called the "line number"
Upper half of the address - called the "page number"

So LDA 0011 gets stored as:

```
0000:  LDA
0001:   11
0002:   00
```

One more point. The op-code (operation code) has to be translated to a numeric code so that: (1) it will fit into 8 bits, and so that (2) the computer will understand it. Every different computer uses a different translation from the "op-code mnemonics" (as LDA or JMP are called) to the code the machine understands.

Figure 2.2 is my try at this flow diagram in three variations:

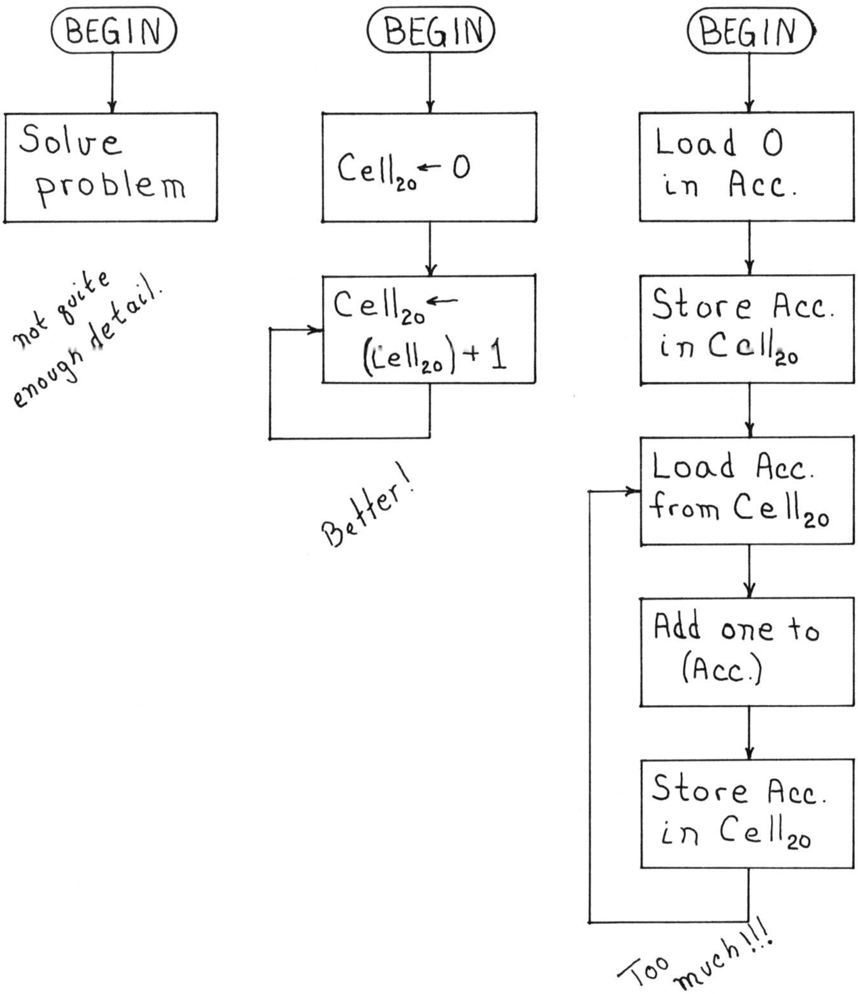

Figure 2.2

For KIM-1 we can translate the op-codes we need for this program as:

Mnemonic	Code
ADD=	6D
JMP=	4C
LDA=	AD
STA=	8D

A complete table for the translation of mnemonics to code will be given in your machine manual.

Now at last we can write down the program ready for entry into the computer:

Cell	Code	Meaning	
0	AD		
1	21	LDA 0021	Clear counter
2	00		
3	8D		
4	20	STA 0020	
5	00		
6	AD		
7	20	LDA 0020	Increment counter
8	00		
9	6D		
A	22	ADD 0022	
B	00		
C	8D		
D	20	STA 0020	
E	00		
F	4C		
10	06	JMP 0006	
11	00		
.	.		
.	.		
.	.		
20	-	The counter	
21	00	Constants	
22	01		

Let's put it in the computer now. Turn on the power. Press RS and see the display light up. Press AD and enter the starting address 0000. Press DA to get into data mode and enter the characters AD. See the display = AD. Press +, enter next word "21", see display "0001 21". Continue entering one word at a time, with pluses between them, until you have entered the word 11 in cell 0011. Press AD to get into address mode. Enter address 0021. Press DA, enter 00. Press +, enter 01 (see display = 0022 01).

Now the whole program is entered. Go back to address mode (AD), and go back to cell 0000 to see whether it went in properly. After you verify that each word says what it should, press + to examine the next word. If you find a mistake, simply go into data mode and type the correct values. The bad ones will be replaced.

A very common error is to forget to press + often enough (before each new word) or to press it too often. Make sure that each cell has the proper thing in it. A good spot-check would be to make sure that cell 0009 contains 6D and cell 000F contains 4C. Then you can be reasonably confident that you didn't make that mistake.

WAIT!

Before you press GO, it would be a good idea to make sure that the stop button will work. You must set the address pointer to 17FA, press DA, enter 00, press +, enter 1C, press AD. That sets up the stop button.

One more thing. There is a so-called "status register" in this machine, which must be cleared to zero before you run this program. Enter 00F1 in the address pointer. Press DA and enter 00. We will explain the status register later.

Now you can enter 0000 in the address pointer. (No harm is ever done by pressing the AD button before entering an address or the DA before entering data. If you are certain what mode the machine is in, then skip it, but, if in doubt, set the mode.)

Make sure the machine is not in single-step mode (switch is to OFF) and press GO. Stand well back. No smoke coming up? You're in good shape. Seriously, it is absolutely impossible to damage a computer by pressing buttons on its console. You can clobber your program but you can't hurt the machine itself.

Now press ST. Does the display light up? It should, and it should say one of the following:

0006	AD
0009	6D
000C	8D
000F	4C

If you get no display at all, then either you forgot to initialize cells 17FA and 17FB so the stop button will work, or you made a mistake entering and verifying your program. Press RS to recover control and go back and re-verify that the stop address is set in 17FA and 17FB and that your program was entered correctly.

If you get some display but not one of the above, then your program is wrong. Re-verify and correct it. Every single character must be correct and in the correct place. No "almost right" allowed here.

Please copy the following onto a large card and tape it over your computer setup:

> All programmers who have written more than one program make mistakes. They make them in verifying, in typing, in translation, and in logic. And lots of other places as well.
>
> IF YOU THINK YOU ARE SMARTER THAN EVERYBODY ELSE IN THE GAME, THEN YOU ARE IN THE WRONG GAME.
>
> If you "never make mistakes," then turn in your computer now

and take up underwater basketweaving or some other hobby. You will save everybody involved a hell of a lot of heartache and frustration by quitting now rather than later.

Most people can learn to accept the fact that they have made an error. They admit it and try a little harder next time. Some people can't do that. Computing is not for them.

So, assuming you have gotten your program to the point where, when you push GO, the display goes out, and when you push ST, the display comes on, with an address that corresponds to the beginning of an instruction, we can go forward.

Stop your program, enter* address 0020 and observe the number stored there. Push PC to recall the program counter. Push GO, then ST, and look in 0020 again. Did the number there change? It should have. Put the machine in single-step mode and push GO. You should observe the next instruction address and op-code displayed. Push GO again a few more times until you end up with 000F 4C on the display. That means you are just about to execute the JMP 0006 instruction and you just stored a new value into 0020. Look in 0020 and see if it has changed. If not, then re-check your code. Either one of your LDA 0020, ADD 0022, or STA 0020 instructions is wrong, or else the number 1 isn't stored in 0022, or else you aren't looking in the right place. Remember, in an instruction, addresses are stored least significant half first but in the address pointer they are entered most significant half first.

Assuming you have that all straightened out and location 0020 is incrementing properly each time around the loop, stop just before executing the jump instruction. Store FF in location 0020. Store 00 in location 00F1 (the status register). Now go once around the loop. You should see 00 in location 0020 because FF + 1 = 100_{16} and there is no place to store the 1 in location 0020. But it does get stored as a "carry" inside the machine in one of the bits of the status register. Since the only "add" instruction in the KIM-1 is "add with carry" (mnemonic ADC not ADD -- O.K., I lied a little), the next time you go around the loop you add 1 (from cell 0022) and 1 from the carry to 00 and get 02. Right?

---

*when you push stop or reset, you are automatically in address-entry mode.

3
MORSE CODE OSCILLATOR

In this experiment we are going to cause a loudspeaker to give out a tone whenever a key is closed, and be quiet when the key is open. This is similar to a conventional Morse code practice oscillator or, if you will, to a doorbell or buzzer.

In order to do this, we have to learn about the input and output ports and about how they are controlled. We also have to learn about counting and testing and the general problem of loop control.

First of all, let us get the general mode of approach specified and then we can get into the details.

To generate a tone we are going to apply a square wave to a loudspeaker. The frequency of the fundamental tone will be given by the reciprocal of the period of the square wave. (Figure 3.1 is a diagram of a square wave.

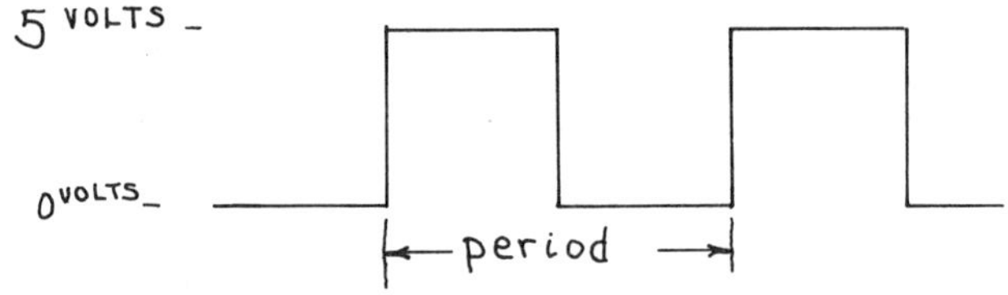

Figure 3.1

If the period is P seconds the frequency will be 1/P oscillations per second. A frequency of 1000 Hertz (cycles per second) calls for a period of 0.001 seconds, or 1 millisecond, or 1000 microseconds. (1 second = 10^3 milliseconds = 10^6 microseconds, or 1 second = 1000 milliseconds = 1,000,000 microseconds.) To generate a 1000-Hertz square wave, we must change the output from <u>zero</u> to <u>one</u>, wait 500 microseconds, change from <u>one</u> to <u>zero</u>, wait 500 microseconds, change back, wait, change, wait, etc., etc.

To put it as succinctly as possible, we must complement the output bit, wait, and then repeat as long as the input key is closed.

Suppose we have the loudspeaker connected to the low-order bit of the output word. Now if we pick up the output word, add one to it, and then replace it, we will succeed in complementing the low-order bit of that word, because odd binary numbers have the low-order bit equal to one and even binary numbers have it zero and, counting up, we alternate between odd and even binary numbers.

If all I want to do is add one to a number, the KIM-1 provides a special instruction called "increment" with a mnemonic of INC.

INC 1234 says to the machine to add one to the number stored in cell 1234 and put the result back in 1234. It is done without regard to the carry bit, so the numbers go FF, 00, 01, 02, etc., in a rational fashion. Carry-out of the high-order bit is simply discarded.

Before reading further, draw a flow diagram for this problem as you understand it now. Begin with a box called "initialize," whose operations we will discuss shortly.

Figure 3.2 is one version of the flow diagram for the Morse code oscillator:

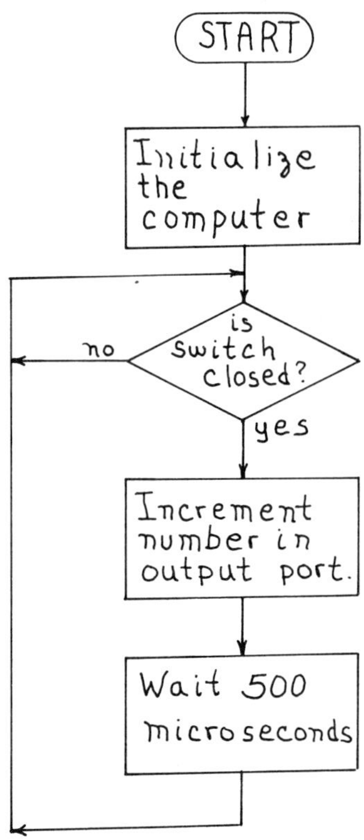

Figure 3.2

We need to discover a way to make the computer wait for 500 microseconds. Since each instruction takes some finite amount of time to execute, we could find, say, a 2-microsecond instruction and write-down 250 of them in a row. That would clearly work, but it would be rather tedious to enter all those instructions, as well as wasteful of memory space. There is a better way: We take a short string of code that requires X microseconds to perform and then perform that short string $\frac{500}{X}$ times. How do we do that? Assume X = 10 micro-seconds, so $\frac{500}{X} = 50$. We arrange a counter with the number 50 in it. We do the string of code and then subtract one from the counter and test to see whether the counter is now zero. If not, we loop back and execute the string again. If it is zero, we don't go back and do it again. What we are going to do is to let the string of code we execute to waste time be the same code that does the testing. Figure 3.3 is a simple flow diagram to explain this:

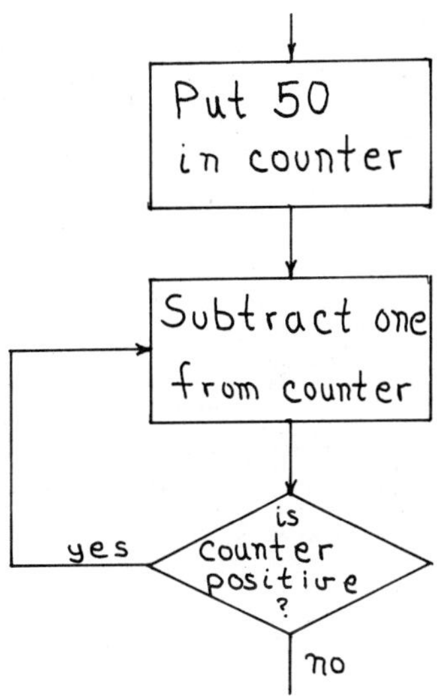

Figure 3.3

Translating Fig. 3.3 into code, we have:

	LDA	CONSTANT	Get the initial value that is to go in the counter
	STA	COUNTER	
WAIT:	DEC	COUNTER	Subtract 1 from contents of counter
	BPL	WAIT	Jump if result is greater than or equal to zero

We have a number of new things here. First of all, we have symbolic names for the cells of memory: "constant", "counter", and "wait", because we don't really care where these cells are just yet. Before we put the code into the machine, we will have to *bind* all these symbolic names: that is, we will have to take some memory cells and decide that that cell is going to hold the counter. Then everywhere the name "counter" occurs we will substitute the address of that cell. Similarly, we don't yet know where this string of code is going to be put, so we just *label* the "DEC COUNTER" instruction, and write that label in the BPL instruction. Again, that label will have to be replaced by a genuine memory address before we load in the program. At this point we don't even know what number we are going to store in this as-yet-unspecified cell we called "constant" because we haven't timed out the loop yet to see how long it takes.

The DEC instruction says to decrement the specified memory cell by *one* and put the result back in the memory cell. The BPL instruction says "branch on plus", which means that, if the result of the most recent move or arithmetic instruction (in this case, the DEC instruction) was positive, we branch (another word for *jump*) to the cell whose name is in the address part of the instruction. Now let us look at the amount of time taken to execute each of these instructions. From the table in the KIM manual we see that time is needed as follows:

Instruction	Microseconds to execute
LDA	4
STA	4
DEC	6
BPL	3 if we do branch, 2 if we don't.

This says the setup time -- the time to put the initial value into the counter -- is 8 microseconds, and each turn around the loop will take 8 microseconds. So if we want a delay of 500 microseconds, we must go around the loop:

$$\frac{500-8 \text{ for set-up}}{8} = \frac{492}{8} = 61\ 1/2 \text{ times}$$

or as a convenient approximation, we will say 60 times. That leaves us 12 microseconds to check the input switch and toggle the output, which is about right. Here we don't need to be too critical, but sometimes we have to get right down to 1 microsecond in timing.

Now that we have decided how many times we need to go around the loop, we need to decide what number to put into CONSTANT to initialize the counter with. Let us suppose we put in the number 2 and see how many times we go around the loop:

Instruction		Value of counter after the instruction is executed
	LDA	?
	STA	2
1	DEC	1
	BPL	1 We do branch
2	DEC	0
	BPL	0 We do branch, 0 is plus
3	DEC	-1
	BPL	-1 We don't branch. Instead we ______ EXIT

That's three times around -- one more than the number we initialize with. So, to loop 60 times, we start off with the number 59_d. We must translate that to hex and, by looking up in the table at the end of the book, we see that $59_d = 3B_h$. Repeat the above example using a BNE (branch if not equal to zero) instruction. If N is the number you start out with, how many times do you go around the loop?

There is one more problem we have to contend with. That is the fact that the branch instructions do not use the same kind of addresses that we have been talking about up to now.

The old scheme is called "absolute" addressing. Branch instructions use a scheme called "relative" addressing. This says what number should be added to, or subtracted from, the program counter, rather than giving the value of a number to put there. Even after you understand what this means, you are going to find it a veritable invitation to errors.

Suppose we have the following set of instructions stored in the computer and we wish to do a branch.

Cell	Word	
100	LDA	LDA 1000
101	00	
102	10	
103	STA	STA 1001
104	01	
105	10	

Cell	Word	
106	BPL	BPL ??
107	??	
108	LDA	LDA 2012
109	12	
10A	20	
10B	STA	STA 2013
10C	13	
10D	20	

Let's assume that, for whatever reason, we might want to jump to any one of the five instructions; that is, to locations 100, 103, 106, 108, or 10B. The offsets of these cells can be obtained by subtracting the address of the cell immediately following the branch instruction, called the zero offset cell -- (in this case, cell 108) -- from the address of the destination. To jump to cell 108 (which in effect turns the branch into a NOP -- or "do nothing" instruction) we would put 00_h in cell 107. To go to cell 10B we put 03_h into 107. To go to cell 106 (which loops back on the branch itself) we would put FE_h into cell 107. To go to cell 103, we put FB in 107, and to go to cell 100 we would put F8 in 107. Summarizing:

Destination	Offset from 107
100	F8
103	FB
106	FE
108	00
10B	03

Remember that "no jump at all" means the next instruction in line (cell 108, in our example) and learn to count in hex, and you are all set -- provided you don't make a mistake. For example, suppose the branch instruction is in cell 1234 and you wish to branch to cell 122A. We subtract 1236 (the zero offset cell) from 122A. A minus 6 is 4 and 2 minus 3 is F. Therefore the offset is F4. To check this, we can write the "count" next to each cell.

Cell		Count
122A		F4
B		5
C		6
D		7
E	- - - - - - - - - - - - - -	8
F		9
1230	- - - - - - - - - - - - - -	A
1		B
2		C
1233	- - - - - - - - - - - - - -	D
4	BPL	E
5	F4	FF
6	(zero offset cell)	00

and count forward to the zero offset cell.

Any offset whose leading bit (leftmost -- most significant) is a one will be treated as a jump backward. An offset with leading bit of zero will cause a jump forward.

Thus the largest positive offset is "$7F_h$" which causes a branch forward of 127 cells, or 40 to 50 instructions, and the largest negative offset is "80_h" which causes a branch backwards of 128 cells from the zero offset cell. Suppose you want to branch to a cell farther away than this? What you must do is branch to an unconditional jump instruction within the permitted range and there you can jump to any cell in storage you like because the JMP instruction has a full 16-bit address associated with it.

There are four branch instructions we need to know at this point. They are:

	(Code)	
BPL	10	Branch if plus
BEQ	F0	Branch if equal to zero
BNE	D0	Branch if not equal to zero
BMI	30	Branch if minus

Remember that the test is applied to the most recent number the machine saw or calculated. If the last instruction before the branch was an LDA, it's the number that got moved. If the last instruction was an increment memory, that memory word is the one that is tested. If the last instruction did an add or subtract, the result of that instruction is what gets tested.

The way this is done is via two bits of the "program status word". These bits are called the Z and N bits. Anytime a word equal to zero is moved or computed, the Z bit is set to one. If the word is not equal to zero, the Z bit is cleared (set equal to zero).

Similarly, when a negative word is moved or computed, the N bit is set. When a positive word is moved or computed, the N bit is cleared.

The branch instructions test these bits and then branch (or don't branch) depending on the value of the bit. For example, the BPL instruction tests the N bit and branches if the bit is zero. BMI branches if N is one.

There are several other bits in the program status word that we will discuss as we need them.

Suppose you want to branch to a far away location if a number we have just computed is positive. If the branch instruction had a long enough "reach", we would say:

```
        BPL FARAWAY
```

but that won't work. What we do is reverse the sense of the text. Branch on Plus is replaced by Branch on Minus and vice versa, and branch-on-equal and branch-on-not-equal are interchanged:

```
        BMI NEXT
        JMP FARAWAY

NEXT:
```

and the branch is just "around" the next instruction which is a jump to FARAWAY. Now if the number is negative, the BMI takes us to NEXT while if the number is positive, we don't take the BMI branch but "fall through" and execute the jump to FARAWAY which is just what we wanted to do in this case. Fortunately, most of the conditional branches we want to use are to nearby locations and we don't have to do this too often, but it is useful to know how when we need it.

Before you can write the program for the Morse code oscillator, you need to know some more about the input and output parts of the KIM-1 or of your own computer. We will discuss the KIM-1 here. The general ideas will be valid for most other microcomputers, but the details may well differ.

As the KIM-1 is set up there are two I/O ports, which we will call PORT A and PORT B. PORT A (KIM manual calls this PAD) may be referenced by addressing memory location 1700, PORT B (called PBD) by addressing location 1702. PORT A has 8 bits labeled A_7A_6 --- A_0 and PORT B has 7 bits labeled $B_7B_5B_4B_3B_2B_1B_0$ ($B_6$is missing). Each of these bits may be treated as an input bit or an output bit and you must tell the computer which way you want them to "face". In the sense of our earlier example of the clerk, he has 15 I/O baskets and, for each experiment, he must label these baskets as IN baskets or OUT baskets. These labels are stored in another pair of cells called DIRA and DIRB, where DIRA is cell 1701 and DIRB is 1703 (the KIM manual calls these PADD and PBDD). DIRA corresponds bit for bit with PORT A, and putting a 1 or 0 in DIRA bit i conditions A_i to be output or input. DIRB conditions PORT B with bit 6 of DIRB having no effect on anything (because B_6 is missing). Contrary to what you might expect to find, a 1 indicates output and a 0 indicates input. (Think of the one and zero as the letters I and O and remember that manufacturers are obtuse and do things backwards).

So to make bit A_0 be an input bit and B_0 be an output bit, we should store 0 in DIRA and 1 in DIRB. This is part of the initialization of the machine that our program must perform. Unfortunately, the bits that are input bits tend to produce <u>ones</u> if you don't tie them to ground. That means that the unused bits of PORT A may be <u>one</u> and hence will confuse your test of A_0 unless you make these other bits be output bits. The way to do this is to store the number "FE" in DIRA so that A_7 - A_1 are output and only A_0 is input. In DIRB we will make all the bits be output bits by storing an FF there.

It saves curses if each program also loads the stop key addresses (17FA and 17FB get 00 and 1C respectively).

The hardware needed for this experiment is as shown in Fig. 3.4.

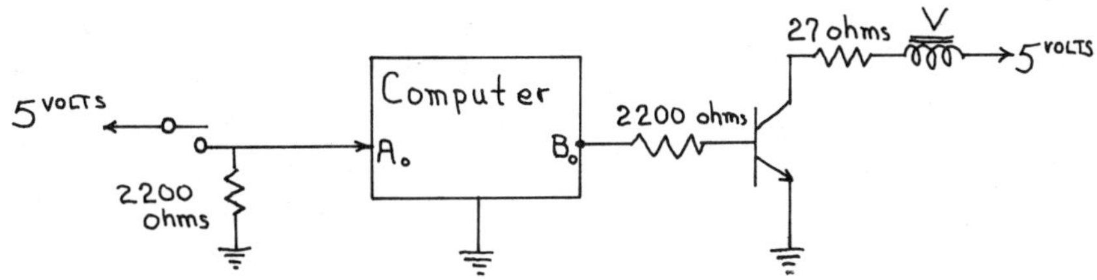

Figure 3.4

When the switch on the input is closed, it pulls A_0 to logical 1. When it is open (not being pushed), the 2.2K-ohm resitor pulls A_0 down to ground. The output circuit connected to B_0 uses a cheap ($2.00 or so) loudspeaker driven by a single transistor amplifier.

Write your program to do the Morse-code oscillator. Ordinary lined paper may be used, or you can construct coding sheets similar to the one in the back of this book, if that is more convenient. Neatness helps a lot here. Things are going to be confused enough when you come to trying to <u>debug</u> your program. (Errors in programs are called "bugs." Getting all the bugs out is called "debugging.")

First, translate the flow diagram to machine instructions. This can be done on scratch paper and should be done in pencil because it is subject to a fair bit of revision. Use symbolic names for variables and for instruction labels. You need to put labels on only those instructions you are going to jump or branch to. Transfer these labels back onto your flow diagram, because that will help you keep track of what is going on. At the end of your program, or in a corner of your scratch sheet, make a list of all the variables as you define them and use them for the first time. If you are going to need some constants, note those as well and write down the number they are to hold. It is amazing how easy it is to forget what JONES is supposed to be equal to. Use descriptive names whenever possible.

After you have written your rough program and "walked" through it a couple of times to be sure that you have the logic correct, you are ready to translate your program into machine code. Look up all the op-codes and write down their translations in the column marked F1 next to the instruction.

Don't try to memorize them. You'll only make mistakes that you don't need. Decide where your program is going to be put in storage. You might as well begin with 0000. Write that in the ADDR column next to the first instruction. Since that will probably be an LDA instruction which requires 3 cells, count off 0, 1, 2 and write down 0003 in the ADDR column for the next instruction (probably a STA?). Count off 3, 4, and 5 for the 3 cells occupied by the STA, and write down 0006 for the address of the next instruction. Continue in this fashion, being careful to count off only 2 for the branch instructions or other 2-cell instructions, and remember to count in hex. The number following 9 is not 10. It is A. 10 follows F. When all the instruction addresses have been assigned, you can begin assigning addresses to your constants and variables. It is perhaps a wise idea to leave a few vacant cells after the last instruction and before the first constant or variable. Each constant or variable gets one cell and may be stored any place you like in the machine. For the purpose of these first few experiments, you may use any address between 0000 and 00EE, inclusive.

Now that all instructions, variables, and constants have been assigned addresses, you can go back and fill in the fields F2 and F3 for each instruction. If there is no third field required for some instruction, skip F3.

If you had an expensive, large "assembler" program it would do this translation for you and you wouldn't have to worry about counting and addresses and so forth. But most people with microcomputers don't have an assembler, so they have to do the translation by hand. Keep the faith; you are getting a first-hand knowledge of how an assembler works and should be able to design one yourself with one hand tied to zero.

Do this much before reading further.

Now pretend that you are the clerk and "walk through" your program once more. You should find that you set up the stop key address (both cells), the direction words for both ports, test for key closure, toggle the speaker. Wait a while in a counting loop, and then go back and test for key closure again. Right?

Now connect the key and loudspeaker to the application connector and then plug the computer board into the application connector.

Now turn on the power. Set the address pointer to the location of your first instruction and begin keying in your program. When it is all keyed in, go back to the beginning and check that you entered what you thought you were entering. As you + through your program, make sure that things went into the cells they were supposed to go into. One way to check this is to look in each cell to which you assigned a label and make sure that the first byte of the expected instruction is stored there.

Set the address pointer to the first byte of the first instruction of your program and push GO. The display should go out. Close the key. If you hear a tone (most unlikely), you did everything right and your program is working as advertised. No tone? Read on and we'll try to help. Push STOP. Does the display come on? If not, one of two things has gone wrong. Push RS to reset and examine cells 17FA and 17FB to see if you have correctly gotten the stop key address in there (00 1C is what you should see). That's O.K., but still no display after GO, ST. Then the most likely explanation is that your program counter has somehow, at some stage, pointed at an address instead of an op-code. Make sure first that all the bytes of your program got in where they were supposed to go. Then check your jumps (to the first byte of the target instruction) and branches -- (count forward from the first byte of the target instruction till you get to the zero offset cell -- come out even?). Suppose you have a display when you push STOP but no tone when you close the key. The address pointer will be pointing to the instruction about to be executed when you stop the computer. Push GO and ST several times alternately, noting where the machine stops. It should be stopping on one of the instructions in the loop where you are testing for key closure. Look at the direction registers; DIRA (1701) should have FE and DIRB (1703) should have 01 in it. Look in 1700 (PORTA) and see what is there. Press the key, and the display of 1700 should change from 00 to 01. If not, your key is not properly connected. Check it. Start the computer again from 0000. Press the key and stop the machine. Start and stop it a few times with the Morse key depressed. Note where it stops. It should be in the waiting loop most of the time. If not, there is a logic error in your program and you are not performing the test of the key properly or else the test of "done waiting." If you are in the waiting loop, check DIRB (1703). It should contain FF. Check PORT B (1702) and note what number it contains. GO and STOP again and look at PORT B again. The number should be different each time because you should be incrementing PORT B each time you exit from the waiting loop. If PORT B is changing almost every time you stop and start the machine, then the problem lies in your loudspeaker circuit. Check to make sure that you are connected to B_0. If all else fails, enter the following program into location 00 A0 and following.

```
00A0      A9 }  LDA # FF
   1      FF }
   2      8D }  STA 1703
   3      03 }
   4      17 }
   5      EE }  INC 1702     Steady-tone generator
   6      02 }
   7      17 }
   8      E8    INX
   9      D0 }  BNE * - 1
   A      FD }
   B      4C }  JMP 00 A0
   C      A0 }
   D      00 }
```

This should, when entered correctly in a KIM and executed, give a steady tone. <u>Remember</u>: Set address pointer to 00A0 (characters appear in that order). Press DA to go into data mode. Enter a character pair. Then press +. Then another character pair. When 00 has been entered in 00AD, press AD to go to address mode. Enter 00A0 in address pointer. Press GO (machine should be in free running condition). If you don't get a tone now, then surely there is an error in your loudspeaker circuit. Look at the transistor. Be sure you have an NPN transistor, not a PNP. Emitter goes to ground. Base connects through a 2K resistor to pin 9 (B0) of the application connector on the KIM. One side of the speaker goes to $+5_V$, the other side to the collector. Make sure the ground of your loudspeaker is attached to the ground of the microcomputer power supply (NOTE: You may use a single 5_V power supply to run both the computer and the loudspeaker). Try another transistor -- the one you have may be bad. If all else fails, find a friend who is familiar with electrical circuits and have him check the circuit for you. Tell him that pin 9 of the application connector should be generating a $1KH_Z$ square wave, about 3 volts Peak to Peak, when the computer is running this program.

Now that you have gotten your oscillator to oscillate, we can perform some experiments with it. Try changing the waiting loop constant -- the value you put in before beginning the loop.

```
       LDA    CONST
       STA    COUNTER
WAIT:  DEC    COUNTER
       BPL    WAIT

CONST: 3B
```

This is part of the code I wrote to solve this problem. The constant I'm talking about is stored in CONST and is 3B to start with. Try making this number smaller (Store 20 in CONST). What happens to the tone?

Try making CONST larger (put a 60 there). Now what happens to the tone? What happens if we put a 90 there? Does the tone go away? That is because the speaker can't follow a very high frequency. Why is the frequency very high for (CONST) = 90 but low for (CONST) = 7F? Would this still be true if we replaced the BPL instruction by A BNE? Why not? With BNE, what constant gives the lowest tone? Explain why.

4
A PIANO KEYBOARD

In this experiment we are going to provide the computer with 13 keys (one octave) and ask it to generate a tone whenever one of the keys is pressed. We will make a different tone for each key and arrange them so that they form a normal, every-day scale of the white and black keys on a piano. We will do this by asking a number of questions:

1. What key is pressed down? if any?

2. What note does this correspond to?

3. What is the time between zero-axis crossings for this note?

4. Has that much time elapsed yet? and is it time to toggle the speaker?

This may be cast as a first-level flow diagram, as shown in figure 4.1. As you will see from looking at the diagram, we are going to find out what key was depressed and then look in a table to find out how long a delay we must allow for the note associated with this key. To do this "table lookup," we going to use index registers. The KIM-1 has two index registers called the x-register and the y-register. As far as we are concerned here, these two registers are similar, and we will concentrate on the x-register for simplicity of discourse.

INDEXING

Many of the instructions of the KIM-1 can be indexed. When we wish to index an instruction, we use a special op-code to tell the computer what to do. For example, load accumulator may be indexed with either x or y: LDA, LDAX, and LDAY. Each of these has a different op-code, which one must look up.

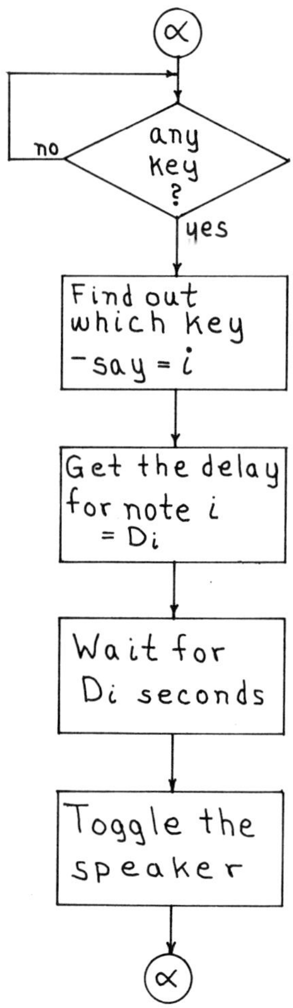

Figure 4.1 First flow diagram for the piano keyboard experiment.

As you know, an instruction like load accumulator has an address associated with the op-code that tells the computer the name of the cell from which to get the information that is to be loaded into the accumulator. For example:

"LDA 1000"

causes the contents of cell 1000 to be copied into the accumulator.

When indexing is specified, the contents of the index register are added to the address field of the instruction to form an "effective address". It is this effective address that is used to go and get a cell from memory.

Suppose index register x has the number 5 stored in it. Then

LDAX 1000 (x)=5

will cause the contents of cell 1005 to be loaded into the accumulator. If we have the number N in register x and we say

LDAX TABLE

then we get the Nth element of the table into the accumulator (see Figure 4.2).

For the octave of 13 notes from C to C' we need a table with 13 entries in it. Figure 4.3 shows two tables with information about these notes. You should observe that, since index registers can contain zero (meaning no offset from the base address of the table), all our tables will start with a zeroth element. This is called "zero-origin indexing".

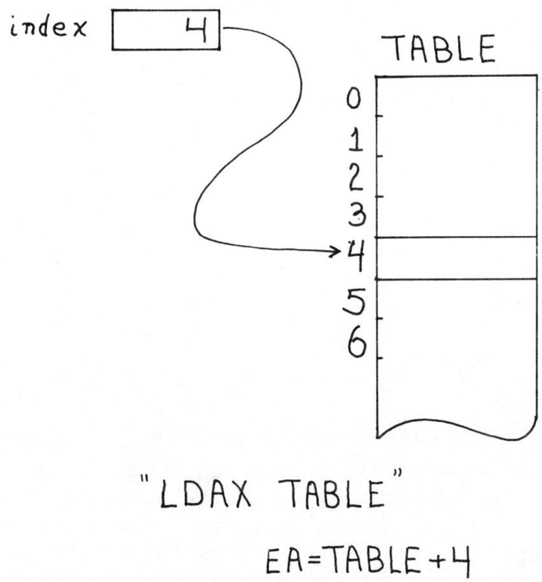

Figure 4.2 The action of an index register. Note that TABLE begins with the "zeroth" element.

	Name of note	PER: Half-period of note
NAME: 0	C	1911
1	C#	1804
2	D	1703
3	D#	1607
4	E	1517
5	F	1432
6	F#	1351
7	G	1276
8	G#	1204
9	A	1136
10	A#	1073
11	B	1012
12	C'	956

Figure 4.3 A table relating to the musical scale. Half-periods are in microseconds for the equal-tempered chromatic scale (American Standard Pitch: A_4=440).

Now, if I knew that the sixth key was pressed, I would know that it represented F# and should go through very nearly 740 vibrations per second (half-period 1351). And if I have the key's number (6) in index register x and say LDAX PER, I will get the number 1351 into the accumulator (unfortunately, 1351 won't fit into an 8-bit word or into the 8-bit accumulator, but that's another problem).

What we are going to need is a table of delays -- one for each note. Assuming that, by magical means, we have the number of the key pressed in register x; then code similar to the following will cause the machine to delay an appropriate amount for each different note:

```
        LDAX    DELAY     Get the delay associated with
                          this note.

        TAY               Transfer the contents of the
                          accumulator to register Y

WAIT:   DEY               Subtract one from the contents
                          of Y

        BNE     WAIT      Branch to wait if result is not
                          yet zero

        INC     PORTB     Toggle the speaker
```

The two instructions "DEY, BNE WAIT" constitute the delay loop. They perform the same function that DEC COUNTER, BNE WAIT did in Experiment 2. The reason we want to use an index register, rather than a location in main store, is because decrementing an index register takes only two cycles to perform while decrementing a main memory location takes six. That means that our delay loop has a smaller "grain" size and we can tune our notes more accurately. The TAY instruction is straightforward. It copies what is in the accumulator into the Y register. It is a member of the group of transfer instructions that include:

TAX	Copy Acc to x
TAY	Copy Acc to y
TXA	Copy x to Acc
TYA	Copy y to Acc

These are one-byte, two-cycle instructions. There are several other instructions that reference the index registers:

LDX *a*	Load register x from memory cell *a*
LDY *a*	Load register y from memory cell *a*
STX *a*	Store register x in memory cell *a*
STY *a*	Store register y in memory cell *a*

It turns out that the load-index register instructions can be indexed but not the store-index register instructions. But there is a restriction. We can index the load of register x only by the contents of register y and we can index the load of register y only by the contents of register x. Thus:

LDXY *a*	Load register x from memory cell *a* + (y)
LDYX *a*	Load register y from memory cell *a* + (x)

Using the LDYX DELAY instruction, we can replace the instruction pair "LDAX DELAY, TAY" shown above. Furthermore, using the LDYX, we do not disturb the contents of the accumulator in case we should need it for something.

Going back to the DEY instruction, there are four instructions of this general type:

DEX	Subtract one from x
DEY	Subtract one from y
INX	Add one to x
INY	Add one to y

-- all two-cycle, one-byte instructions.

The index registers of the KIM-1 are each 8 bits long so they can hold numbers between 0 and 255_d inclusive. When performing address modification (indexing), their contents are always treated as positive numbers; so a table beginning with entry zero may reach as far as entry 255, having a total of 256_d entries. But when incremented or decremented or moved or loaded or stored, their contents are treated like any other 8-bit number; the leftmost bit is considered to be the sign bit and you can test to see if the number is positive or negative. But this is only for the purpose of testing. When you add one or subtract one or use the number for address modification, the number is "unsigned binary" and $127_d + 1 = 128_d$.

IMMEDIATE ADDRESSING

Quite often we wish to get a number into the accumulator (or an index register) whose value is known in advance -- indeed, known at the time the program was written. Such numbers are called "constants" and we have handled this problem in the past by loading the accumulator from some memory cell in which we store the constant. This takes four memory cells to accomplish: one for the op-code, two for the address, and one for the constant. Further, there is the problem of deciding where to put the constant and then getting the right address into the instruction without making a mistake. This loading or using of constants is so frequent that the inventors of the KIM-1 provided a special form of addressing that circumvents the problem. It is called "immediate addressing." In immediate addressing, you use an alternative form of the op-code (designated by a # following the mnemonic) and then put the one-byte constant in place of the first byte of the address. The second byte of the address is not needed, so it disappears. For example, to set up the stop button address, we may write:

```
LDA #00      Put 00 in Acc
STA 17FA     Store in cell 17FA
LDA #1C      Put 1C in Acc
STA 17FB     Store in cell 17FB
```

This translates for KIM into:

```
A9 00
8D FA 17
A9 1C
8D FB 17
```

Most instructions that specify getting something from memory can use immediate addressing:

```
LDA#    A9
LDX#    A2
LDY#    A0
ADC#    69
```

Those that put things into memory (STA,STX,STY) may not.

OTHER ARITHMETIC INSTRUCTIONS

To carry out this experiment, we are going to need two more instructions that perform arithmetic or logical operations on the contents of the accumulator. Since there are only a few instructions in this group, we might as well do them all at the same time.

The first of these instructions is the "arithmetic shift left" (ASL). The word specified by the op-code is shifted left one bit position. This is equivalent to multiplying the unsigned binary integer by two. Bit 0 goes into bit 1, bit 1 goes into bit 2 and so on. The result replaces the old word. Then, if we start with:

0 0 1 0 0 1 1 0

we get: 0 1 0 0 1 1 0 0

Two questions arise: What goes into bit 0 and what becomes of the bit shifted out of bit 7 to the left? The answer to the first question is zero. With ASL we shift in zeros on the right end. That is consistent with the interpretation of the operation as a "multiply by two." The bit shifted out of the left end of the word goes into a special bit called the "carry" bit. This bit may be tested for being zero or one by the instructions BCC -- branch on carry clear (zero), and BCS -- branch on carry set (one). The carry bit is another bit in the program status word.

Ah, you say, but what happens to the old value that used to be in the carry bit? Well, that is thrown away; it evaporates. (Some people say that old used carry bits are collected in a "bit bucket" and just as new baseball players are sent to find the key to the pitcher's box, so new programmers are sometimes sent to empty the bit bucket.)

Logical Shift Right (LSR) causes the contents of the word to be moved one bit position to the right. This time zeros come into bit 7, bit 0 gets copied into the carry bit and again the old value of the carry bit gets thrown away.

Rotate Left (ROL) is more parsimonious than either of these two instructions. It finds a use for the old value of the carry bit. Namely, it puts that value into bit 0. Otherwise, it is just like ASL.

Rotate Right (ROR). Same as ROL, but in the opposite direction.

Summing up these four instructions with a picture, we have Fig. 4.4.

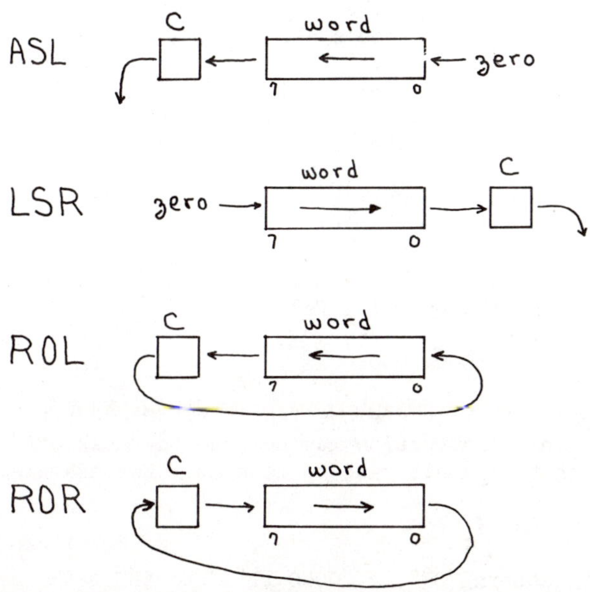

Figure 4.4 The rotate and shift instructions.

These three instructions may refer to any cell in main memory.

```
ROR   a
ROL   a
ASL   a
LSR   a
```

They may be indexed with index register x but not y:

```
RORX  a
ROLX  a
ASLX  a
LSRX  a
```

or they may refer to the accumulator:

```
RORA
ROLA
ASLA
LSRA
```

In each case the designated word is shifted or rotated and then put back in its place.

The next instructions we will consider are the logical instructions. These instructions do not consider words to be numbers, but as a collection of 8 bits. What they do to a particular bit does not influence what they do to an adjacent bit. For these instructions, we take a group of bits from memory and another group from the accumulator. We perform the required operation and put the result back into the accumulator.

AND. If bit M_i and bit A_i are one, then the result is one. Otherwise the result is zero. The symbol for AND is $\wedge$.

$$A \leftarrow M \wedge A$$

If the initial bit patterns are

Acc 0011 0011

M 0101 0101,

the result of an AND operation is

Acc 0001 0001

Only where both bits are one (as in bit 0 and bit 4) do we end up with a one. This instruction may be used to "mask off" bits in the accumulator that we don't want to look at. For example:

```
AND # OF
```

uses the bit pattern "OF" or "0000 1111" to AND with the contents of the accumulator. It guarantees that the four high-order bits of the accumulator will be _zero_ and the bottom four will remain the same. This instruction may be immediate addressed (AND#), directly addressed (AND), or indexed by either _x_ or _y_ (ANDX, ANDY).

_OR_. The OR instruction called "ORA" leaves a _one_ in the accumulator wherever there was a _one_ in A or in M (or for that matter in both). Its symbol is $\vee$, which is the AND symbol inverted. This inversion of the symbol is quite reasonable since with AND you get a _one_ only if both operands were _one_ and with OR you get a _zero_ only if both operands were _zero_.

Applying the ORA to the bit patterns

```
Acc   0011 0011

M     0101 0101,
```

we get

```
Acc   0111 0111
```

This instruction has the same options as AND:

```
ORA#
ORA
ORAX
ORAY
```

The _exclusive or_ instruction EOR gives us a _one_ wherever the two operands differ and a _zero_ where they are the same. Thus:

```
Acc   0011 0011

M     0101 0101
```

under the EOR instruction gives

```
Acc   0110 0110
```

Again, its addressing options are the same as for AND:

```
EOR#
EOR
EORX
EORY
```

and its symbol is $\neq$ or sometimes $\oplus$ (called "ring sum").

EOR may be used to complement the bits of the accumulator and replace _ones_ with _zeros_ and _zeros_ with _ones_. This may be done conveniently by using:

```
EOR# FF.
```

After executing any one of these three instructions, you may test for all zeros in the accumulator (BEQ or BNE), or you may test to see whether the leftmost bit (bit 7) is zero or one (BPL or BMI, respectively).

EXTERNAL CONNECTIONS

Now that we have these instructions out of the way, we are ready to get on with designing the experiment. We need 13 normally open switches and one loudspeaker with amplifier. Counting eight I/O lines in PORTA plus seven in PROTB, we find we will have one line left over. I choose to connect things as shown in Figure 4.5. Notes C through G are connected to PORTA -- lines A_7 through A_0. Note G# is connected to B_7 and notes A through C are connected to B_5 through B_2. The loudspeaker amplifier is connected to B_0. Therefore, we must make all PORTA lines be input (place the pattern 00 in DIRA); and, to make the upper six bits of PORTB be input while the lower two are output, we place the pattern 03 in DIRB. Note that we will assume that the nonexistent B_6 is an input bit and will have to allow for this later.

The way the keys are arranged, they are normally zero and go to one when pushed. So we will pick up the word from PORTA, put it in the accumulator, and see whether it is all zeros. Suppose it is not all zeros. Then one of the keys C-G has been pressed. Right away we can test bit 7 of the accumulator to see if that was the key pressed. If not, we will shift the accumulator left one position and check that bit. If still no, we keep on shifting till we get a one in bit 7. We are guaranteed that this will happen because we know that not all the bits of the accumulator are zero. Everytime we shift, we will keep count of how many shifts we have done in index register x. Once we have identified which key was pressed, we can jump off to a place named FOUND to look up the delay associated with that key. We will wait out the delay, toggle the speaker and go back to see if any key is down.

If we didn't find a key in PORTA, we will look in PORTB to see if any of those was pressed. To get rid of the phantom key (B_6) and the lower two bits of PORTB that are output bits, we can mask off those positions using an AND immediate instruction. Better do that before testing B for nonzero. If B is all zeros (after masking), we can go back to test A again. If B is not all zeros, then one of the keys G#-C' was pressed. We repeat the shift and count instructions (remembering to start the count with 8 this time so we don't confuse G# with C, etc.) until we identify the key. Then we can go to FOUND to look up the delay, do the wait and toggle the speaker.

Note that, in our counting procedures, we must test and count the phantom key (B_6), so entry 9 of our delay table will refer to B_6 while entries A-D hex refer to the higher real keys (A-C').

Before reading further, draw a flow diagram of this program.

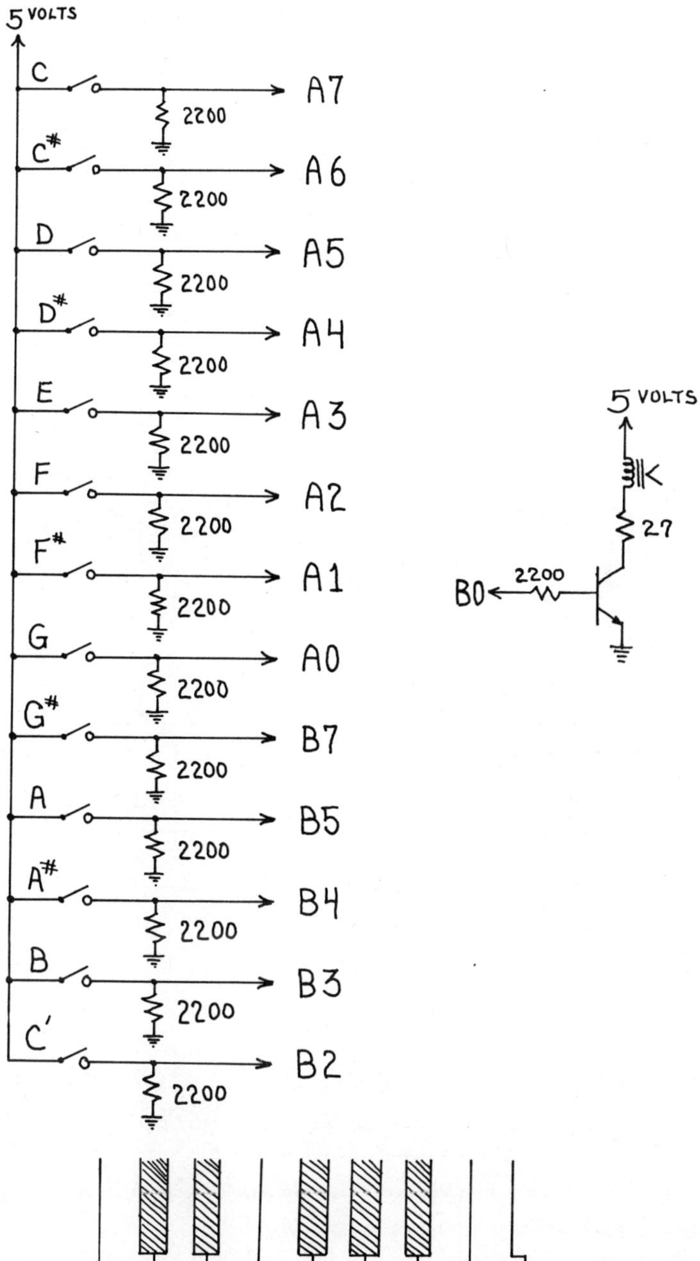

Figure 4.5 Connections for the piano keyboard experiment.

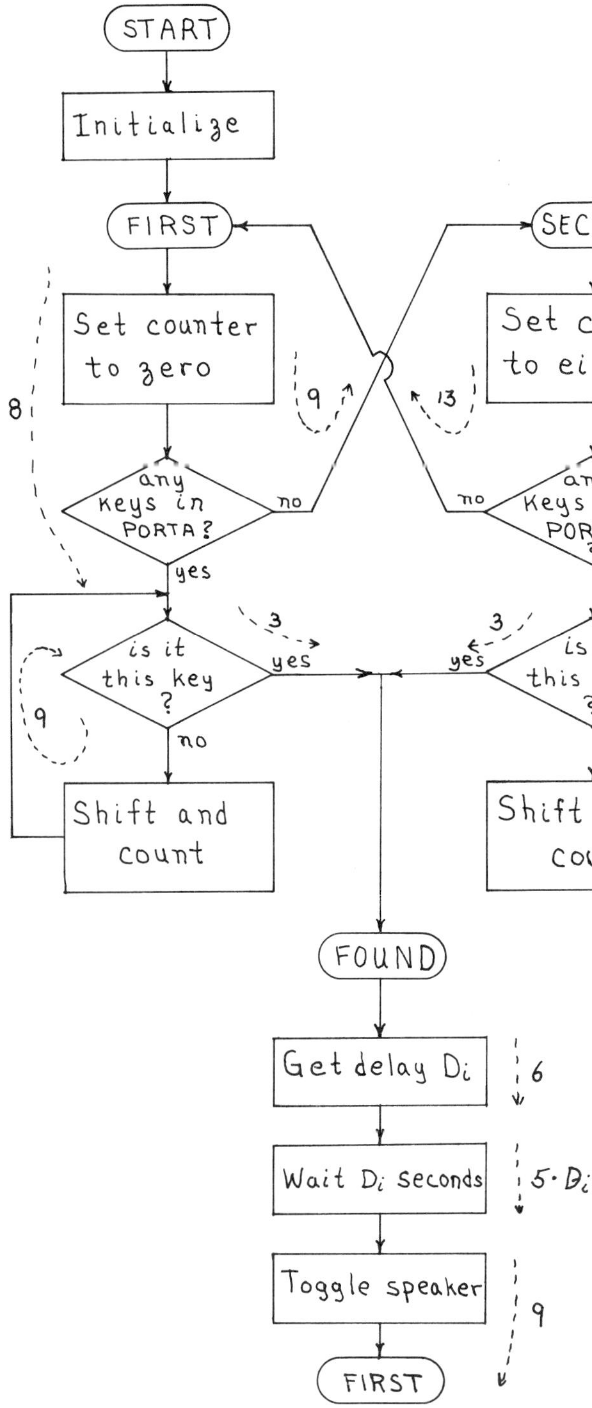

Figure 4.6 Flow diagram for piano keyboard.

Figure 4.6 shows my flow diagram. Given the discussion that we have just gone over, I don't think we need to spend any more time on this diagram. Taking one of the flow diagrams (mine or yours), proceed to write the code for this program, and be sure to fill in the number of cycles each instruction takes because we are going to need that information to compute the delays.

Each cycle represents one microsecond (one millionth of a second -- 10^{-6} sec) of time. Remember that a branch takes three cycles if you do branch and two if you don't. Counting up cycles for various pathways, as shown next to the paths on the flow diagram, we find that it takes a minimum of 11 microseconds (cycles) to get from FIRST to FOUND if the note was C and 9 microseconds more for each note higher between C and G.

If the note is in PORTB, it takes 9+12+3 or 24 microseconds to determine the first note G# and 9 extra microseconds for each succeeding note (including the phantom). Getting the delay value, toggling the speaker, and jumping back to the beginning (at FIRST) takes another 15 microseconds in my program. Yours, of course, may be different in its details.

Adding all these times together, we have the following base values that need to be subtracted from the delay times for each note.

		Fixed delays
	C	26
	C#	35
	C	44
Port A	D#	53
	E	62
	F	71
	F#	80
	G	89
	G#	39
	phantom	48
Port B	A	57
	A#	66
	B	75
	C'	84

Using a single index register, we can loop around our delay code up to 256 times. My first program took 5 microseconds per loop, or a maximum delay of 256 x 5=1280 microseconds (cycles). Finding the first key (C) takes 26 microseconds, so, with a full delay, I could wait 1280 + 26 or 1306 microseconds between each toggle. That was too short a time, so I added a three-cycle instruction to my loop, which then looked like:

```
WAIT: JMP W1

W1  : DEY

      BNE WAIT
```

The jump to W1 is inserted just to use up 3 microseconds. That makes the basic loop time 8 microseconds. Taking the half-period of C of 1911, less the fixed delay for C (26), we get 1885 microseconds. At 8 microseconds per loop that means

$$\frac{1885}{8} = 236 \text{ times around the loop.}$$

Computing (by hand, of course) the number of loops for the other notes, we get the following table:

Note	Half-period	Fixed Delay	Time in loop	Number of loops* in decimal	8 microsec/ loop in hex
C	1911	26	1885	236	EC
C#	1804	35	1769	221	DD
D	1703	44	1659	207	CF
D#	1607	53	1554	194	C2
E	1517	62	1455	182	B6
F	1432	71	1361	170	AA
F#	1351	80	1271	159	9F
G	1276	89	1187	148	94
G#	1204	39	1165	146	92
Phantom key	----	48	----	---	--
A	1136	57	1079	135	87
A#	1073	66	1007	126	7E
B	1012	75	937	117	75
C'	956	84	872	109	6D

* Note all numbers of loops are rounded to the nearest integer. It is hard to go around a loop a nonintegral number of times.

The final column translates the number of loops into a hex number.

Naturally enough, if your code differs from mine substantially, you will get different values for the delay constants and, consequently, the number of loops.

DEBUGGING

Now you have written your code and walked through it by hand (pretending to be the clerk), and translated it into machine code and checked _that_ twice, and remembered to put the least significant portion of the address in field 2 and the more significant portion in field 3, and typed it in and checked that by stepping through with our + key, and found no mistakes and checked that the last instruction ended up where you thought it was going to. And it doesn't make pretty music like it was supposed to. What do you do now? Now you find out that at least one of the above statements is in error.

First, let's check the hardware so we can be sure of that before going on. You can check the loudspeaker by the same code you used to check it in experiment 2. Load in 00A0 - 00AD the hex numbers: A9, FF, 8D, 03, 17, EE, 02, 17, E8, D0, FD, 4C, A0, 00, and transfer to 00A0. That should generate a steady tone and will indicate that the speaker is O.K.

Go into single-step and execute the first few instructions of your program that set the stop key address and initialize the direction registers. Look in DIRA (1701). It should have "00". DIRB (1703) should have "03". Yes? Now look in 1700 (PORTA) and press the keys one at a time and see:

No key	00
C	80
C#	40
D	20
D#	10
E	08
F	04
F#	02
G	01

In 1702 (PORTB), you should see:

No key	00	
G#	80	
A	20	Remember the phantom key
A#	10	
B	08	
C'	04	

You may find the low-order two bits are either (or both) one (depending on how you toggled last), so do a mental AND operation to wipe them out. For instance, if no key gives you the pattern 03, then G# will be 83, B will be 0B, and C# will be 07. If you find that hard to do, just store a "00" there. Push DA and 00.

There are too many things that could have gone wrong to try to go through them one by one. You will have to narrow down things a bit on your own.

Do some of the keys work and the others give sour notes?

Then you probably made a mistake calculating your delay constants. Check them.

Do the keys on PORTA work but not PORTB? or vice versa?

Then look at the section of code that doesn't work. Compare it with the section that does. Did you remember to mask out B_6,B_1, and B_0, using AND# and BC?

No sound at all?

Look in 1702 (PORTB), observe the pattern in the low-order two bits. Run your program a few seconds with a key pressed. Look in 1702 again. The low-order bits different? Then you are toggling the speaker once in a while but not at an audible rate. Change the JMP FIRST instruction at the end of FOUND to be a JMP FOUND. Now when you push the stop key you can examine (and/or change) the values in the index registers by looking (and/or depositing a new value) in cells

00F4	Contains y
00F5	Contains x

Try putting some numbers in there, starting your program at FOUND, and seeing whether those numbers change.

Try replacing the first instruction of FOUND by what is called a "dynamic halt" -- that is a jump to itself -- in this case.

```
FOUND:  JMP FOUND.
```

Now begin your program from the beginning. Don't press any keys yet. Stop the program. It should have stopped in either FIRST or SECOND looking for a key. Restart the program and press key C. Stop the program. You should be executing the dynamic halt at FOUND. Anywhere else is a mistake. If you are in the right place see what the index register you were using as a key counter says. In my program, 0 corresponds to C, 1 to D, etc. Does it work for both ports? Note G# gives you 8 and A gives you $A(10_d)$.

Did you remember to load the index register first and then get the contents of the port? The test instructions operate on the last piece of data moved or computed, so the LDA PORTA (or PORTB) must just precede the BEQ or whatever.

Puzzle hard. It's probably some simple idiotic error. When I wrote this program, I mis-translated an op-code and fell into FOUND through a side door that wasn't supposed to exist. It took me half an hour to find the error.

As a last resort, compare your code with mine (see Appendix) and see if I did any thing you forgot to do. See if you can understand exactly why I used each instruction. Believe me, there was a reason. Then look at your code again to see what the differences are.

Good luck!

5 KEYBOUNCE

Everyone is familiar with what happens if one holds a rubber ball a few feet above a hard floor and lets it go. It bounces. And if you leave it alone, it bounces a few times with decreasing amplitude and then lies quietly there on the floor. Most people know that, when you close an electrical switch, you bring two pieces of metal together so that current can flow between them. Few people know, or for that matter, care, that these two pieces of metal will bounce off each other a few times before coming to rest in firm contact. All "snap action" switches (like wall switches) and most pushbutton switches exhibit this behavior every time they are closed. The reason that this has remained unknown to the general public is not due to a conspiracy to hide a product defect on the part of the United Switch Makers of America. Rather it is due to the fact that, for most switches, the last bounce is over in less than a couple of milliseconds. If a switch took a second to settle down, you could see the lights flicker; but the normal human being can't see a fluorescent tube go on and off at 120 times per second, and that is on the order of <u>ten times slower</u> than the flicker introduced by bouncing contacts.

But to a computer operating with a one microsecond clock, a millisecond is a long time, and the average human key-push, which lasts between a tenth of a second and one second, seems like forever.

We use key closures in two ways when we communicate with a computer. In the first way, we use the key closure to trigger off some event. We use it as a start signal. Once we detect the closure of the key, we take off and do something and never come back to look at that switch again -- or at least not for some great while. In this case we couldn't care less about switch bounce or the duration of the push. The first sign that the switch closed is all we care about.

But consider the case where we are monitoring a calculator keyboard within a computer. When we detect a <u>new</u> character being entered, we shift all the old characters left one place, and put the new character in on the righthand end of the "accumulator." If it is a function key, we jump off and execute the function. Since the computer is very much faster than the human key-pusher, it can do what it has to do and get back to look at the keyboard again long before the human can get his finger off the key. Well, clearly we want each key press to enter just one character, so when the computer comes back to scan the keyboard again we don't want it to say, "Aha! <u>Another</u> seven!" and enter <u>that</u> into the right end of its accumulator. But on the other hand we must allow for the individual, strange as he may be, who does want to enter the number 77. We can't require that each digit accepted be different from its predecessor in order to be recognized.

What is usually done is to require that, in order to enter the number 77, the user must push the key, release it, and then push it a second time. This way the computer can "see" a seven, enter it once and then ignore that "most recent key" until it goes back to zero. Only when it changes from open (zero) to closed (one) will the machine treat the <u>one</u> as representing <u>another</u> character to be entered. What we have said here can be summed up in a flow diagram (see Fig. 5.1). When we detect the fact that no keys at all are now being pushed, we make the "state" of the machine be "clear." Perhaps we store a <u>zero</u> in a cell called STATE. Then, when we detect a key, the first thing we do is examine STATE. If it is <u>zero</u>, we know this is a "new" key closure and we should do something about it. The first thing we should do is make the state be "busy" -- perhaps by storing a <u>one</u> in STATE. Then we accept the key closure, do whatever is required by the character the user entered, and then go back to scan the keyboard again. If the sluggardly user still has his finger on the key we ignore him until he releases it. We can refine this just a bit if we so desire. In STATE we can keep not just a record of the fact that "some" key was pushed but a record of <u>what</u> key was pushed. We can, in fact, store the "most recently accepted character" there. Then, when we go back to scan the keyboard, we will accept any key <u>except</u> the one stored in STATE. If we can do this (and, depending on how the keys are connected to the computer, we may or may not be able to handle two keys pushed at one time), we are said to have "two-key roll-over."

Now what does all this have to do with key bounce? Well, look back at your code for experiment 3 (the piano keyboard) or consider the following brief segment of code:

```
                                        # of cycles

      SCAN:      LDA     PORTA          (4)    Get the keyboard
                 BNE     GOT A KEY      (2/3)  See if it is all zero
                 STA     STATE          (4)    Yes it was, clear STATE
                 JMP     SCAN           (3)    Go scan again
   GOT A KEY:    LDA     STATE          (4)    Get the state
                 BNE     SCAN           (2)    If busy go to SCAN

                                                      Accept the key
```

It takes seven microseconds to arrive at GOTAKEY, and 13 to detect all-zero keyboard and clear STATE, and maybe another 50 or so to "accept" the character. If the key is bouncing along merrily, sometimes closed and sometimes open for a millisecond, we are practically guaranteed to come back, find it open, declare the keyboard "clear," and then catch it as a "new" key on the next bounce.

To avoid this problem we should insert a delay after accepting a character and before going back to scan again. If we delay long enough, we won't get back until after the bounces are all over; but if we delay too long, the keyboard will be sluggish and exasperating to use. So it would be nice to know how long the average key bounces

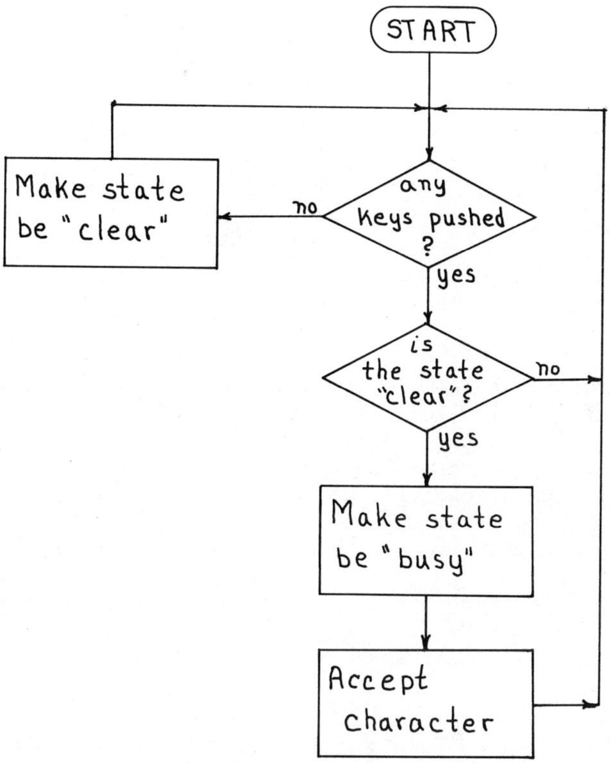

Figure 5.1 A flow diagram for a keyboard scanning routine.

so we can select a reasonable delay. If we insert such a delay, or if we remove the bounces by electronic means, we are said to "debounce the keyboard."

Since the computer can detect key bounces (otherwise we wouldn't be concerned with them), let us use it as a tool to discover how long the bouncing continues.

We will hook up one key into any of the inputs of PORTA or we can use the notes C-G of the hardware of Chapter 4. The key might be hooked up as shown in Fig. 5.2.

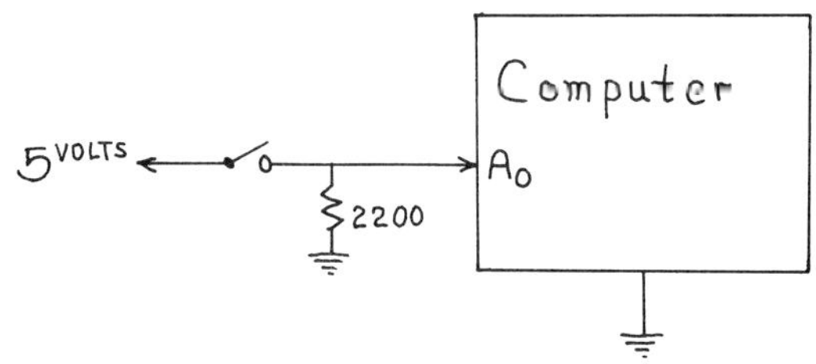

Figure 5.2 The circuit for a key.

First, of course, we should initialize the stop address and make PORTA be an input port (at least the key we want to look at). Next we should wait until the key goes first to one, because there is no point in collecting data while the operator is out for coffee. Once we see the first sign of closure, we should start recording (in the computer's memory) the state of the switch at regular time intervals until we run out of space or until all the action is over.

Before reading further, draw a flow diagram of this process.

Now examine the flow diagram in Fig. 5.3.

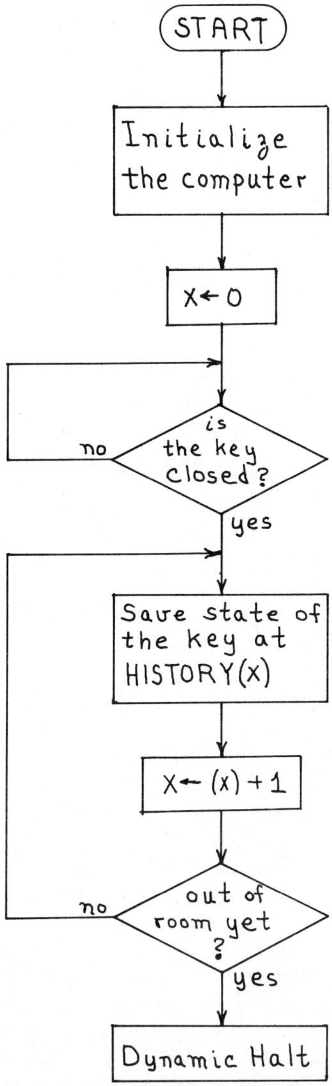

Figure 5.3 Flow diagram of the program to capture the history of key bouncing.

Since the bounce occurs very quickly, we would like to take samples as close together as possible, and we should take as many as possible so that we can be sure that we have caught the last bounce.

We need to write a fast sampling loop, and we need to know how much memory is available in KIM-1 for recording information.

KIM-1 MEMORY MAP

In order to get some limits on how much data we can collect and on how much space our program can take, we need to know how big the KIM-1 memory is and what it is used for.

The advertising brochures tell you that KIM-1 has 1K bytes of memory. The K here stands for 2^{10} or 1024. KIM-1 has 16 address lines so it can reference one of 2^{16}, or 64K, cells of memory. The names (addresses) of these cells would be 0000_h through $FFFF_h$. But the KIM-1 you are working with probably has much fewer cells than this. The standard, off-the-shelf KIM-1 has 1K of read/write memory cells assigned to locations 0000 through 03FF (see Fig. 5.4). Of these cells, the ones between 00EF and 00FF are reserved for the KIM-1 operating system, and should not be used by the programmer, in the ordinary course of events. Of this set, the ones we might be concerned with are the cells in which the machine context is stored:

00EF	Program counter low byte
00F0	Program counter high byte
00F1	Status register
00F2	Stack pointer - described later
00F3	Accumulator
00F4	Y index register
00F5	X index register

Beginning in cell 01FF and working downward toward cell 0100 there is the "stack." We will discuss some uses of the stack in the next section, and other uses will be postponed to the next experiment. At this point it will suffice to say that, if the user avoids subroutines, interrupts, and stacking operations, he can use page 1 (0100-01FF) to hold instructions or data as he sees fit.

All of page 2 (0020-02FF) and all of page 3 (0300-03FF) are always available to the programmer.

The reason memory is broken into "pages" of 256_d bytes is that addresses are stored in two bytes of memory called the page number of the line number. An additional 108 bytes of read/write memory are available at addresses 1780 through 17EB, inclusive, in case you need them. They are just like the bytes in 0000-03FF and may be read or written at will. 17EC through 17FF are reserved for the KIM-1 system.

We are already familiar with the input-output ports A and B and the port direction registers that occupy the four cells from 1700-1703. There are two additional ports (C and D) that occupy cells 1740 through 1743 for PORTC, DIRC, PORTD, and DIRD. C has 8 bits and D has 7, missing D_6 just as B_6 was missed. These two ports are used by the system to scan the hex keyboard and drive the 7 segment

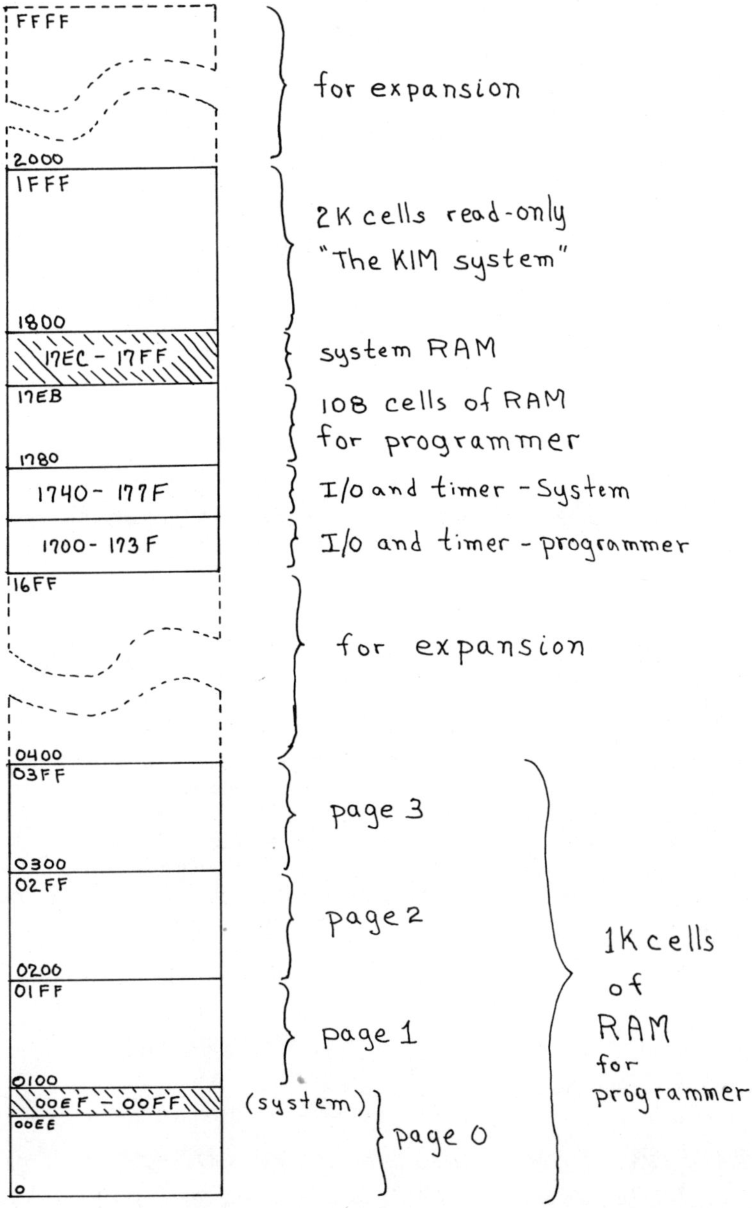

Figure 5.4 The KIM memory map.

displays, but may be used by the programmer if these devices are taken into account or if he wishes to use the displays or onboard keys.

In cell addresses 1704-170F there is an interval timer that we will discuss later, and in 1744-174F there is a second timer.

In cells 1800-1FFF there are 2K cells of read-only memory. These cells hold the KIM-1 operating system. This system is made up of many subroutines and some of these subroutines can be used by the ordinary programmer to great profit. (see Appendix B)

The remaining addresses (0400-16FF and 2000-FFFF) are not connected to anything in a regular KIM-1. Don't use them. Some of them decode as "real" addresses and will clobber your programs.

Looking back at fig. 5.3, we see that 0000-03FF are available to the user (you). But the KIM people stole cells 00EF-00FF and, in return, gave you cells 1780-17EB. Why didn't they make life simple, leaving that block in page zero for the user, and eating up a few of the cells in page 17 instead? The answer to that question is contained in the next section.

ZERO-PAGE ADDRESSING

Normal absolute addressing requires three bytes to hold the op-code, the low byte of the address, and the high byte of the address, as, for example:

```
AD )
03 }   LDA 0103
01 )
```

Now all machines can become too small for the programs we wish to put into them. As an aid in compressing your KIM-1 programs the designers included something called "zero-page addressing," which takes only two bytes instead of three; but it requires that the cell addressed be in page zero -- as you might have figured out from the name. Like the other addressing options, this requires a different version of the op-code for each instruction, but it does save one byte per instruction and one cycle of execution time.

```
LDAZ      03 means the same thing as:

LDA       0003
```

but the first translates as:

```
A5
03
```

and the second as:

```
AD
03
00
```

All the loads, stores, and arithmetic/logic instructions have this address option, which we will symbolize by adding a Z to the instruction mnemonic. We can also index (register x only) this by adding the letters ZX to the mnemonic.

I do not believe that the beginning programmer, or indeed most programmers, should use these options because it is just one more thing to remember and the Lord knows there is already more than enough. So if you want to use these options look up the op-codes for them in your machine manual.

But in writing the operating system, they were faced with strict limits on the amount of space available. They chose to use page-zero addressing to save space. That is why the cells from 00EF through 00FF belong to the system.

If you think you are going to be crowded and you can't afford more read/write memory (sometimes called RAM), then go with God and have a good time.

SAVING THE HISTORY OF THE KEY BOUNCES

If you can remember that far back we were looking for a place to store the history of the key bounces -- and we wanted to take samples fast.

Suppose, for openers, we decide to keep the history in page 3. The following code will surely capture the history, but it has some severe drawbacks.

```
        LDA PORTA
        STA 0300
        LDA PORTA
        STA 0301
        LDA PORTA
        STA 0302
           .
           .
           .
        LDA PORTA
        STA 03FF
HERE:   JMP HERE
```

It is fast. No doubt about that; LDA takes 4 cycles and STA the same, so we can get a new sample every 8 microseconds. But each instruction pair takes up 6 bytes of storage, and 256 pairs will eat up 1536 cells -- about 500 more than we have available. Never mind the tedium of punching all those characters in. We could probably write an "echo" program that would start with one copy of the pair of instructions and make 255 more copies -- each with a proper storage address. If we plan to capture 256 samples, we have only 768 cells (not counting the forbidden cells) in which to put our program. Using page-zero addressing and moving the history down to page-zero would speed things up to 6 microseconds per sample, and cut the size down to 4 bytes per sample, or 1024 cells for instructions. Better, but not good.enough.

So let's try indexing. That will save space and programming time, at the expense of execution time.

Assuming an initial value of 0 in x:

```
                              time
LOOP:  LDA       PORTA         (4)
       STAX      0300          (5)
       INX                     (2)
       BNE       LOOP          (3)
HERE:  JMP       HERE          14
```

will do the job and take 14 microseconds per pass. Each time we go around the loop, it is called a "pass" or, more formally, an "iteration."

Can we speed things up any? Yes, if we are willing to learn about the stack; but don't be too disappointed if the gain (in the end) doesn't seem worth the effort.

THE STACK

A "stack" of information is just what it sounds like. Imagine one word written per index card and a pile of cards on the table. When we want to enter a new word in the stack we obtain a clean unused card, write the word on it, and put it onto the pile on the table.

If the pile is stacked up neatly, the only word we can read is the top one. The others are hidden. We can add new cards to the stack (with new words on them, presumably). This is called "pushing the stack." Or we can take cards off the stack and throw them away. This is called "pulling the stack."

In the KIM-1, the stack is stored in page 1. For reasons known only to Oog, the original Neanderthal computer designer, stacks are always stored "backwards" in memory, beginning with a high address and working down to a low address. There is an 8-bit control register called the "stack pointer" (abbreviated "S"), which points to the next free space on the stack. This register begins in cell 01FF and works down to 0100, but the user may change the value in S whenever he wants.

Of course, you may address the cells of page 1 in any of the normal ways we have discussed before, but when treated as a stack, communication is via the accumulator. The instruction "Push accumulator on stack" (PHA) takes 1 byte of storage and 3 cycles to execute. Operation is as follows:

PHA The contents of the accumulator are copied into the cell of page 1 pointed at by the stack pointer S.

<u>Then</u> the stack pointer is decremented by one:

$$(Acc) \rightarrow M_S, \quad (S)-1 \longrightarrow S$$

Since the stack pointer is decremented <u>after</u> being used, it is always pointing at the next empty cell of the stack. Supposing I load the accumulator with the number 1 and push it onto the stack. Then I load the number 2 and push that onto the stack, and so on, until I have pushed six numbers onto the stack. Then Figure 5.5 shows what the stack will look like.

If I were now to push the number 172 onto the stack, it would go into cell 01F9 and the stack pointer would be changed to F8.

To get things off the stack and back into the accumulator, we use the "pull accumulator from stack" instruction (PLA). It behaves like this.

PLA Add one to the stack pointer. <u>Then</u> copy the contents of the cell of page 1 pointed at by S, into the accumulator:

$$(S) + 1 \longrightarrow S, \quad (M_S) \longrightarrow Acc$$

If we were to "pull" from the stack of Fig. 5.5, the stack pointer would be changed to FA and then the contents of cell 01FA (that is, "6") would be copied into the accumulator.

<u>Note</u>: If the user tries to push more than 256 elements onto the stack, the stack is perfectly willing to accept them. But since it can only address cells in page 1, it has to overwrite some of the earliest elements in order to store the new ones. Supposing the stack pointer is initialized to FF; then the first element put on the stack goes in cell 01FF. The 256th element added (no pulls in between times) goes in cell 0100. The 257th element goes in 01FF over the first, and the 258th goes in 01FE, etc. So you can store a maximum of 256 elements in the stack. You can do thousands of pushes and pulls without getting into trouble, provided you never get more than 256 pushes ahead.

When you put items on the stack or take them off, it is the <u>last one put on</u> that gets pulled off first. For this reason, stacks are sometimes called LIFO Stacks (last-in-first-out).

In addition to pushing and pulling the accumulator, one may push and pull the status register. Since we haven't yet studied the status register in detail, we will simply note that fact and move on.

There are two instructions that allow the user to load the stack pointer or to get it into position so that he can see it. These are:

TXS transfer <u>x</u> to stack pointer

and TSX Transfer stack pointer to <u>x</u>.

To put all this together, we need one more item of information. The KIM-1 operating system also uses the stack. It uses 8 bytes of the stack whenever you push the stop button. We'll see why in the next experiment. We don't want those 8 bytes written over our history. So the thing to do is to count down the number of entries in an index register and, if we begin with $256-8=248_d$ in the index register, we will quit while there is still room for KIM to use the last (0107-0100) 8 bytes of page 1. Some code to use the stack to

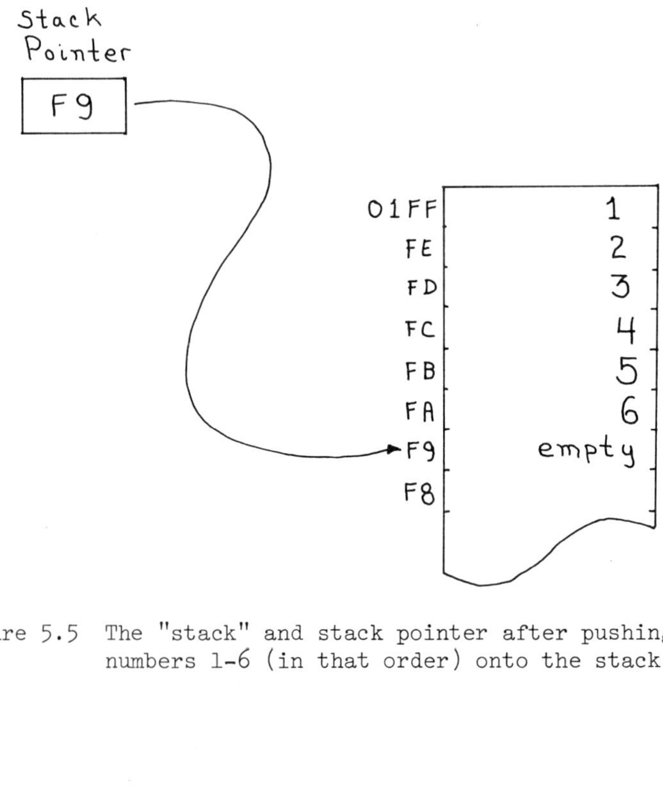

Figure 5.5 The "stack" and stack pointer after pushing the numbers 1-6 (in that order) onto the stack.

store history looks like this:

```
INITIAL:  LDX# FF
          TXS             Set stack pointer
          LDX# F8         (248 decimal)

LOOP:     LDA 1700           (4)
          PHA                (3)
          DEX                (2)
          BNE LOOP           (3)
                            12 cycles
```

This takes 12 microseconds per sample, and is not much faster than the scheme we used before. But you were warned about that.

ADDED FILLIPS

Another handy thing to do might be, after you have recorded the history, to look back upward along the history to find the last zero. You could use X to do that search and find the value of X in cell 00F5 after you push stop.

When you are reading the history out it will be convenient to use the + key. Remember the stack will be stored inverted, earliest entries at 01FF and later ones downward in store.

- Write the program to perform this experiment -

Don't forget to initialize the stack pointer to FF.

Time your sampling routine to see how long it is between samples. This will calibrate the time of the last "open," which is what you want to know.

Record on paper the history of opens and closeds for several button pushes. Try teasing the button closed as slowly as you can. Try pounding it home smartly. Try several times with medium strength. If you have more than one button hooked up, try using a couple of them to see if they all bounce alike.

Allowing, say, a 50-percent safety margin, how long should you wait if you wish to avoid false opens (debounce these switches)?

EXTRA CREDIT

As long as you have this nice button-watching routine set up, you might modify it so that you can test humans to see in how short a time they can get on and off a button. For starters, I suggest a 1-millisecond interval between samples.

6
A COMBINATION LOCK

In this experiment, we are going to simulate a combination lock. There will be four push buttons to act as inputs and four lights to display the "state of the system." In order to get lots of input combinations, we will allow the user to push several buttons at a time. We start off with light A on and B, C, and D off. The user presses some combination of buttons. If it is "wrong," nothing happens, If it is "right," light A goes out, light B comes on, and we wait for a new input. Now, correct input advances the state to C and wrong returns us to A. Similarly in C, correct advances us to D (door open), and wrong drops us back to A. From state D, any input at all sends us to A (door closed and locked).

It is possible to draw a "state diagram" to represent these transitions, of which Fig. 6.1 is an example.

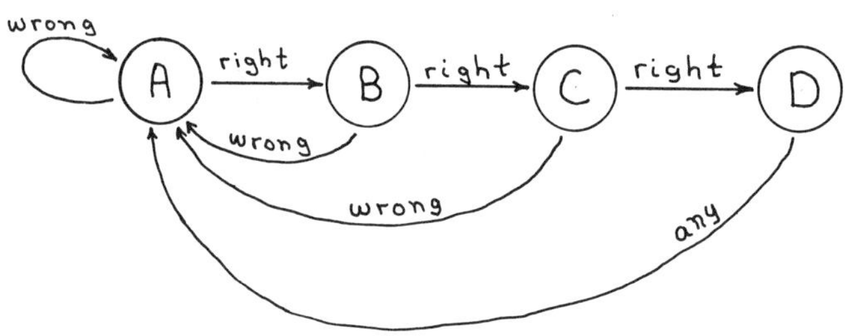

Figure 6.1 A state diagram of the combination lock.

You will immediately notice the similar "feel" of state diagrams and computer flow diagrams. The state diagrams tell us <u>what</u> is supposed to happen, whereas the flow diagrams tell us <u>how</u> it is supposed to happen. Good programming technique calls for the use of both types of presentation. When approaching a problem, you should first write down in words, or using a state diagram, or both, what it is that you are trying to accomplish. Once you have a clear statement of the problem, with all possible pathways included, then you are ready to begin to consider how to accomplish these goals. I find flow diagrams helpful. Many other professional programmers do, but many do not.

When you have a situation with complicated transfer of control from one section of a program to another, then flow diagrams are most useful. If you have straight-through control flow (one path), then perhaps a prose statement of what is to be done (or a mathematical equation) is more concise and meaningful than a long column of boxes with cryptic notes containing "shorthand". The point is that even very simple-sounding programs can become too large to hold in your head in their entirety, so you need a way of keeping your ideas on paper. This is intrapersonal communication -- "you to yourself." Next, you may want to describe your program to another person -- this is interpersonal communication. Finally, you may want to have a description of your program so that you can refer to it next week or next year. You say that you could never forget how cleverly you solved this gorgeously complex problem? Are you sure? Tell me what this piece of code does:

```
0020: BD
   1: 24
   2: 00
   3: A8
   4: 88
   5: D0
   6: FC
   7: EE
   8: 02
   9: 17
```

Not too clear? Perhaps a note or two in the margin might be of some help? We just went over it in Chapter 4. Try page 42.

When your flow diagram (or whatever) is complete, then and only then should you get out the coding sheets and begin writing instructions.

As you grow more sophisticated at programming, you will, of course, look ahead in the process and have a fairly good idea of what the code is going to look like, long before you start to write it. You may even have scribbled, on the backs of old envelopes, some parts of the code. Very often some feature (or lack of a feature) in the machine you are using will allow you to write more compact or faster-executing programs if you just structure your data in fashion B rather than the "obvious" fashion A. In the beginning you won't see these things until you get into the coding process. When you do see them, you have to choose whether to continue on or to back up and start over. Both answers are acceptable. In this book, we are much more concerned with getting a problem solved than we are with providing an elegant solution. There will be times, however, when speed and size (of program) are important. Then you must use the best approach you can think of, find, steal, or otherwise obtain. The best morals for the programmer are:

1. Think first -- code later.
2. Simple is beautiful.

Look back at Fig. 6.1; it should be fairly obvious how you should go about constructing a flow diagram. But before we do that I want to introduce the concept of a subroutine, which will greatly simplify the program. We are going to use one subroutine to monitor the input pushbuttons and another to delay a fraction of a second after the first button-push to allow closure of any other buttons the user wants to push for this particular input combination.

SUBROUTINES

A "subroutine" is a small program designed to perform a specific task that is needed by another program called the "main program." Typically, the main program will need this task performed several times, from different places in the main program. One example is a "delay subroutine," that would wait a certain amount of time and then return control to the main program. This subroutine might be called from several places in the main program. Typically, each place that calls the subroutine would like a different amount of delay. In order to cause this to happen, the main program must have a way of telling the subroutine how long a delay it desires. This is called "parameter passing." We will look at some alternative methods in just a moment.

Most microprocessors have a hardware stack and KIM-1 is no exception. This stack is used to store the return address. If we transfer control to a subroutine from point A of the main program, and from point B of the main program, the subroutine must be able to go back to point A in the first instance, and back to point B in the second. Two instructions are provided, which utilize the stack to achieve this purpose. They are:

JSR Target

Jump to subroutine. The address (two bytes) of the last byte of the JSR instruction is pushed onto the stack. Then the Target address is placed in the program counter so that the next instruction will be taken from the Target cell -- presumably the beginning of the subroutine.

RTS

Pull the two-byte address off the top of the stack and place it in the program counter. Then increment the program counter by one.

Let us consider how these are used. Suppose that, in location 1000, we wish to jump to a subroutine in location 1234. When we have finished executing the subroutine, we want to return to location 1003 -- the address of the instruction following the JSR. Suppose there is another call for the subroutine in location 1010 (see Fig. 6.2). We wish to execute the instructions in the main program in order, with two "sidesteps" to execute the instructions of the subroutine. We could achieve the same effect by leaving out the JSR and RTS and just copying the subroutine code into the main program twice, once at point A and again at point B. Of course, the total amount of code we would have to write would be greater; and, if space is at a premium, we would be wasting storage space.

When we execute the JSR in cells 1000, 1001, 1002, the machine first puts the return address (1002) onto the stack. If this is the first use of the stack and we initialized it to FF, then it would store:

01FF	10
01FE	02
01FD	Next free cell on the stack

Then the JSR will put 1234 into the program counter, so the next instruction fetched will be the first instruction of the subroutine. The subroutine will continue executing one instruction after another until it gets to the RTS.

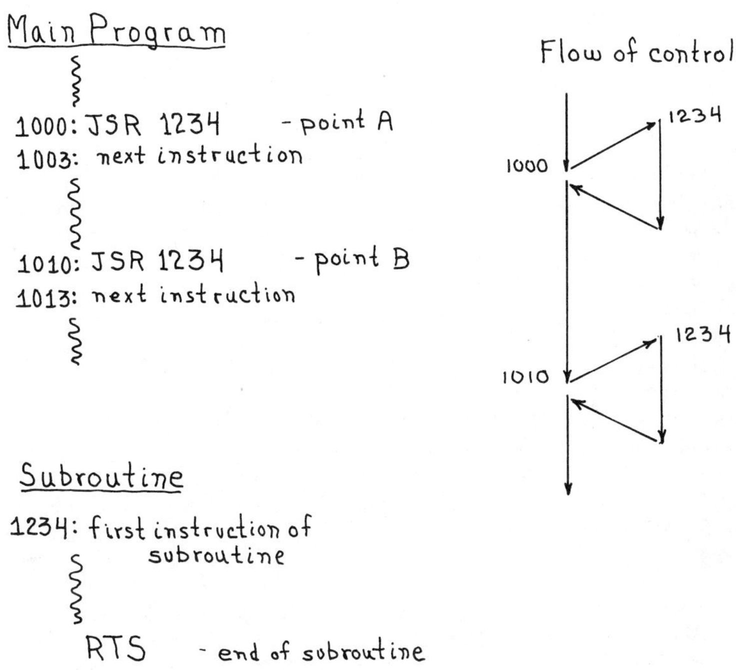

Figure 6.2 Example of a main program with two "calls" to a subroutine beginning in cell 1234.

This will pull the two top cells off the stack and put them in the program counter and then increase it by one; so the program counter will contain 1003 and the stack will look like:

01FF Next free cell.

Now execution continues from cell 1003 and goes on until we reach the next JSR, located in cell 1010. This time the <u>return address</u> placed on the stack is:

01FE	10
01FE	12
01FD	Next free cell

and again, 1234 is put in the program counter. Execution of the subroutine continues as before, and when the RTS is encountered, it pulls 1012 from the stack to put into the program counter and bumps it to 1013, so execution of the main program continues from cell 1013.

Using a stack for storing return addresses allows us to have nested subroutines; that is, our subroutine may call on another subroutine, which may, in turn, ..., ad infinitum (almost). Successive return addresses get added onto the stack with each JSR and peeled off in order by each RTS.

PARAMETER PASSING

Now that we have discovered how to call a subroutine and how to return from one, we must look at various ways of telling the subroutine what we want it to do. This is called "parameter passing."

Our particular case is very simple. The best way to handle it is to load the number of units of delay we desire into the accumulator and then jump to the subroutine. The subroutine will expect the number to show up in the accumulator, so it will store A in a convenient local counter and count down the requisite number of times before doing a return. As a matter of fact, since it is going to be counting, perhaps we should pass the count in an index register. Either way is good.

If the subroutine is supposed to calculate something for us, it needs to return its answer to the main program. Again, the accumulator is the natural place to pass back the result.

Some subroutines require more than one parameter. For example, the subroutine might be designed to calculate A times B. In that case, we could pass A in the accumulator and B in index register X, and, if we wanted, return the product as Y. There are three registers in KIM-1 (A,X, and Y) so we can pass up to three parameters that way.

If we have more than three parameters, we could agree to pass them in some known fixed locations. The subroutine might expect its first parameter in cell 00F0, its second in 00F1, and so forth. Before each JSR to this subroutine, the main program will need to make sure that cells 00F0 and so forth contain the right values for the subroutine to work on. Another subroutine might expect its parameters in cells 00E3 through 00E6 and calls to that subroutine would be preceded by setups of cells 00E3-00E6. Of course, results can be returned in any cell or cells of storage that are agreed upon by the subroutine and its calling program.

Yet a third way exists of passing parameters. This consists of putting the list of parameter values after the subroutine call. If, for example, we have a subroutine SMITH that needs 5 parameters A,B, C,D, and E, a call to SMITH from cell 0362 would look like:

```
0362:      JSR      SMITH
0365:      A
0366       B
0367       C
0368:      D
0369:      E
036A:      Next instruction of the main program.
```

with cells 0365-0369 containing the values of the parameters A-E. This is a particularly useful method of transferring parameters if the values to be used are known when you write the program. Then you just write them down and don't have to have code to set them up. Some subroutines have a variable number of parameters. Each call must specify how many there are going to be <u>this time</u>. In that case, the conventional way to tell the subroutine how many parameters to expect is to put that number in the first position following the call -- in our case, in 0365 as the value of A. Including A itself, there are 5 parameters here, so the value of A would be 5.

When one of these two methods is used, the subroutine must do a bit of extra work to locate the parameters. When we enter the subroutine, the last two words on the stack point to the cell holding the third byte of the JSR instruction. If we could get that address and add one to it, it would point at parameter A. Larger computers provide convenient ways of doing this (which accounts for the widespread use of this method of passing parameters), but it is possible to do it in a micro using indirect addressing, which we have not yet examined.

THE PROGRAM

Let us assume we are in state A. We look up the "correct" code for the A-to-B transition and call the "key watch" subroutine. This subroutine looks for a key depression, waits a fraction of a second, then reads in the complete picture of what keys are closed and which are open. It compares this pattern with the "correct" pattern, and returns to the calling routine with a 0 in the accumulator if there is no match and a 1 if there is an exact match.

The main program looks at this 0 or 1 and either branches back to the beginning or goes forward to the next state. That will require us to turn off the "old" light and turn on a "new" one -- we can do this with a subroutine also -- and wait until the keyboard is clear (goes back to 0000) before looking for the "correct" input for this state.

We have then, four subroutines so far:

Keywatch	Look for the "correct" input.
Delay	Called by Keywatch to waste a half second.
Light	Turn on the requested light and turn off all others.
Clear	Wait until the buttons go to 0000.

Keywatch requires one parameter -- the correct combination;
Delay can be fixed so it doesn't require any;
Light needs to know which light to turn on, and
Clear needs no input because it knows what to look for.

Keywatch returns a single bit (0 or 1). Let us agree that all communication will take place via the accumulator.

Draw a flow diagram of the combination lock problem at this point.

Figure 6.3 shows my first attempt at a flow diagram. It will do the job, but there are several things that could be improved. To begin with, Delay is only called from one place in Keywatch, so there is no profit in making it a subroutine; but let us pretend that this is only part of a larger program that might want to use a Delay somewhere else, so we will leave that as shown.

The next point is that Light and Clear could be combined into one subroutine rather than two. We would then check for 0000 keyboard in state A and could drop the Clear check from state D. Third, in Keywatch, we do a test, set a flag and return. Then the first thing we do after every return (except for state D) is to test that flag. We could combine the test and branch inside Keywatch. A failure would return to state A, which could begin by clearing the stack. A successful comparison would do a normal return. How about state D? Well, "failure" sends the system back to state A, but so does success, so there is no problem here. Let us try again to draw a flow diagram with these changes. See Figure 6.4 after you try for yourself.

Well, Fig. 6.4 is better than Fig. 6.3, but it is still pretty complex for such a simple problem. Let us try again. This time we will put a number from 0-3 into the accumulator to represent the present state. We will call one subroutine that will find, from a table, which light to light and light it, then wait for a clear keyboard. Then it will look up the input combination required to move to the next state, wait for an input, compare it with the input, and either branch back to the beginning (if it doesn't match), or do a return if it does compare. Try that one, then look at Figure 6.5.

Now we have a flow diagram that will fit on one page and there is some hope that we can understand it, if not in a glance, at least within a minute or two of examination.

HARDWARE AND SOFTWARE

With four buttons and four lights, we have a lot of freedom in the way we connect to the computer. Figure 6.6 shows one way of connecting things that is reasonably simple.

Since no particularly new programming techniques except the use of subroutines have been introduced, I don't feel that you should need too much help to get this one going. If you have trouble, look in 00F2 to find the stack pointer, and then examine the stack to see what return address is stored on it. That should tell you where you came from. With this program as shown, the stack should never have more then one pair of bytes (one return address) on it. If you have more than that, you are probably forgetting to re-initialize the stack in state A.

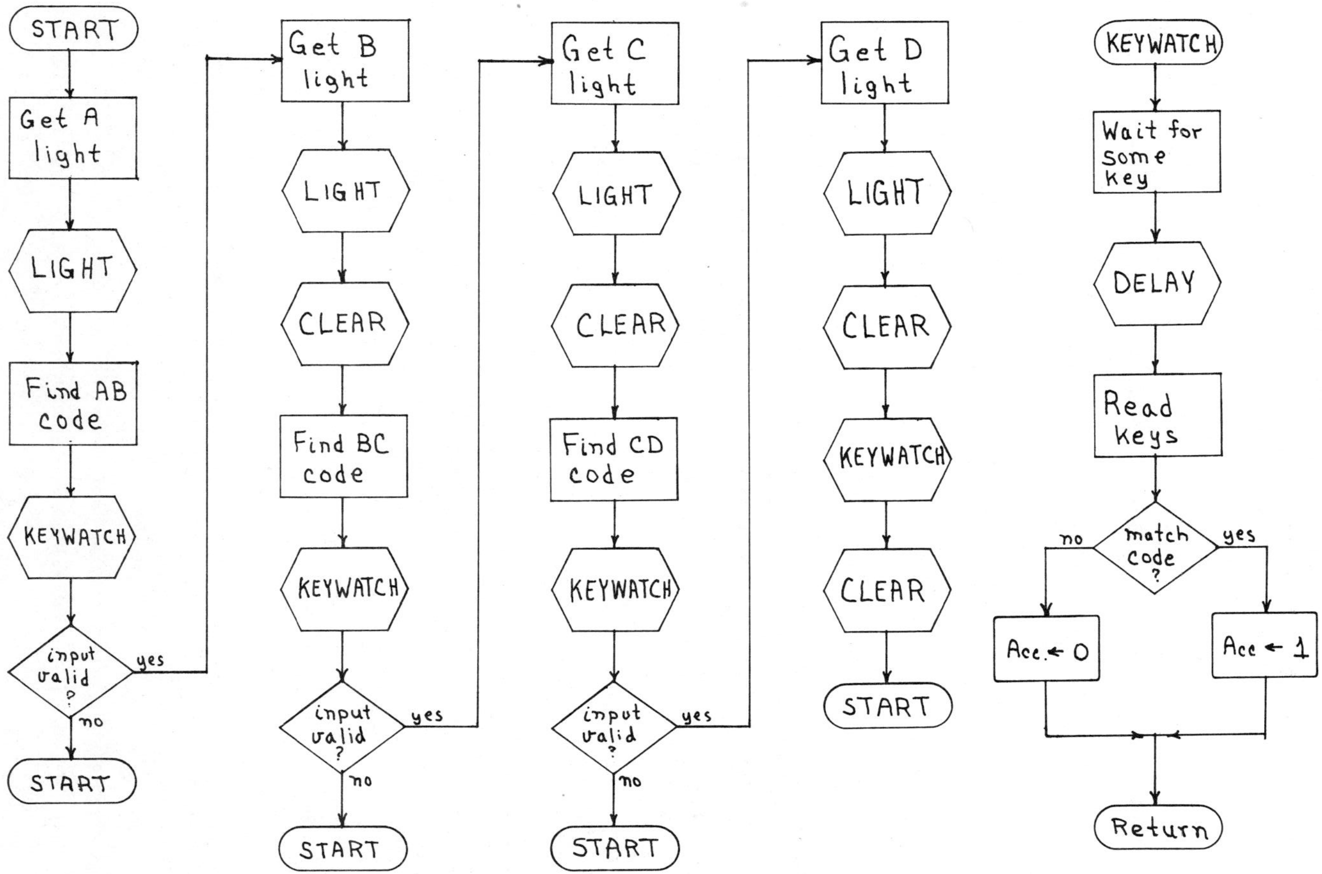

Figure 6.3 First flow diagram of combination lock problem.

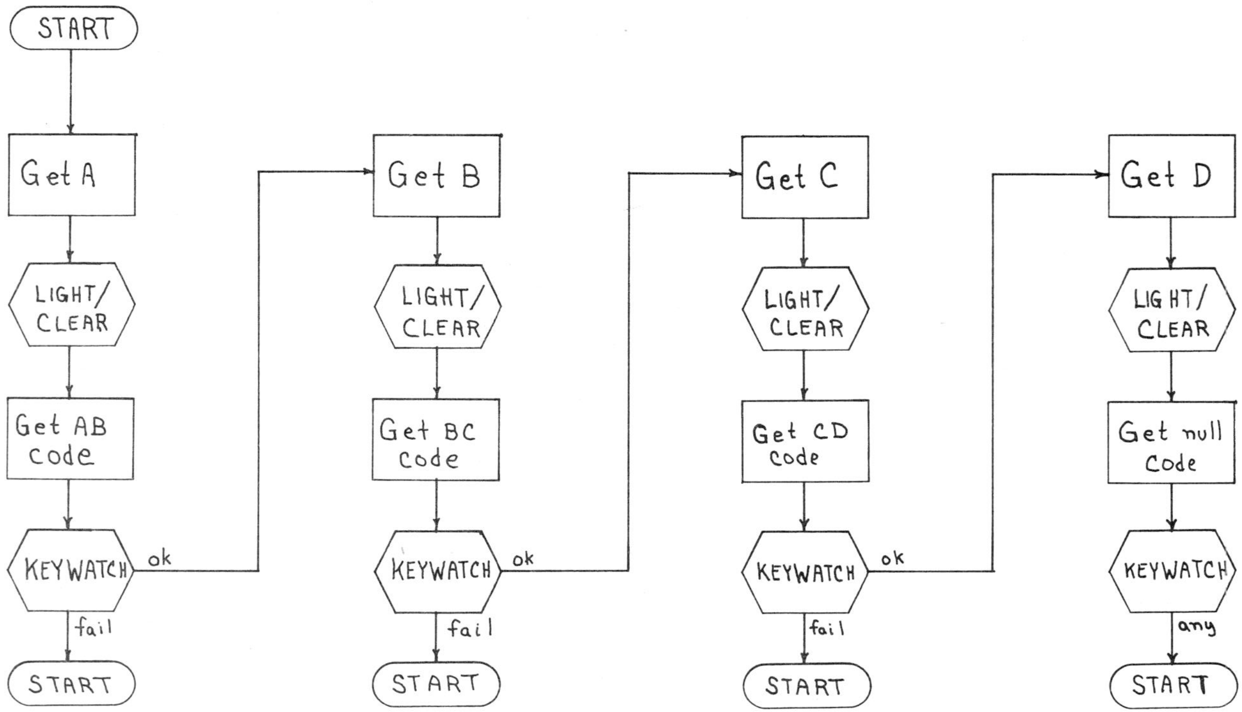

Figure 6.4 Improved flow diagram for combination lock.

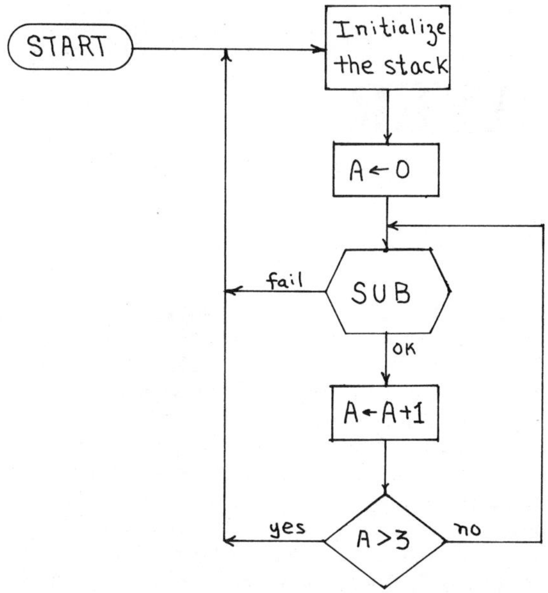

Figure 6.5 A better flow diagram yet. Better in the sense that it is simpler and thus easier to understand.

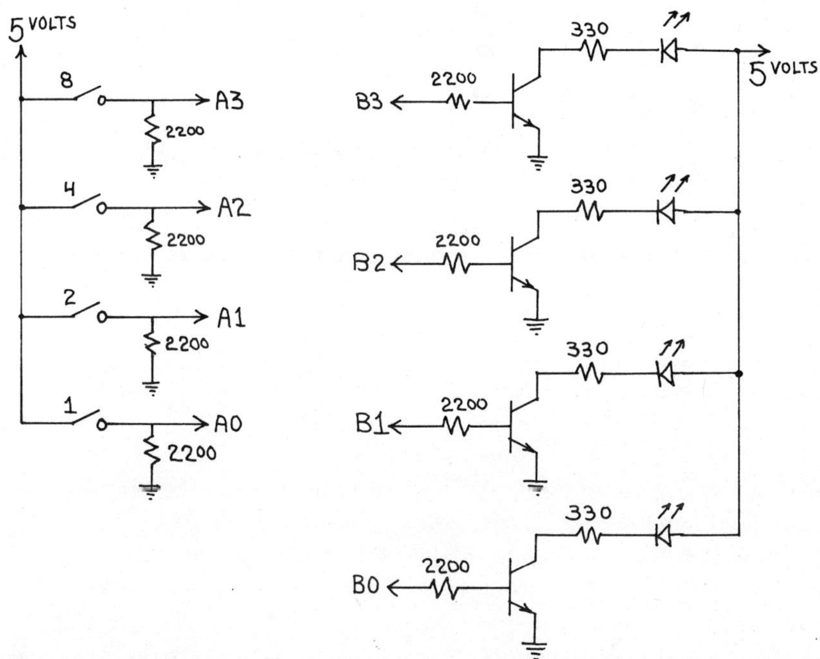

Figure 6.6 Connections for the combination lock problem.

7
TUNE PLAYER

Let us return to the subject of music. This time we want to store a couple of tunes inside the computer. When somebody comes up to the machine and pushes button N on the console, we will select the Nth tune from our repertoire and play it. We will need a loudspeaker and, if you are not using the KIM-1, you may need some pushbutton switches.

Our program is going to take somewhere around half a page (128 cells) of storage. Let us be safe and estimate that it takes all of page zero. That leaves us the order of 750 memory cells to store tunes. After some cursory analysis, I have discovered that most popular songs run around 75 notes in length. Many of them are written in the key of F (one flat: B flat) and are confined to the 1-1/2 octaves reaching up from middle C to E'. The duration of the notes in popular songs are from whole notes to eighth notes, with the dot or "add 50% to the duration" being fairly common. Taking the eighth note 𝅘𝅥𝅮 as being of unit length we have the most common durations to be:

𝅘𝅥𝅮 = 1	𝅗𝅥. = 6
𝅘𝅥 = 2	𝅝 = 8
𝅘𝅥. = 3	𝅝. = $12_{10} = C_{16}$
𝅗𝅥 = 4	

The rest (silence) will be called note zero. We can encode the scale as:

0 = rest
1 = C
2 = D
3 = E
4 = F
5 = G
6 = A
7 = B^b
8 = C'
9 = D'
10 = E'

Given these restrictions, we can pack one note with its frequency (4 bits) and duration (4 bits) into one cell. Then, at 75 notes per song, we will have room for 10 different songs inside the computer. Each cell will contain the duration of the sound (in units of eighth notes) plus the numeric name of the note. We will have to look up the half-period associated with this name somewhere else.

As in the piano-keyboard case, we want to toggle the speaker once every half-period but now we want a longer time period -- the order of a quarter second -- to be the base duration. We will use a counting loop as before for the basic toggle, but we are going to use one of the KIM timers to generate the major duration cycle.

KIM TIMERS

The KIM-1 has two timers built into it which the programmer may use.

The first of these occupies the address 1704-170F and the second one the addresses 1744-174F. That is not to say that each timer has 12 registers. Rather, when the address 170X is sent out, the X is decoded by the 6530 device to select one of several possible actions. In actuality, the two ports PORTA and PORTB and the two direction registers DIRA and DIRB are part of this scheme. The low-order hex character of the address consists of four lines labeled $A_3A_2A_1$ and A_0.

A_2 is used to determine whether the timer or the I/O ports are being addressed. If $A_2 = 0$, it is the I/O ports, and then the two low-order bits of the address A_1A_0 select whether PORTA (00), PORTB (10), DIRA (01), or DIRB (11) is being addressed. When $A_2 = 1$, we wish to talk to the timer, and the meaning of bits A_3, A_1, and A_0 is as described below.

A_1A_0 -- Determine the <u>size</u> of the time intervals to be counted by the timer. The timer has one counter register and, when we store a number in the timer, we put that number in the counter register. For example:

```
LDA#  A0 puts 160 in the accumulator
STA timer puts 160 into the counter register
```

This means that the timer will count down 160 time intervals before it is finished. By selecting A_1A_0 appropriately, we can vary the size of the interval being counted.

If A_1A_0 take on the following values, the size of the time interval is:

A_1A_0 =	00	1 microsecond intervals
	01	8 microsecond intervals
	10	64 microsecond intervals
	11	1024 microsecond intervals

A_3 determines what happens when the timer counts down to zero. If $A_3 = 0$, nothing happens except that, when zero is reached, the time interval is set to 1 microsecond and the timer keeps on counting down 00, FF, FE, etc. If $A_3 = 1$, then when you load the counter (or read it, for that matter), PORTB bit 7 (B_7) is set to one. When the timer counts out, B_7 is cleared to zero and remains zero. The timer then counts downward in 1-microsecond intervals. It is necessary to make B_7 be an input port in order for this to work properly. You do that by storing a $7F_h$ in DIRB (or anything with a leading zero).

To lay all this out in tabular form, we imagine that we have gotten a decimal 10 in the accumulator via a LDA#0A and now we are going to put that 10 into the timer, using one of the addresses 4 through F, as follows:

If the accumulator contains 10_d, then

	Time delay before counter shows zero	Clear B_7 at end
STA 1704 -	10 microseconds	no
05 -	80 microseconds	no
06 -	640 microseconds	no
07 -	10,240 microseconds	no
0C -	10 microseconds	yes
0D -	80 microseconds	yes
0E -	640 microseconds	yes
0F -	10,240 microseconds	yes

Addresses 1708-170B are not used.

For our purpose we would like to be able to test the count down to zero when we want to, so we will use one of the addresses C-F. To get a convenient-sized time interval for an eighth note, we will LDA#A0 (160 decimal) and STA 170F, which gives a time delay of 160 x 1024 or 163,840 microseconds (or approximately 1/6 of a second). Then, to speed up the playing of a song, we can replace A0 by a smaller number, or slow it down by using a larger number.

The second timer is located at 174X and is exactly similar to the one described above except that 174C-174F addresses cause D_7 (the leftmost bit of PORTD -- 1742) to be cleared, rather than B_7. The KIM-1 system uses the timer at 174X, so some caution is warranted if you plan to use both the timer and some of the system subroutines.

INDIRECT ADDRESSING

In order to be able to point into one of several different songs, we need to introduce the concept of indirect addressing.

In the KIM there are two forms of indirect addressing. The first one is called "indexed indirect" and is indicated by adding an XI to the instruction mnemonics. Only X may be used as the index register. We say:

```
LDAXI    12
```

This takes the number 12, adds the contents of X to it ((X) + 12), and uses this as the address of a cell in page zero. If X contains the number 6, the address computed will be 18. From cells 18 and 19 we get the low-order and high-order bytes of an address, respectively. Suppose (0018) = AC and (0019) = 02. The address is 02AC and it is from cell 02AC that we load the accumulator.

If cells contain the following numbers:

```
   X: 6
0018: AC
0019: 02
02AC: 0B
```

we get the number 0B into the accumulator when we say:

```
LDAXI  12
```

The other form of indirect addressing is called <u>indirect indexed</u>. It requires use of register Y and we indicate it by adding IY to the mnemonic. In this mode we do indirect reference first and then indexing. If we write:

```
LDAIY  05
```

and cell

```
05: 64
06: 03
```

and Y: 1

then we first pick up the 16-bit address at 05, 06, then add the contents of Y to that, getting 0365, and then use that as the address of the operand to put into the accumulator. By incrementing Y, we can step through the list of values or notes stored in 0364, 0365,...

PLAYING THE NOTES

Let us suppose that we have the address of the start of our song stored in cells 00ED and 00EE (low-order byte first, of course) and that we are using index register Y to point to the note we wish to play. When we pick up that note from the song table (using indirect addressing), we will find a duration (in eighth notes) in the left-hand four bits and the name of the note in the righthand four bits.

The first thing to do is to "unpack" (pull apart) these two nibbles (4-bit packages) and set them up for use by the playing routine. We can extract the name of the note by a simple mask operation, and by moving the nibble into an index register, we can then look up the duration of a half-period in a table. We will store this duration in a fixed named cell because we will need it many times before the note is finished, and thus we will save all this extraction and look-up procedure each time we need it. Next we get the note again and, by shifting right four times, get the duration down to the low-order end of the accumulator so that we can store it in another convenient cell. We can count down on that cell to see how many "time outs" we should have.

When we have finished playing one note we should go back and get another and so on and on until we get to the end of the song. How can we tell when the song is over? One way would be to store as the first "note" of the song a count of how many real notes there are and keep track of how we are progressing. Another way would be to store the song backwards in memory and count down to zero on index register Y. Yet another way, and the one I choose, is to use a "flag" at the end of the song. We take some unused note/duration pattern, say, FF_h, and when we see that we know the song is over. No need to count. We just look for this particular pattern and call it our "end of file" or "end of record" or "end of song" indicator. Of course, we have to test each note/duration pattern to see if it is that special pattern, but there is a compare operation provided in KIM which makes this easy to do.

As a matter of fact there are three compare operations: compare A, compare X, and compare Y (CMP, CPX, CPY). To take the first of those, since they all work the same, CMP subtracts the operand from the accumulator. The difference is not put into the accumulator but is discarded. However, the subtaction sets the N (negative) and Z (zero) bits of the status register if the difference is negative or zero, respectively. Immediate, direct, zero-page, indexed, and indirect addressing are allowed. Following a compare, one of the test instructions can be applied to discover whether the result of the comparison was positive (accumulator greater than operand), negative, zero, or nonzero.

Only immediate, direct, and page-zero addressing are available for the CPX and CPY instructions.

In order to decide which tune to play, we will wait for the user to push a key. Let us say that we number the tunes 0-F. Since the KIM already has these keys built into it, we should look at how these keys are connected, so that we can use them.

THE CONSOLE KEYBOARD AND DISPLAY

If we ignore the Stop, Reset, and Single-step buttons, we can consider the rest of the keyboard. If you remember, the system has its own timer and I/O ports. The KIM manuals refer to these ports as A and B without distinguishing them from the A and B we already know and love so well. We will call them C and D in this discussion so we don't continually have to mention which A or B we are talking about.

PORTC is location 1740
PORTD is location 1742
DIRC is location 1741
DIRD is location 1743

Four of the bits of PORTD (namely D4,D3,D2, and D1) are used to drive a chip called a "decoder." It is a 74145 (if you care) and it has 10 output lines (called Row 0-Row 9) (see Fig. 7.1), which are all high ($+5^V$) except the one being addressed by the number in D_{4-1}. That one row selected is pulled to ground.

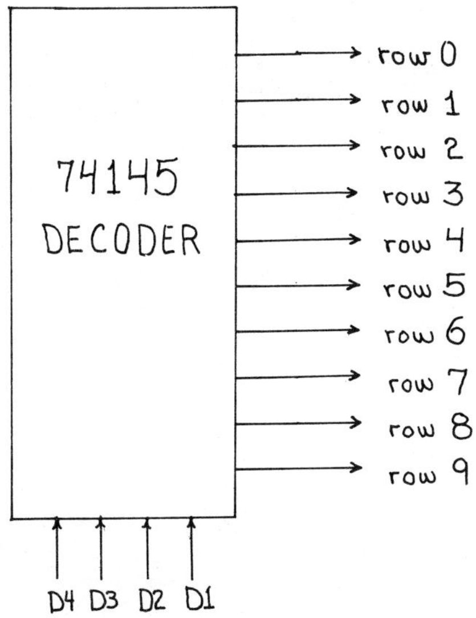

Figure 7.1 Decoder chip to select one of 10 rows.

In the technology used in the KIM-1, input lines which are left to themselves tend to go to $+5^V$ (logical one). The decoder's rows 0, 1, and 2 go to select which of three rows of buttons will have one side pulled to ground. These buttons are arranged in three rows of seven buttons, each as in Fig. 7.2.

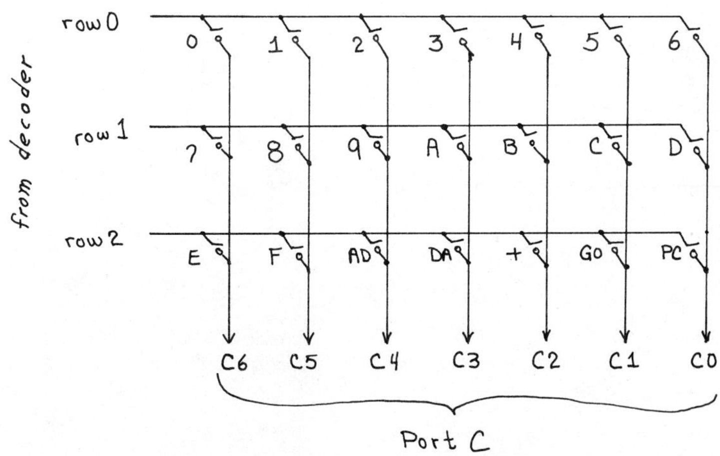

Figure 7.2 Three rows of seven switches as connected on the KIM Keyboard.

So if we make Port C be input and D be output, then if we put the number 4 in Port D and if button DA is pushed, we will find an F7 in Port C (all bits are <u>one</u> except the bit pulled to <u>zero</u>). By putting the numbers 0, 2, and 4 in D and examining C, we can tell which, if any, buttons have been pushed.

But the KIM system has to do this also, and presumably the KIM system programmers have gotten the routine down pat. They thoughtfully wrote their key-scanning program as a subroutine which we can use by doing a

```
JSR    1F6A
```

<u>A word of warning</u>: This subroutine uses A, X, and Y and preserves none of them. It returns with a number in the accumulator which corresponds to the key depressed or the number $15_h = 21_d$ if no key was pushed. The numbers (in hex) they have assigned to keys are:

Key	Value in A	Key	Value	Key	Value	Key	Value
0	0	6	6	C	C	+	12
1	1	7	7	D	D	GO	13
2	2	8	8	E	E	PC	14
3	3	9	9	F	F	No key	15
4	4	A	A	AD	10		
5	5	B	B	DA	11		

Since the code which they wrote is fairly subtle, I will not encourage bad habits on your part by reproducing it here.

TUNE PLAYING

At this point you are ready to try your hand at a flow diagram for the tune-playing portion of the program. You should wait for a key push, get the address of the start of that tune from a table, play the tune a note at a time, and then, when the terminal flag comes up, go back to wait for another key push.

If once you have found a key, you then ignore the keyboard until after the tune is over, you will have no problems with key bounce. After completing your flow diagram, compare it with Figs. 7.3 and 7.4.

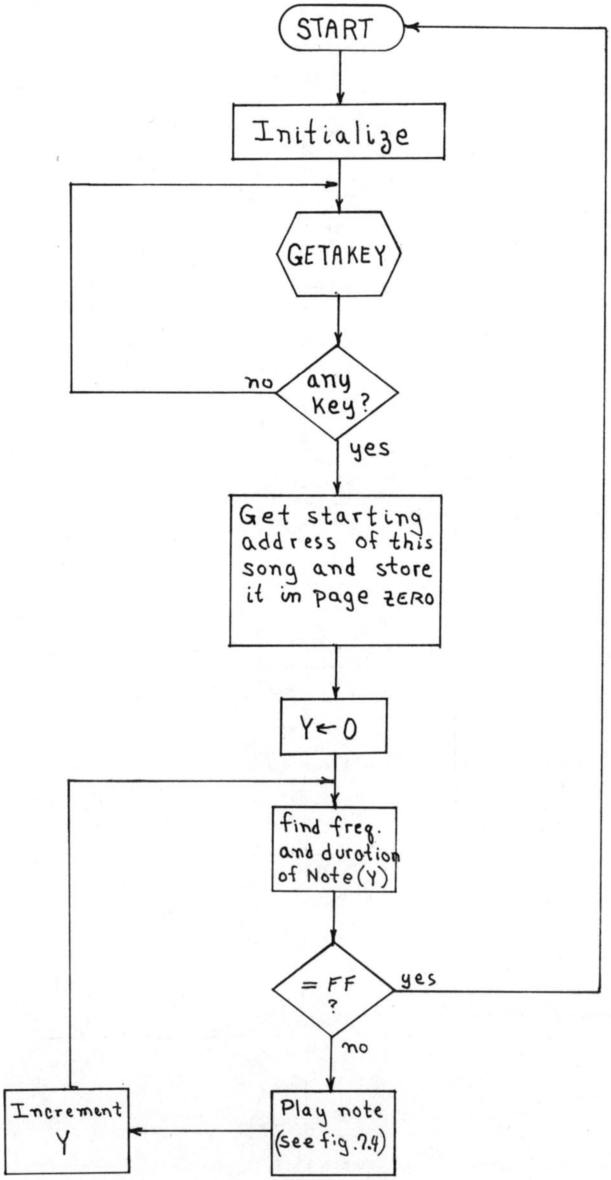

Figure 7.3 Overview of tune player

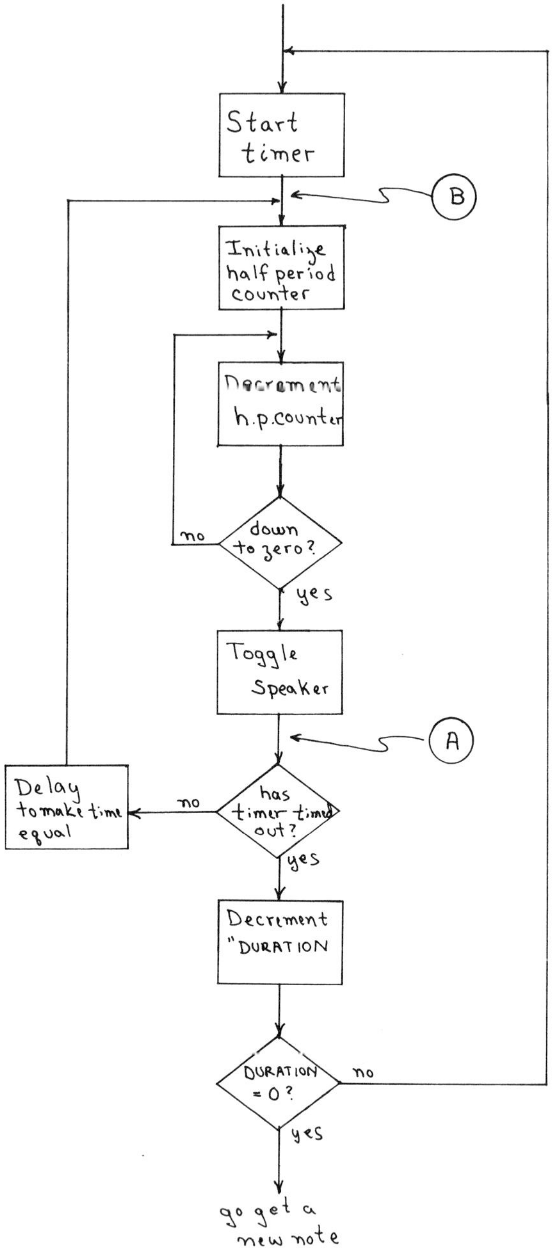

Figure 7.4 Details of playing one note

THE PROGRAM AND HARDWARE

For this experiment we need only a loudspeaker. I reused the speaker-switch box from Chapter 3 (Morse code) in order to save time, money, and energy. Figure 7.5 reproduces the circuit required to drive the speaker.

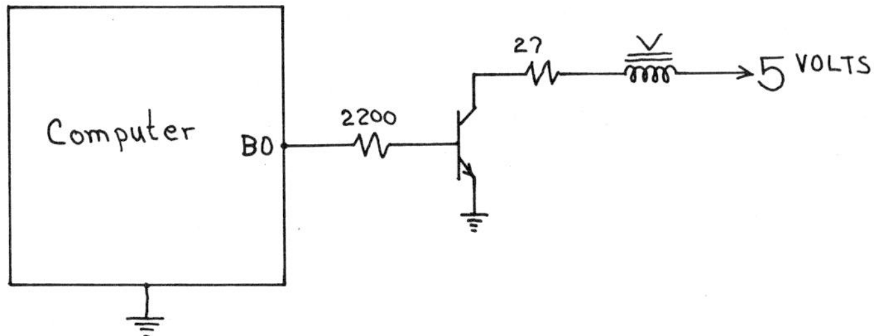

Figure 7.5 Circuit to drive a loudspeaker from the KIM.

It is connected to pin BO so we can use the same old technique of incrementing location 1702 to toggle the speaker.

Figure 7.4 shows the details of playing one note of a song. We have an inner loop which counts a half-period counter to zero and establishes the basic frequency that is to be sounded. Around this there is an outer loop which uses the KIM timer to measure the duration of the tone. If the timer has not "timed out," we go back and do another half-period (lefthand path). If the timer has timed out, we see whether we have done enough "eighth-note" intervals and if not, go back to start the timer once more (righthand path). Thus, there are two paths from point A to point B. In order to keep the tone from "ticking" at eighth-note intervals when we take the righthand path, we need to insert a delay in the lefthand pathway. There are many ways to waste time in a computer. One of the easiest is a string of instructions that do nothing. For reasonably short delays such as we need here, it is not worthwhile to put in a loop, although that can frequently be of use. A set of "jump to the next location" instructions can use up time in 3-microsecond increments. NOP's (no operations) take 2 microseconds each and only one byte each. Combinations of the two allow us to get any desired number of cycles of delay. In my case I needed 12 microseconds delay, which I got by writing:

```
JMP  *+1
JMP  *+1          *+1 means "the present instruction
JMP  *+1          plus one (instruction)"
JMP  B
```

To start the timer we can write:

```
LDA # 80
STA   170F
```

which gets an eighth note of about 1/10 of a second. Testing for time out is done on B7, with one meaning "not yet over" and zero meaning "it is done." Most of the other techniques required have either appeared before or been discussed earlier in this chapter.

The following table is the encoding of three songs in a form suitable for the program as described above. Tones are derived the same way as those of the piano keyboard with the obvious differences due to different timing.

"0" Red River Valley

21	24	46	10
26	25	44	25
24	22	64	10
24	21	24	46
10	26	10	26
48	27	26	C5
21	24	46	10
26	10	26	44
25	26	28	67
10	27	20	22
10	22	41	24
25	46	25	10
25	84	10	24
FF			

"1" British Grenadier

21	24	21	24
25	46	25	16
17	28	24	16
15	14	13	64
21	24	21	24
25	46	25	16
17	28	24	16
15	14	13	24
20	16	17	38
19	28	27	36
17	28	24	32
12	18	17	16
15	44	23	11
11	24	21	24
25	46	25	16
17	28	24	16
15	14	13	64
FF			

"2" Nearer My God To Thee

C6	85	44	84
32	10	C2	C1
84	46	B5	10
85	40	C6	85
34	10	84	32
10	C2	81	44
83	45	B4	10
84	40	C8	89
38	10	88	46
B8	10	C8	82
31	10	81	46
C5	C6	85	34
10	C4	32	10
C2	81	44	83
45	B4	10	84
FF			

8
DIGITAL CLOCK

In this experiment, we are going to make our microcomputer function as a digital clock displaying hours, minutes, and seconds. The problem breaks down into four distinct but interacting parts, which we will take up one at a time. They are: measuring a second, counting and converting, displaying the time, and setting the clock. We will begin with the display.

DISPLAY

There are several ways that one can design a display; your choice will depend on your relative wealth, electronic abilities, the microcomputer itself, and the time you have available.

Perhaps the simplest, from a construction point of view, is what we will call the binary coded decimal (BCD) display. There is a clock called "Binatime" which is commercially available and which uses this form of display. Its major drawback (attraction?) is that it requires some training to read. Consider four bits holding a binary number between 0 and 15. If we put these four bits in an output port and connect a light-emitting diode (LED) to each bit, we can display this binary number as is and let the user convert from binary to decimal. To display hours, minutes, and seconds, we need six digits or 6 x 4 = 24 bits. That is more than we have output bits available on most microcomputers, so we will have to do something clever. What we should do is to invert the scheme we have used previously for reading a matrix of switches and build a matrix of lights. Figure 8.1 shows what we have in mind. We put one of the character lines at logical <u>one</u>, the others at logical <u>zero</u>. Since the transistors invert as well as amplify, the single selected vertical line will be held at <u>zero</u> volts and the other five will be allowed to float up to plus five volts. Now if we want to show the pattern 0101 in this character position, we put 0101 on the "bit" lines. Those lines are connected through noninverting emitter-followers to the horizontal lines. So the lines with <u>one</u> on them are clamped to plus five volts, and the lines with <u>zero</u> applied to them are allowed to float. Now, at any intersection where the vertical line is clamped to <u>zero</u> and the horizontal line is clamped to plus five volts, we have a potential difference of five volts and the light-emitting diode across that intersection will light up. All other intersections will have one side or the other floating and no potential difference will appear there; hence, their diodes will not conduct and will not give off light.

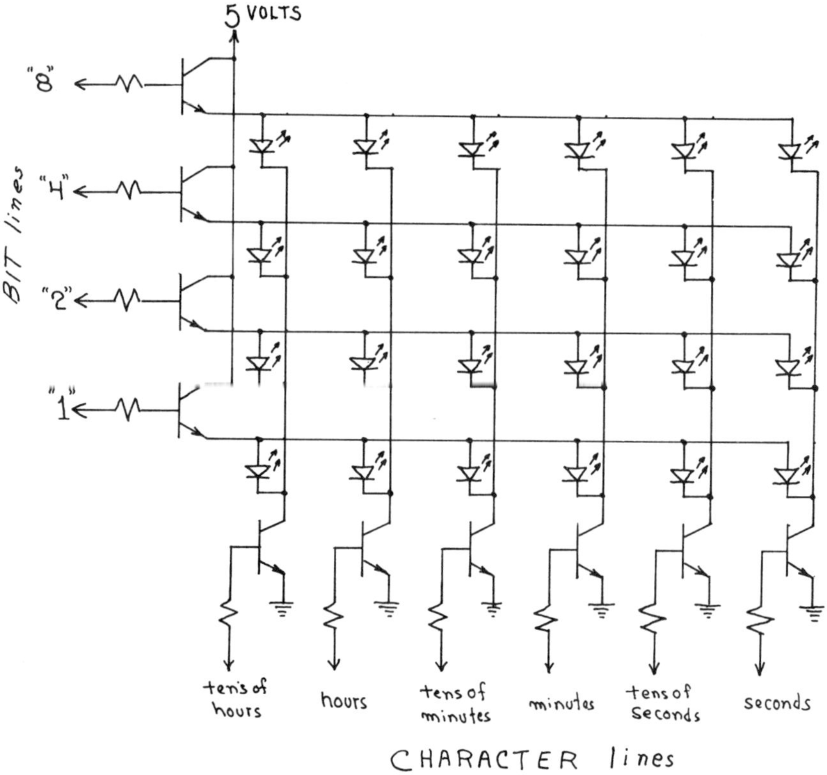

Figure 8.1 An LED matrix of six characters each of four bits.

This scheme allows us to display one digit at a time, but we have six digits to display. To accomplish this, we are going to rely on a characteristic of the human eye. If a light is turned on about 50 times per second, it appears to an observer as a steady nonpulsating light. The frequency at which this happens is called "flicker fusion" and varies somewhat from person to person, but 50 pulses per second is above the fusion point for most people. So what we will do is to display character one, then character two and so forth, making sure that we get back to display character one again before 20 milliseconds have gone by. This is called <u>display commutation</u>. With six characters to display, this means that we can turn on a character, wait up to 3 milliseconds, turn that character off and proceed to the next character. Of course, each character is only going to be one sixth as bright as if it were on continuously, but that can be compensated for (up to a point) by driving the lights harder -- by putting more current through them. You will note, in Fig. 8.1, that we have no resistors in series with the diodes. That is to allow more current to flow when they <u>are</u> lit. Our friendly delay loop generates a time interval of about 2 milliseconds. This will be good enough for our purposes.

A somewhat more sophisticated form of display is the so-called "seven-segment display" unit. This consists of seven bar-shaped, light-emitting diodes arranged as shown in Fig. 8.2.

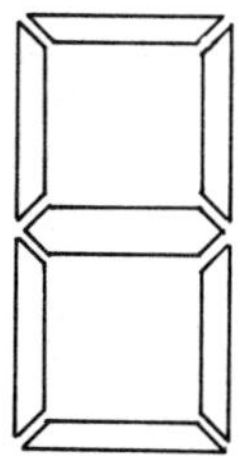

Figure 8.2 A seven-segment display unit.

These are available with either the negative terminals tied together (common cathode) or the positive terminals of the seven diodes tied together (common anode). If they are to be used in a circuit similar to that of Fig. 8.1, we would want common cathode units.

Within the computer we store a table which translates four-bit binary numbers to seven-bit on/off patterns. These patterns are:

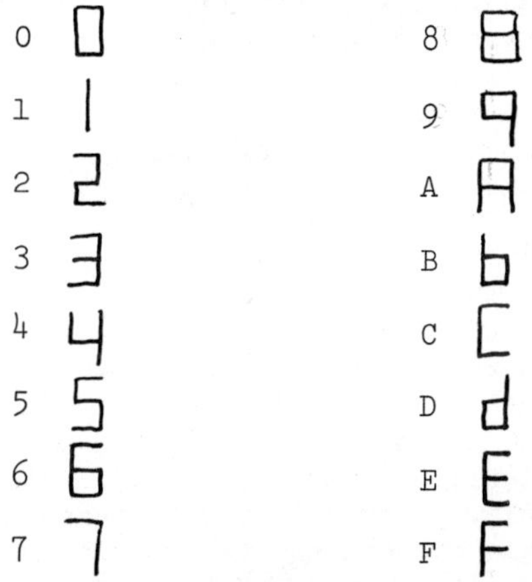

Note the similarity of B and 6. It leads to lots of confusion.

The KIM-1 has six such display positions built into it and the table for translation of characters is stored in the ROM at locations 1FE7 through 1FF6. To select a display position, we store an even number between 8_h and 12_h in location 1742, where 8 is the leftmost character, A the next, then C,E, 10, and 12. To select what character to show, we store the translation of that character in location 1740. We must make sure that ports C and D are output ports by storing FF in 1741 and 1743.

In our discussion of the KIM-1 keyboard, we mentioned the 74145 demultiplexor. Four bits (D4,D3,D2, and D1) select one of ten lines and pull that line to ground. The other nine are all at plus five volts. If you are building your own display, you can use one of these chips to select which character you want to have turned on, and you may thus have up to ten characters. Other demultiplexors are available that have four inputs and 16 outputs, or three inputs and eight outputs. Some are available to drop one line and hold the others high (as we just mentioned), and others will raise one line and drop all the others.

For our clock problem, the display routine is going to be the main routine. We will write it as an endless loop just as if it were the only program in the computer and as if displaying the time were the only task to accomplish.

Figure 8.3 shows a flow diagram for the display program, but you might want to try drawing one yourself before looking at it. In this case, the code is shorter than the flow diagram.

COUNTING THE SECONDS

As you no doubt may remember, there are 60 seconds in a minute, the same number of minutes in an hour, and 24 hours in a day, but only 12 on the usual household clock. At one time it was proposed to divide seconds into 60 parts called "thirds" (the third division of an hour). At the height of the decimalization craze of the French Revolution, some clocks were made with 10 hours per day and 100 minutes per hour, but that didn't catch on. From the point of view of a binary computer, this usual 12, 60, 60 division is somewhat inconvenient. 16,64,64, or better, 16,16,16,16 would be ever so much easier to handle, but that probably won't catch on either, so we have to find a way to handle the present scheme.

Rather than trying to re-organize the world, let us accept the current scheme for telling time and figure out a way to make our computer comply with it.

Suppose we have a counting routine and arrange to enter it once every second. We count up to 59, reset to 0, and generate a carry; count carries up to 59, reset that count to 0, and generate a supercarry. We can then count supercarries up to 12, at which point we reset the supercarry count to 1. This will give us a count of seconds, minutes, and hours in conventional style (12 o'clock is followed by 1 o'clock, <u>not</u> 11 followed by 0).

In order to keep the display program simple, we assumed that the six digits for display were all decoded and ready. The only time we need to change one of these digits is when we increment the corresponding counter. But the counters count up to 12 or 59, not to ten, so we need a subroutine that will take a binary number and convert it to a decimal number. 100000 should come out as 0011 0010. We will call this subroutine CONVERT and examine it in a moment. First, let's draw the flow diagram for the counting routine (see Fig. 8.4). Remember, when you change the hour you will have to change the minutes and seconds also.

Now we are ready to look at CONVERT. We will enter with a number between 0 and 99_d in the accumulator and return with the answer

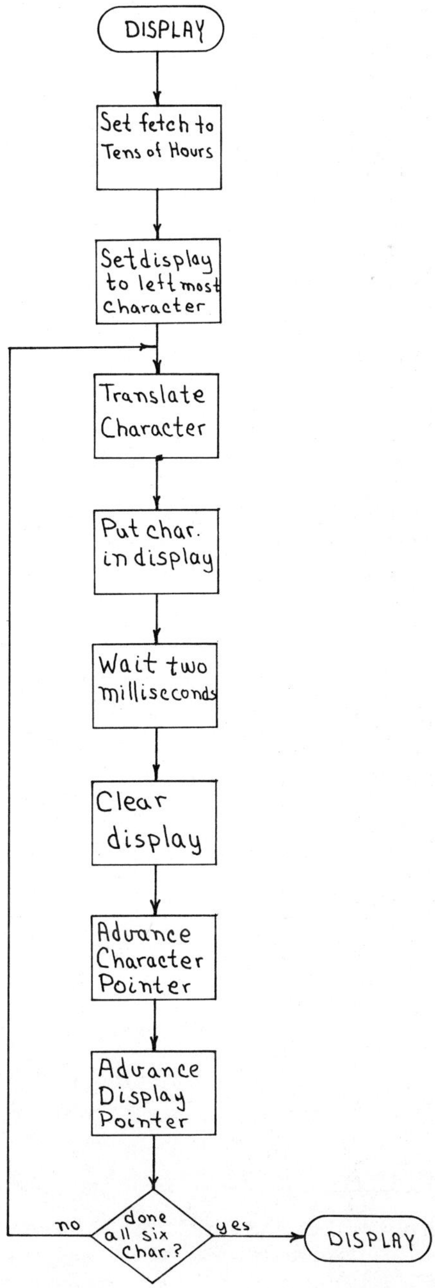

Figure 8.3 The display routine for a digital clock

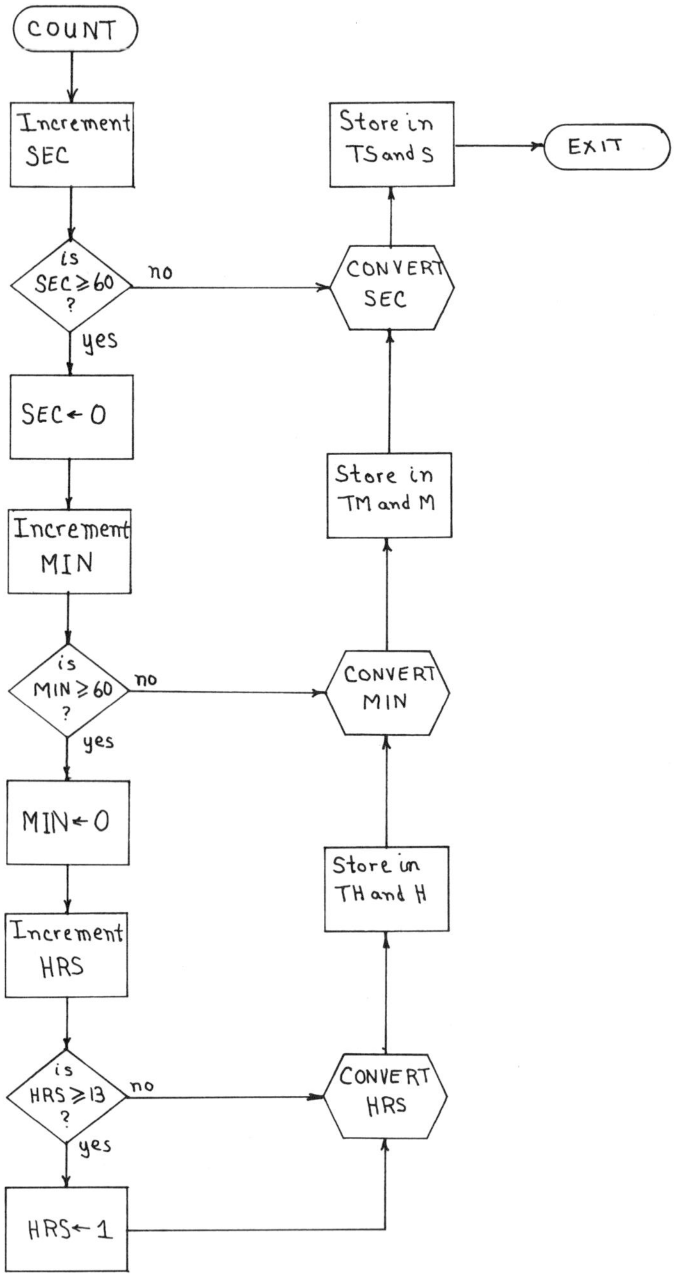

Figure 8.4 The routine for counting hours, minutes and seconds

stored in X(tens) and A(units).

We begin by clearing X and setting the carry bit (so that subtraction will work properly) and then subtracting 10_d from the accumulator until it goes negative. We will increment X once for each subtraction (except the last one). Finally we add back in 10 and the units are in the accumulator (see Fig. 8.5). It's not what you might call elegant, but it works.

TIMING AND INTERRUPTS

Now we need a timer for one-second intervals and a way to get into the counter routine from the display routine, which has no exits. Both of these will be accomplished via interrupts, which we must now examine.

In the KIM-1 there are two types of interrupt: NMI and IRQ (non-maskable interrupt, and interrupt request). NMI is the simpler of these so we will discuss it first; but most machines have interrupts similar to IRQ so we will discuss that as well.

Suppose you are sitting in your office having a conversation with a colleague. The phone rings; this is an interruption. You stop talking to your friend, say "Excuse me," and answer the phone. When you hang up you turn back to your friend and say, "Now, where were we?", and go on with your conversation. An interrupt in a computer is exactly the same.

Whenever the NMI line goes from logical one to logical zero (it is the transition that matters), an interruption is generated. As soon as the currently executing instruction is finished, the following things happen:

1. Store program counter (high byte first) on the stack.

2. Store processor status register on the stack.

3. Turn ON the I bit in the processor status register.

4. Load the program counter (low byte first) from 17FA and 17FB.

Steps 1 and 2 save the program counter and the status register so that when we want to resume our regular program, we will know where we left off. Step 3 inhibits interrupts from IRQ (but not from NMI) (see below), and step 4 transfers control of the computer to the program whose address is stored in 17FA and 17FB. That pair of addresses should be familiar. That's where we stored 1C00 in order to make the "stop" key work properly. And that is just as it should be. The stop key drives the NMI line to ground, generating an interrupt. 1C00 holds the beginning of the KIM-1 display/entry routines. So when we press stop, we interrupt the executing program and transfer control to the display routine. The address of the next instruction the computer was going to execute (and would have done had we not pushed stop) is saved on the stack (and in the KIM-1 it is also loaded into the display). If we want something else to happen when

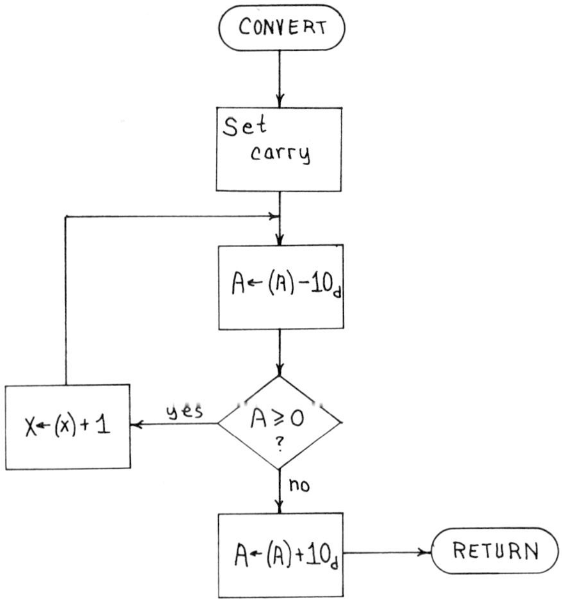

Figure 8.5 Subroutine to convert binary to two digit decimal. X will hold tens digit and A & 6 units digits.

NMI goes to ground, we write an appropriate program to make that happen and put its starting address in 17FA and 17FB. Note that if you use NMI as an interrupt line, the stop button won't work. That is quite inconvenient.

Typically, such an interrupt-handling program will end by going back to the main program. It does this by executing an RTI (return from interrupt) instruction. This loads the processor status register and the program counter (in that order) from the stack. This gets you back to where you were just before the interrupt occurred, ready to go forward. But what about the other registers, A,X, and Y? The main routine was probably using them for something. Since we don't know when (relative to the main program) the interrupt is going to occur, we have to assume that they were in use. And the interrupt routine has to have some registers to work with. It is therefore good practice to save A, X, and Y even if you don't plan to use them in the interrupt routine. Plans have a way of changing. To do this we may write:

```
SAVE:   PHA     Push A onto the stack
        TXA       (X)—→A
        PHA     Save X on the stack
        TYA       (Y)—→A
        PHA     Save Y on the stack
```

We should do this right at the beginning of the interrupt routine before we forget and before we use any of the registers for anything else. Saving the registers on the stack allows us to handle "nested" interrupts if they should happen. Remember that NMI can't be blocked. Should another event pull NMI to ground another interrupt will occur even if we haven't finished handling this one. So (a) save machine context on the stack so it doesn't get clobbered, and (b) be careful about what you connect to the NMI line.

At the end of the interrupt routine, we want to restore all the registers and go back to the main program. We can do this by:

```
RESTORE:  PLA       Load A from stack.
          TAY       Transfer to Y
          PLA
          TAX       Get contents of X back.
          PLA       Get contents of A back.
          RTI       Return to main program.
```

The RTI restores the program status register and the program counter. Everything else is up to the programmer. Note that the program status register is saved before the I bit is set, so when it is restored by the RTI, the old value of I is restored.

The IRQ line of the KIM-1 is similar to the NMI line with the following exceptions:

1. As long as IRQ is at ground, it will try to interrupt the computer (with NMI it is the change that matters, with IRQ it is the level).

2. An IRQ interrupt is possible only if the interrupt-inhibit bit I of the processor status register is <u>zero</u>.

3. Upon IRQ interrupt, the program counter is loaded from cells 17FE and 17FF.

By setting the I bit to <u>one</u>, we can inhibit interrupts on IRQ (mask them out). If IRQ goes to <u>zero</u> while I = 1 and then I is cleared before IRQ goes to <u>one</u>, an interrupt will occur as soon as I is cleared.

This type of interrupt is similar to that found on most microcomputers. In order to use it properly, you must have some external circuitry that will ensure two things, first that the IRQ line will stay down at ground until the computer gets around to handling the problem, and, second, that the line goes back to <u>one</u> before returning to the main program. This is most readily accomplished with a flip-flop (see Fig. 8.6) that is set by the event and cleared by the computer. The output bit (perhaps B5?) should be unique to this flip-flop. It must be raised to <u>one</u>. This will clear the flip-flop and allow NMI to go to one. Then it should be brought back to <u>zero</u> so another event can set the flip-flop.

If more than one external event can cause an interrupt, then it will be necessary to decide which of these events caused a particular interrupt. It is for this reason that the output of the flip-flop is shown as being connected to an input pin (one for each flip-

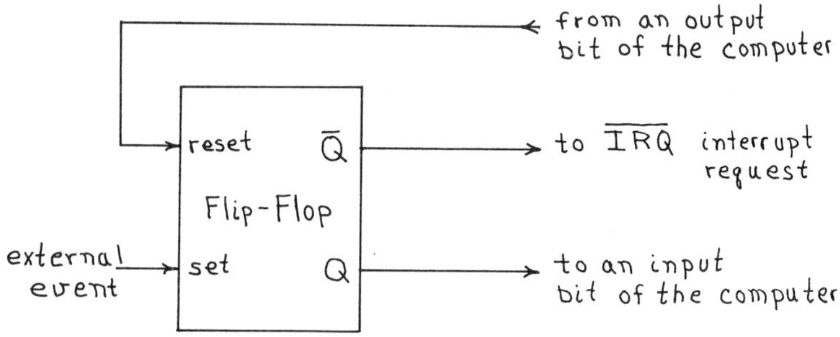

Figure 8.6 A flip-flop for storing (latching) the occurrence of an external event for interrupt with the connections for clearing the flip-flop and for sensing its state.

flop) so that the computer can test the flip-flops to see which one is on.

For our problem of generating a timing interval, we have several choices available. The most general solution is shown in Fig. 8.7. By amplifying a 60-cycle sine wave, we can get a square wave that is alternately zero and one. If we are going to connect this to the NMI line of a KIM-1, we could eliminate the flip-flop and connect the output of the inverting amplifier directly to the NMI line. This circuit will generate an interrupt 60 times a second (once per "third"), and we can count these up and give control to the second-counting program every sixtieth time. Both the "less than 60 thirds elapsed" and the exit from the counting routine should go back to the display program with an RTI when they are done. While the power-line frequency does wander somewhat during the day, the utility companies are aware that many people run synchronous clocks from the power line and they arrange, each night after midnight, to speed up or slow down their generators so that exactly (more or less) 24 x 60 x 60 x 60 cycles take place in a 24-hour period, thus keeping the clocks "on time" within reason. Figure 8.8 shows a sample interrupt routine for counting thirds.

If you have a KIM-1, I recommend that you use the IRQ interrupt from one of the timers built into the KIM. By loading 255_d (FF) into location 170E, we generate a delay of 255 x 64 = 16,320 microseconds, and 61 of these delays are very nearly a second. Using 170E we will clear B7 when the timer times out. We take a cliplead or a piece of wire and connect B7 to IRQ. Then when the timer times out, our program will stop whatever it is doing (probably displaying a character) and jump to the routine whose starting address is in location 17FE, 17FF.

Since the crystals that generate the one-microsecond cycles on the KIM are not of necessity very accurate, we can expect some variation in the speed of our clocks. The one I programmed gained one

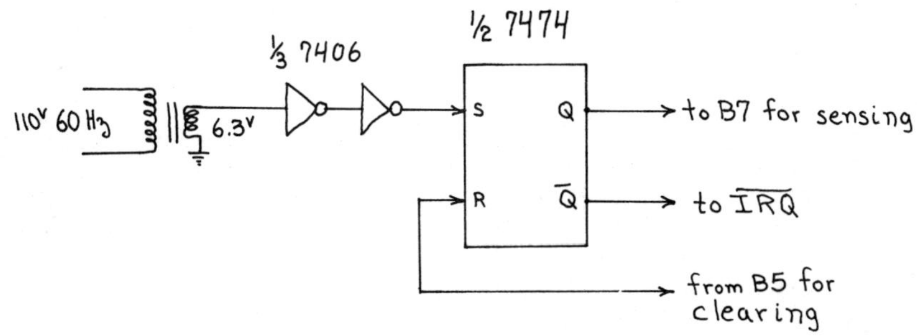

Figure 8.7 The circuit to generate an interrupt 60 times per second.

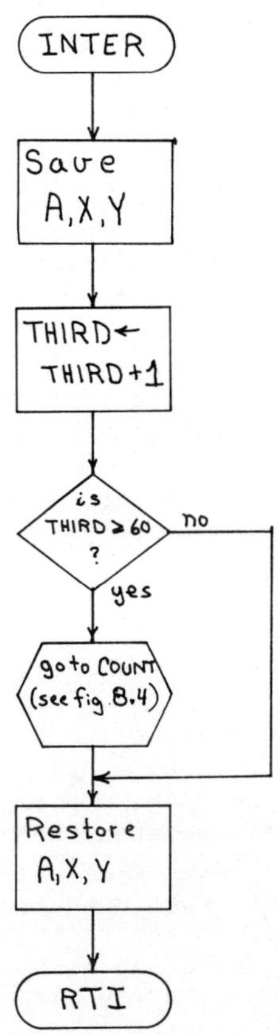

Figure 8.8 The line clock interrupt fielding routine.

hour in 4 days -- about 1 percent fast, which is acceptable for the instruction timing of a computer and for us, even if not for a commercial clock.

SETTING THE CLOCK

Given the best of all possible clocks, sometimes the power fails and we have to be able to reset the clock. Since, under those conditions, we would have to reload the clock program, and the cassette-reading routines leave us ready to run at location 0000, we should begin our clock-setting program there and put everything else wherever it may fall. Besides, 0000 is easy to remember in case we come in some morning and find the clock running but wrong.

What we would like to be able to do is to enter characters one after another and have them march across our display from right to left until we had the proper HHMMSS in, and then to send the computer off to translate this to binary and start the clock running. That seems a little complicated for an auxiliary routine, although you may choose to do it if you like. Let us compromise and store the tens of hours (TH) in location 0, the units of hours in location 1, and so forth, with a binarizing routine beginning in cell 6. That way we can enter the time conveniently in decimal and be set up to take off once it is properly in.

The binarizing routine will pick up pairs of digits (from 0,1 and 2,3 and 4,5), multiply the first one by ten, add it to the second element of the pair and store the result in HRS, MIN, or SEC, as necessary.

How do we multiply by ten in a machine that has no multiply instruction? Very simple. We note that

$$10\ N = 2 * (4*N + N)$$

and we can multiply by two by shifting left. So we pick up the first number, shift left twice, (multiply by four) add in the number and shift left one more time. Then we add in the second number. If the whole operation is done using an index register to get the digits, we are home and dry, quite conveniently. Figure 8.9 shows a flow diagram to set the time.

GETTING IT TOGETHER

At this point, you may be able to put the program together. Start with the set time, drop into the display section, and get that part working. Then write the seconds counter and converter. Transfer to it manually and see that it updates the values in TH, H,TM, M, TS, and S properly -- try a time of 9:59:59 and see if you get 10 o'clock.

Finally, enter the interrupt code and connect the interrupting event (external line clock or timer) to the NMI (or IRQ) line. Remember to initialize the stack and to set the address of your interrupt routine into 17FA and 17FB (or 17FE, 17FF).

Figure 8.10 gives an overview of how your complete program is going to look. SETTIME binarizes the input and starts the timer so

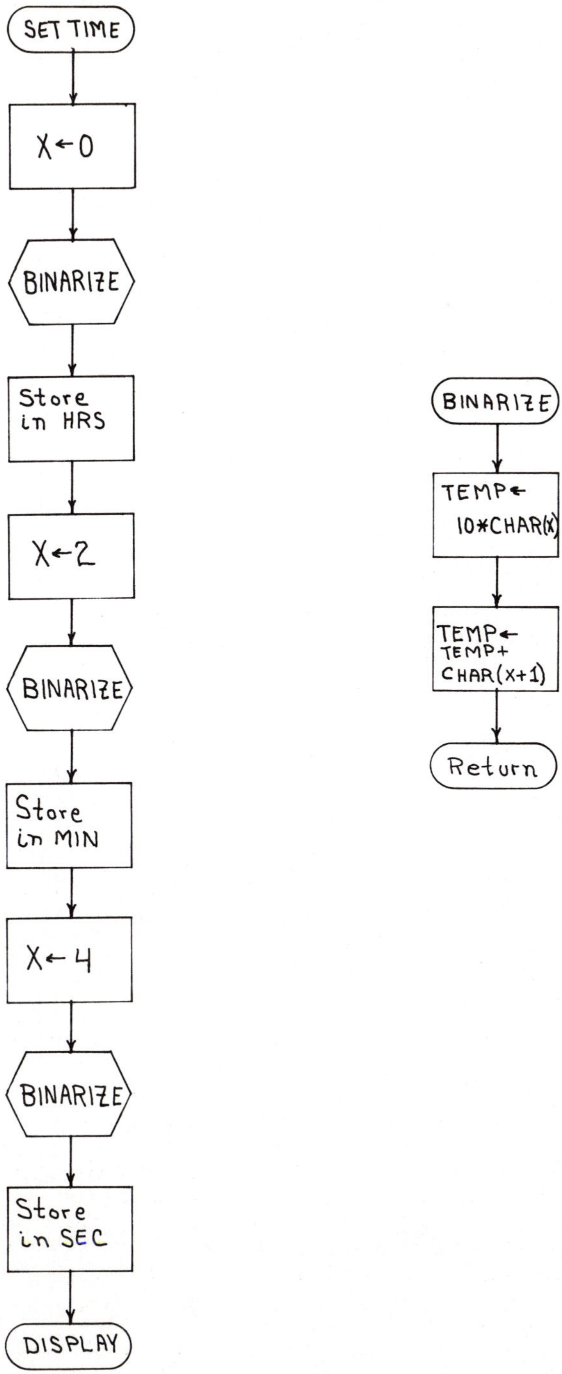

Figure 8.9 The Settime routine.

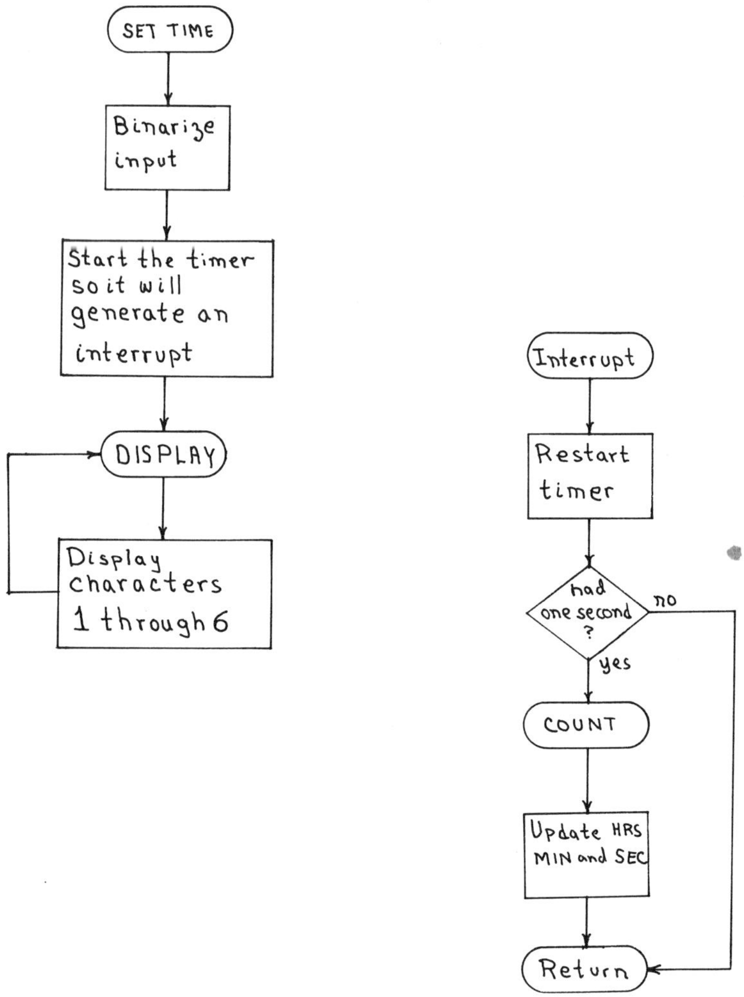

Figure 8.10 Overview of clock programs.

that it will generate an initial interrupt. Display puts the six characters of the time up on the display and does it forever. When the timer times out, the computer is somewhere in the display loop. It saves its place and goes off, via 17FE, 17FF, to the interrupt routine, where it restarts the timer so another interrupt will occur later and looks to see if a second is up. If not, it returns directly. If it is up, it updates the hours, minutes, and seconds counters as necessary, and converts those counts to display characters. Then it returns to the display program. The next time out, and the next and the next, will cause a repetition of the action. Between time outs, the display keeps chugging along, showing the characters to the admiring world. Seriously, programming interrupt is hard to understand and harder to get right. You will feel very proud when the program works.

Since these programs are difficult to make work, allow me to suggest a debugging technique that may be of some assistance. Using * to indicate the present instruction address, we can write

```
JMP * + 1
```

meaning "jump to the next instruction". As written, this merely takes up time and space and does nothing for you. But, if you change it to

```
JMP *
```

it becomes a trap or dynamic halt. The program hits it and goes no further. But if you scatter these judiciously throughout your program they will allow you (by changing them to JMP *) to make your program stop in various places so you can see what is going on. For example, a JMP * + 1 between the binarize input and the starting of the time allows you to see whether the decimal time you entered was properly converted to binary. In the display loop you can examine index registers and so forth to find out why no display at all is shown (or whatever else happens). One at the beginning of the interrupt routine will allow you to discover if that routine is ever entered, and one at the beginning and at the end of the counting routine allows you to check that out. To be sure, it is rather clumsy to set these back and forth from "do nothings" to "traps", but they are a lot easier to stick in when you are first writing your program and they do no harm at all if left in, in the do-nothing position. On most microprocessors there is a "break" instruction which is a one-byte interrupt-generator that can be used instead of the JMP * +1, but I am not going to try to explain that while you are still sweating out simple interrupts. Read up on it yourself.

9
TRACKING

An operator sits in front of a meter. His job is to keep the needle centered. As it moves off to the right, he turns a knob counter-clockwise and brings it back to center. As it moves left, he corrects with a clockwise turn of the knob.

Perhaps he is keeping the Enterprise's phasors centered on a Klingon ship. Perhaps he is controlling the depth at which a nuclear submarine is sneaking into an enemy harbor. Whatever he is doing he is observing an analogue signal, the meter movement, and generating an analogue response, the motion of his control knob.

ANALOGUE AND DIGITAL

Up to now we have been dealing with a purely digital world -- a light is either on or off, a button is either pushed or not -- but, as we all know, many aspects of the real world are not of this type. The brakes of a car are not either on or off; the driver can push the pedal down with infinite gradations of force. So, too, with an accelerator, or a steering wheel. In the Navy the supposedly standard response to any emergency is to shout "right full rudder," but in most situations the helmsman moves the wheel in a continuous fashion, a bit to the left (sorry, port) or the right, as occasion demands. The position of the wheel corresponds to the position of the rudder which, in turn, corresponds to the rate of turn of the ship.

In this chapter we are going to explore how to connect a discrete digital device like a computer to an analogue world. Specifically, we are going to consider how to build simple inexpensive analogue-to-digital converters (ADC's) and digital-to-analogue converters (DAC's), and how to set up a tracking problem like that described in the opening paragraph.

In a tracking problem we have a situation similar to that shown in Fig. 9.1. There is an input or command signal. The actions of the human (the knob position) are subtracted from the command and the resulting difference is called the error signal -- the amount by which the response fails to match the command. The human observes the error signal and changes his response in such a way as to reduce the error.

The response is an analogue signal -- a voltage generated by a potentiometer -- which must be changed to a digital representation in order for the digital computer to be able to handle it. On the output side, the error signal (command - response) must be converted from a binary number (digital) to a meter movement (analogue repre-

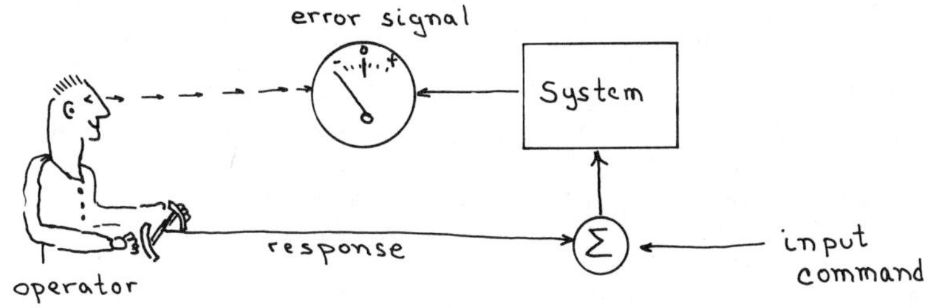

Figure 9.1 A human operator in a closed loop.

sentation). Since this is the easiest part, let's tackle it first.

DIGITAL TO ANALOGUE CONVERSION

Many computers (large or small) that must interface with the real world must generate analogue signals from internal binary representations of numbers. What is almost always done is to convert the digital signal into a voltage and then convert the voltage into some other form by auxiliary devices outside the computer. One convenient way to make a voltage visible to a human is to use a voltmeter. What I have in mind is one of the old-fashioned kind where the meter has a needle like the one on a speedometer, that swings over to the right as the voltage increases and to the left as it goes to zero.

Ordinary inexpensive (< \$100) voltmeters usually consist of a 50-microampere meter (full-scale deflection if 50 microamps flow through the meter) in series with a resistor. See Fig. 9.2.

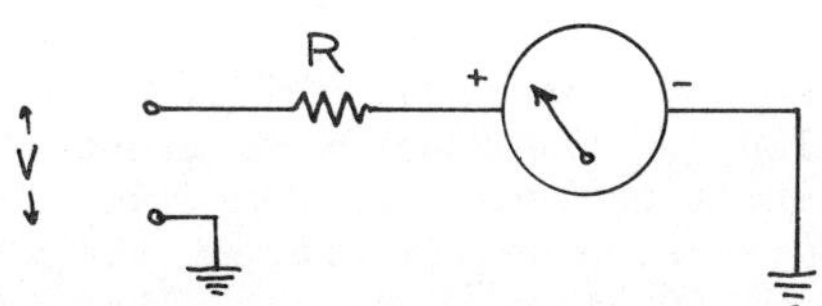

Figure 9.2 A typical voltmeter.

There is usually a switch to allow us to change the size of the resistor R and thus change scales, but we have left that out for simplicity.

Now every stableboy (who has studied high-school physics) knows that voltage is what pushes current through a resistor. The more voltage, the more current; the higher the value of the resistance for a given voltage, the less current will flow. In fact, a gentleman by the name of Ohm summed it up neatly by remarking that:

$$V = IR$$

where V is voltage measured in volts, I is current measured in amperes (amps, for short) and R is resistance measured in Ohms (he wasn't that conceited; the name was coined after he died).

Now suppose we want the voltmeter to show full-scale deflection if 5 volts are applied across the terminals. To make the meter deflect all the way to the right, we need 50×10^{-6} amperes, or 50 microamps, flowing in the plus side of the meter and out the minus side. Since V = IR, it must be that:

$$R = \frac{V}{I}$$

or the resistance in the curcuit should equal $\frac{5}{(50 \times 10^{-6})}$ or 100,000 ohms -- abbreviated 100K

Since our computer may not generate a full 5 volts at one of its output bits, let us make the resistor be variable and use a potentiometer in place of a fixed resistor. Then we can adjust full scale on our meter to our own convenience.

Let us look at an output bit. If it is turned ON, it will output V volts, where V depends on the machine being used. For the KIM-1, V $\approx$ 5 volts (read "approximately equal to"). If the output bit is OFF, it will put out about 0.1 or 0.2 volts (say, 0 volts). Suppose we have a program that turns the bit on and off in such a way that it is on half the time and off half the time. We could easily turn it on and off 1000 times per second (or even much faster if we wanted to). But the meter can't move that fast. It is sluggish. It might take half a second to go from zero to full scale and back to zero again. So what does it do? It displays the average value of a rapidly changing input. In this case it would display 2.5 volts or mid-scale.

That's how we are going to make a D-to-A converter. The more we turn on the output bit (percentage-wise), the higher the average value will be and the higher the meter will read. Let's look at the program.

We will run a counter down from 127 to 0, one step every few microseconds. As long as the counter is greater than NUMB, we will output a zero. When it is less than NUMB, we will output a one. At 50 microseconds per step we will repeat the whole cycle every 6.4 milliseconds, or 156 times a second. That is so frequent that the meter won't even wiggle. Figure 9.3 shows several ways of hooking up such a meter. The nearer NUMB is to zero, the less time we output a one and the more time we output a zero. Thus the average output voltage will be proportional to NUMB. Time lost at the end of the cycle resetting things merely lowers the maximum value of the output and all other readings proportionately. (If you don't have a potentiometer (variable resistor), you can use this method of adjusting full scale.)

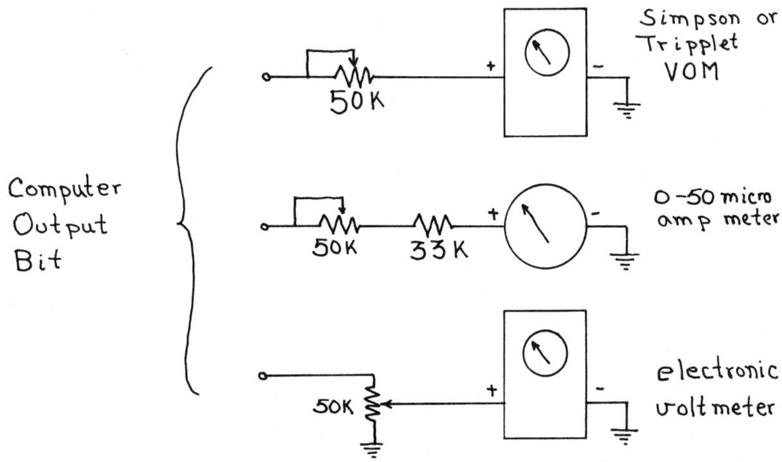

Figure 9.3 Several ways of making a voltmeter to display the output voltage.

Figure 9.4 shows a flow diagram of an output loop, together with a delay loop for adjusting full scale; V is the value to be put out.

If V = 0, then we never put out a 1, and the average value of the output is identically zero. Suppose V = 127 and suppose, further, that it takes T microseconds to go around the upper loop once. Now we will output a one each time around, and we will spend 128T milliseconds in the upper loop. We will spend D milliseconds in the "wait" state putting out a zero, so the average value of the output (P) will be

$$P_{ave} = \frac{128T}{128T + D} \cdot 5 \text{ volts}$$

By increasing D, we can lower the average value of the output so that the meter reads full scale for V = 127. In order to make this work properly, we need a full-scale voltage of less than 5 volts. Many meters have 2½-volt or 3-volt scales built in. If you are designing your own meter, a full-scale (50 microamps) of 2½ volts is reasonable. This calls for a 50K-ohm resistor; 47K is a standard value. Since we are going to adjust the full-scale reading anyway, accuracy of the resistor is not critical.

If you need high-frequency response on the output, then you should not use this extra delay to adjust full scale because that will decrease the number of output samples you can generate per second, and hence decrease the frequency response. In that case, you should use a variable resistor. For our tracking problem this delay method is entirely satisfactory.

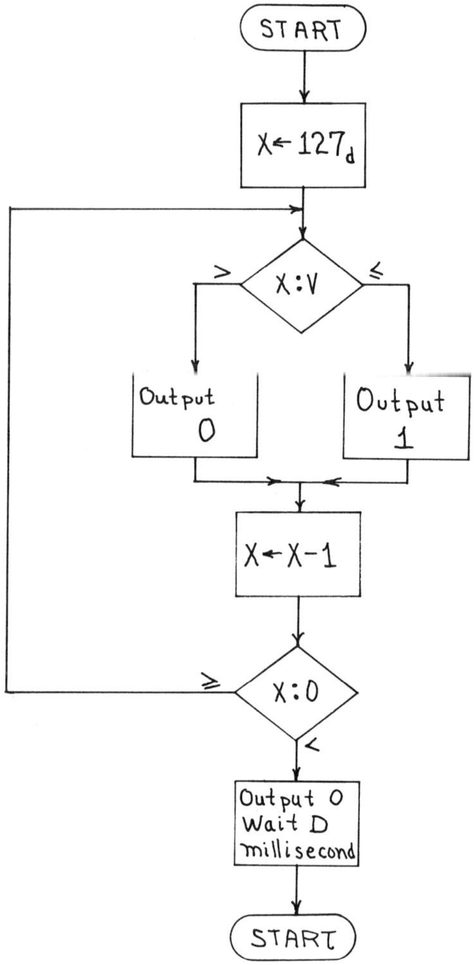

Figure 9.4 Output loop to put out the value V. D is a delay used to adjust full-scale reading.

Obviously this scheme can be generalized, and several outputs can be driven by one microcomputer. For many situations this system will be adequate for displays that do not have to change rapidly. For example, one might use it to control the speed of a model train by feeding the output voltage to a dc power amplifier.

In many situations, however, the low rate of response of this scheme will preclude its use. For example, we might want to plot points on an oscilloscope with a 60-hertz sweep. Then we must arrange to be able to change the output value 200 times or more per 60th of a second so that we can paint arbitrary wave shapes or lines on the screen. To do this, we must use a more conventional D-to-A converter.

These work in parallel, rather than letting a time average of the output generate the voltage. Suppose we want to display a point in analogue fashion with an accuracy of one part in 256. This will require eight output bits. We load the binary number to be converted into the output bits and connect them to a circuit similar to that shown in Fig. 9.5. Resistors of increasing value (and decreasing accuracy requirements) are connected to the bits, starting with the most significant. The circuit works by summing up currents. Suppose the most significant bit is a one and is at +5 volts. Through the 1K resistor it will inject $(5 - V_{out})/1000$ amperes, or $(5 - V_{out})$ milliamps. If the second most significant bit is one, it will inject $1/2\ (5 - V_{out})$ milliamps, and each less significant bit will put in half as much current as the preceding one. If a bit is at zero, it will withdraw $\frac{1}{R} \cdot V_{out}$ milliamps from the junction of all the resistors. Now, V_{out} will adjust itself so that the amount of current flowing into the junction is equal to the amount flowing out. Consider a 4-bit version of the device holding the number 1010. We have input currents of

$$(5 - V) + 1/4\ (5 - V)$$

and output currents of $1/2\ V + 1/8\ V$. Since these are equal, we may write:

$$(5 - V)\ (1 + 1/4) = V(1/2 + 1/8).$$

Solving for V, we get:

$$V = 3.33 \text{ volts},$$

which is 2/3 of 5 volts, just as the number 10_d is 2/3 of 15_d, the maximum possible 4-bit number.

A TO D CONVERTER

To convert an analogue signal to a digital representation, we are going to use a DAC as an output and add it to the unknown input. We will increase the output until the sum of the two reaches some known voltage called the "trigger voltage."

Since we know the output voltage (V_{out}) and the trigger voltage (V_{trig}), we can cleverly figure out the unknown voltage (V_{unk}) by subtraction:

$$V_{unk} = V_{trig} - V_{out}.$$

To add two voltages, we use a circuit similar to the one shown in Fig. 9.6.

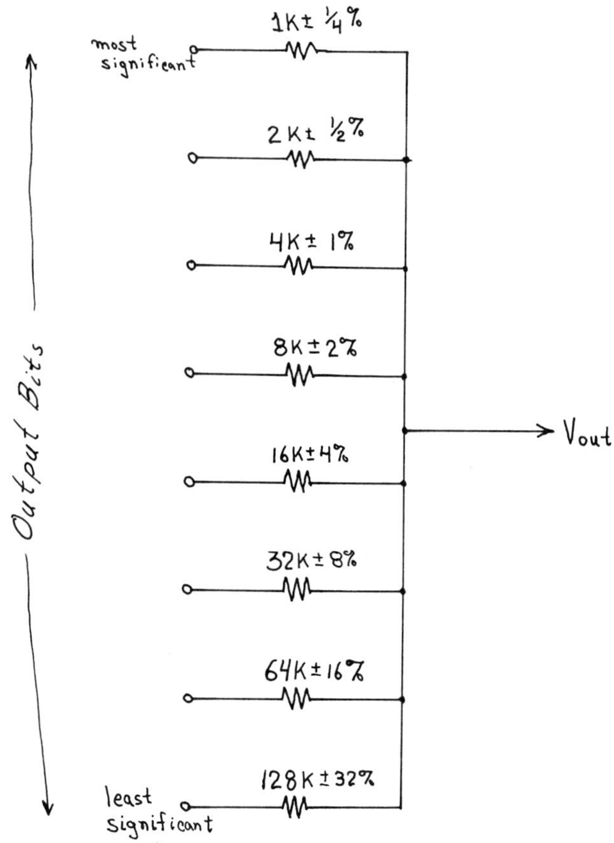

Figure 9.5 A conventional D to A converter (DAC).

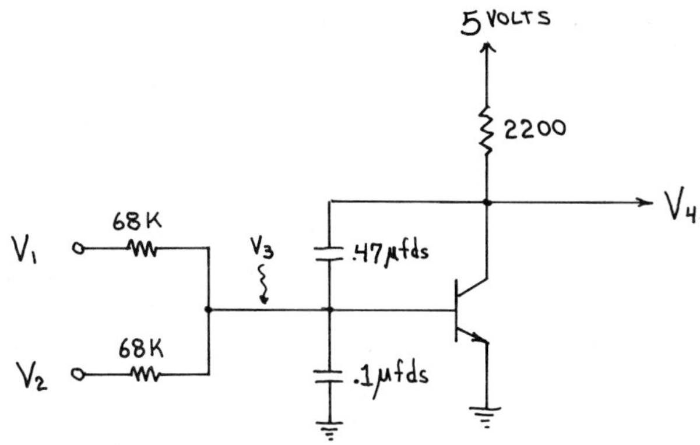

Figure 9.6 A voltage adder and decoupler.

Consider first the voltage V_3 at the junction of R_1 and R_2. Ignore the capacitors and the transistor. By the same conservation-of-current arguments we used above, as long as $R_1 = R_2$, then

$$V_3 = 1/2\ (V_1 + V_2),$$

which, except for the factor of one-half, is the sum of V_1 and V_2. The capacitors are there to prevent rapid changes in V_1 or V_2 (as, for example, might be caused by a simple DAC described above) from affecting V_3. It smooths out or averages the resulting sum. We can connect V_4 to the input of any microcomputer without worrying about the computer loading down the suming circuit and destroying its accuracy. When the voltage of V_3 is "high," V_4 will be "low" and vice versa, because the transistor inverts the signal applied to it.

As we increase the voltage applied to an input bit of a microcomputer, there will come a critical voltage at which the computer changes its mind about whether it is seeing a <u>zero</u> or a <u>one</u>. This is the <u>trigger voltage</u>, and it will vary from one type of computer to another and even between two examples of the same type. My KIM-1 has a trigger voltage of 1.35 volts. Connect a voltmeter from V_4 to ground and, with V_4 connected to an input bit of your computer, see if you can measure the trigger voltage. Is it the same for all input bits on this port? On another input port? Note that you may need to write a very short program to be able to see the input bit. With a KIM you just "look at" 1700 for port A and remember to put 00 in 1701 so port A is an input port.

Now we have the principles of the ADC worked out we need to look at the details. Suppose we measure V_4 and the computer senses a <u>one</u>. then we know that V_4 is greater than the trigger voltage and that V_3 is too low. We have to increase the average value of the voltage V_2, so we output a <u>one</u> on that bit. We come back 100 microseconds later and observe that V_4 seems to be <u>zero</u> now. We have fallen below the trigger voltage and V_3 is too large, so we make V_2 be a logical <u>zero</u>.

If we keep on doing this regularly, the average value of V_4 will be just equal to the trigger voltage (V_{trig}) and the average value of V_2 will be equal to

$$V_2 = 2V'_{trig} - V_1,$$

where V'_{trig} is the voltage at the base of the transistor that will generate V_{trig} at the collector. If V_1 is derived from a potentiometer controlled by the operator, then we have a measure of where he has put his control knob. Figure 9.7 shows a circuit to derive V_1; V_2 is connected to some convenient output bit, say B0.

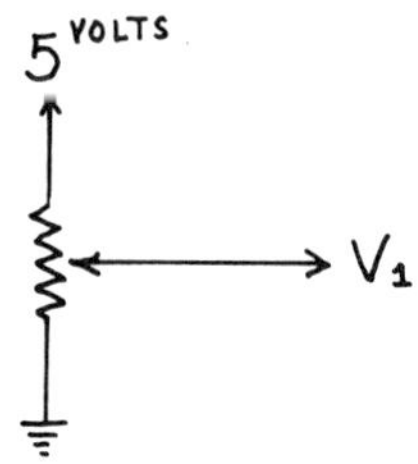

Figure 9.7 The operator's control. He moves the arm of the pot.

We have generated V_2 but we don't have any record inside the computer of what we have done; that is, we don't know the average value of V_2. We are going to go around a loop 128 times to generate an output voltage for the meter. If, each time we go around, we increment N if we made $V_2 = 1$ and don't increment it if V_2 is zero, when we eventually exit from the loop we will find N is a number between 0 and 128, depending on what percentage of the time we output a 1 to the ADC.

If we clear N before we re-enter the loop, when we exit we will find N is a good estimate of V_2 and it will do for our experiment.

COMMAND SIGNAL

If we just take the input signal and program it across to the output, the user will quickly center the needle and then perhaps begin to lose interest in the experiment, since there is not much else to do. What we want to have is a command signal that will cause the needle to move around on its own, and the operator's task will then be to cancel out these variations.

What task shall we set the operator? The classical tracking task uses a sine wave as the command signal. This has a drawback: It is hard to compute in a system without a multiply instruction.

Let us choose a simple triangular wave that goes from 0 to 63 and back to zero again, in some time period like 15 seconds. That means a change of 10 units per second or one unit roughly every tenth of a second. In my program I go around the meter output loop about once every 5 milliseconds. We will start at zero and, roughly every 20th time through the output cycle, we will add a one to COMMAND until it gets to 63. Then we will turn around and start subtracting one from COMMAND until it gets down to 0. Again we reverse and count up. This will give COMMAND a triangular shape with a period of something like 12 seconds.

If we want to generate a more complex command signal, we might do it by storing a string of 0's, +1's, and -1's, and running through this list, adding the string element to COMMAND, say, 10 times per second. For a 15-second period we would need 150 values. Plenty of room to store them, but a little tedious entering them. One should be certain to make the number of plus ones equal to the number of minus ones, lest the value of COMMAND gradually increase or decrease without limit. Using this scheme we, in effect, integrate (sum up) the values over time, and at time i,

$$\text{COMMAND} = \sum_{t=0}^{i} \text{Element (i)}$$

$$= \text{element (0)} + \text{element (1)} + \ldots + \text{element (i)}.$$

We can, using this scheme, generate almost any arbitrary wave form we might like. I choose, for simplicity, to use the triangular wave described earlier, but if you want to, you could try the other scheme.

We will compute the ERROR signal as being the COMMAND plus half the operator's RESPONSE. If each number ranges from 0 to 63, the sum of the numbers will range from 0 to 126.

ERROR = COMMAND + 1/2 RESPONSE

If we add the command and the response, we can't get into any complications due to negative numbers. This just "inverts" the apparent knob position. Since the response ranges from 0-128, we will divide it in half so that it is equal in range to the command, and the total is not larger than the largest number we can display (128).

I think we are about ready to draw a flow diagram, so why don't you try before looking at Fig. 9.8?

We need to assign I/O bits now. Let's put the meter output bit as B0. We need to sample and test the response input bit so let's make it be A7 so we can test for 0 or 1 conveniently. The V_2 output bit can go in A0.

The user's task will be to keep the output meter needle at exactly mid-scale. One more point: Life being what it is, a clockwise movement of the control knob will more than likely cause a counterclockwise motion of the meter needle. That is not very good human engineering, so if this problem occurs, we can "fix" it by interchanging the "output 1" and "output 0" after we compare X to the ERROR.

MORE COMPLICATIONS

Once you have learned to track a signal as shown above, you may be ready for more challenging pastimes. In what we did above, the response knob generated a signal that was added to the command directly. This is often called "first-order" or "position" control. Suppose, instead, we wanted the knob to control a velocity -- a rate of change. We can do this by integrating the response as follows:

N is our measure of the response. N - 32 is a zero-centered transformation of that response. Let NPRIME be equal to the sum of N over time. Then, each time we get ready to compute the error signal ($\alpha 2$ in Fig. 9.8), we let

NPRIME←NPRIME + (N-32)

and

ERROR←COMMAND + 1/2 NPRIME

We will have to be careful to limit NPRIME to the range 0-63 so that the error doesn't become impossibly large (positive or negative). Now a knob displacement seems to control the rate of correction. Large knob positions will cause the needle of the meter to swing rapidly. Small (near the center) knob positions will cause slow changes. This is a much more difficult tracking task and usually holds peoples' interest for some time. One can, of course, go further and integrate N twice so that the knob position controls the acceleration of the needle. To do this we compute:

NPRIME←NPRIME + (N-32)

NDOUBLE←NDOUBLE + NPRIME

and ERROR←COMMAND + 1/2 NDOUBLE

but if you are really interested in this sort of thing perhaps you should first get a book on servomechanisms and study that.

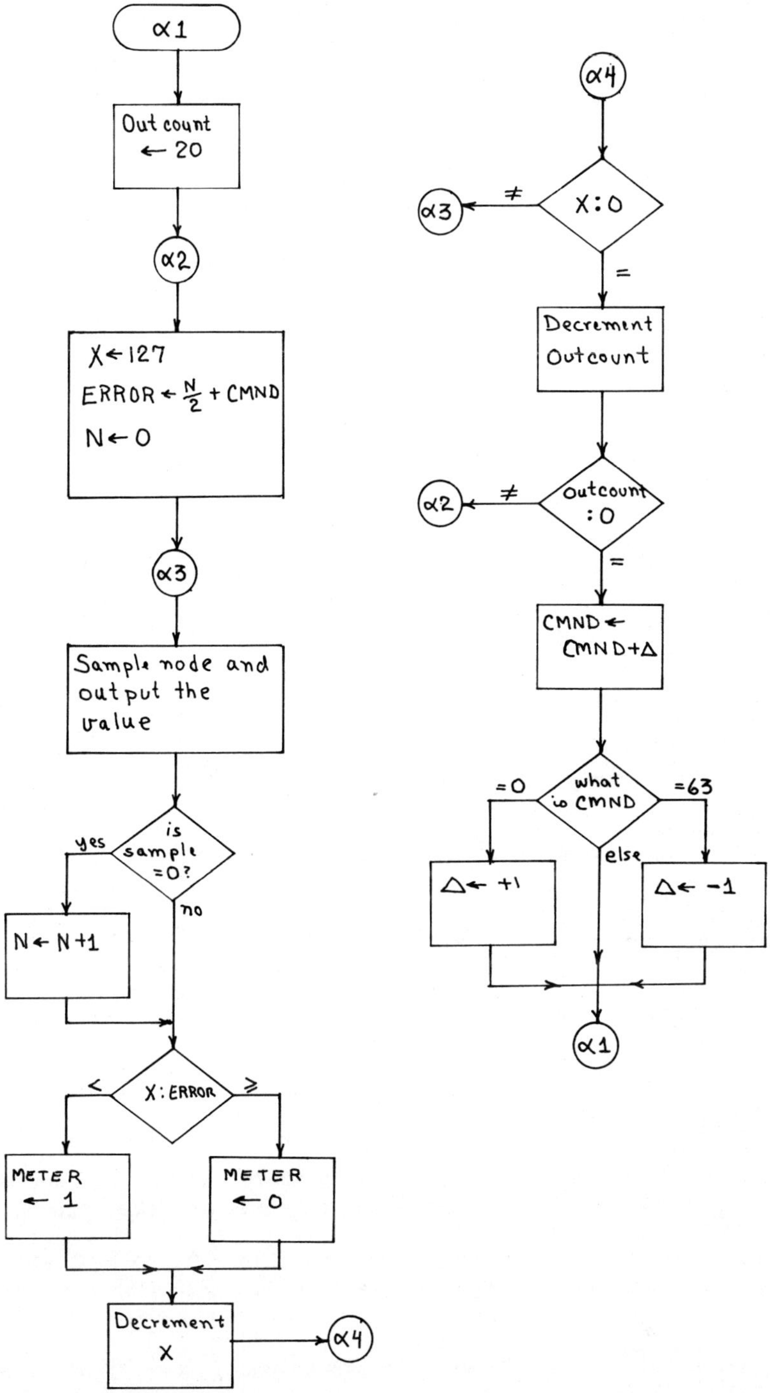

Figure 9.8 A flow diagram for the tracking problem.

10
MICROBART

In this chapter we are going to construct a model railroad simulator and eventually get two "trains" running around on a figure-eight "track" without having them collide with each other at the crossing.

To start off, let us describe the "track" layout. This will look like Fig. 10.1.

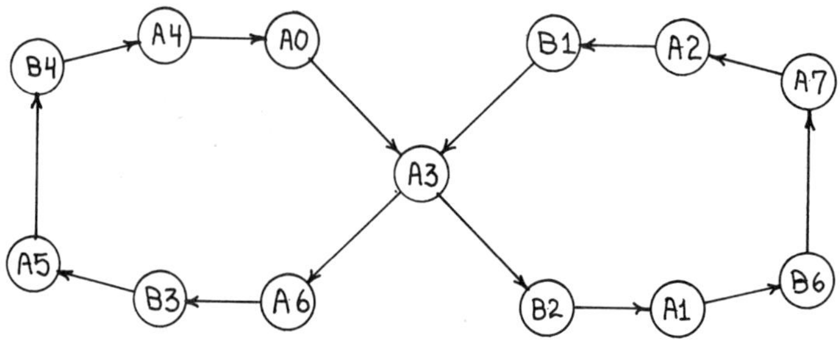

Figure 10.1 A "track" consisting of 13 lights laid out in a figure 8.

Each light will be connected to one of the output bits of the computer A0-A7 and B0-B4. As you will note, the person wiring up the track had a macabre sense of humor and no rational scheme seems to have been employed. But we will persevere and overcome this apparent idiocy by means of a linked list, which will be described immediately.

LINKED LISTS

When a train travels over the track shown above, it might start on the track section called A0. Moving in the direction of the arrows, it will proceed to A3, then B2, and eventually get around to A4, from whence it returns to A0. We will simulate this journey by lighting the lights in turn, each for perhaps a second. Note that we pass

---

* BART is the Bay Area Rapid Transit system and is the first major electronically controlled transportation system. It has had some problems getting operational.

through A3 twice, once coming from the upper left and once from the upper right. Let us call these sections A3L and A3R. If two trains are present on the track simultaneously, we must be sure that only one train occupies a track section at a time. Since A3L and A3R are merely different names for the same section, we must take care to have, at most, one of them occupied at any one time.

One of our problems is that the track blocks don't come in order. Let us look for a moment at Fig. 10.2.

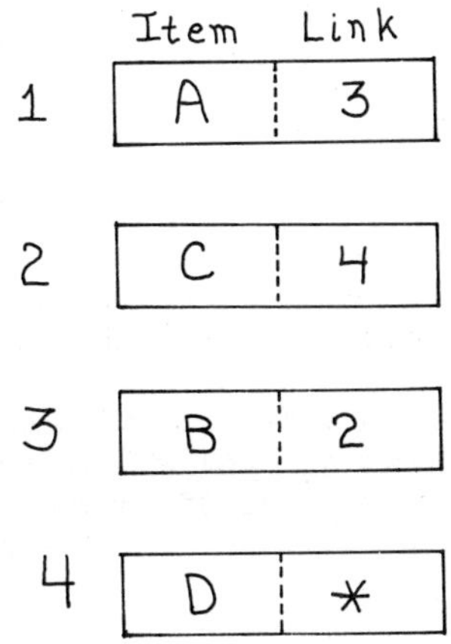

Figure 10.2 A linked list

We have the first four letters of the alphabet (A,B,C, and D), but they are not stored in order. They are stored in "slots" in the machine with A in slot 1, B in slot 3, C in slot 2, and D in slot 4. How can we link them together so they may be read out in order? The second half of each slot contains the number of the next slot to look at. Beginning in slot 1 we are directed to slot 3, then 2, then 4, and there the * tells us we are at the end of the list. The ITEM portion of each slot tells us the letter associated with that slot. Sometimes there are several items, sometimes there are none, and only the list itself is of interest. We can store all the words of one slot together. For example, slot 1 might occupy words 0200 and 0201 while slot 2 occupied 0202 and 0203, etc. Or, conversely, we can store each kind of field in one array (thus 0200 holds A, 0201 holds C, (0202) = B, and (0203) = D, and the links are in a second array:

```
(0218) = 3
(0219) = 4
(021A) = 2
(021B) = *        often represented by zero or a
                  negative number
```

Let us look first at the links we need to tie the blocks in the proper order. We will store these links like this:

Name of block	Storage address	Index of next block
A0	0200	3
A1	1	8
A2	2	9
A3L	3	A
A4	4	0
A5	5	C
A6	6	B
A7	7	2
B0	8	7
B1	9	D
B2	A	1
B3	B	5
B4	C	4
A3R	D	6

To find out what block comes after A6, we look in entry 6 of the table and find a "B". Entry B of the table is associated with block B3.

Each block is identified with a particular piece of track, with the complication that blocks A3L and A3R (representing the crossover) are identified with the <u>same</u> piece of track. To make this simple for our program to remember, we will have a "track section table" as shown below:

Block name	Storage address	Section number
A0	0210	0
A1	1	1
A2	2	2
A3L	3	3
A4	4	4
A5	5	5
A6	6	6
A7	7	7
B0	8	8
B1	9	9
B2	A	A
B3	B	B
B4	C	C
A3R	D	3

In locations 0220-022D, we will build a table of showing which light should be lighted in PORTA if a train is in a given block, and in 0230-023D a similar table for PORTB.

Block name	Storage address	ALITE	Storage address	BLITE
A0	0220	01	0230	0
A1	1	02	1	0
A2	2	04	2	0
A3L	3	08	3	0
A4	4	10	4	0
A5	5	20	5	0
A6	6	40	6	0
A7	7	80	7	0
B0	8	0	8	01
B1	9	0	9	02
B2	A	0	A	04
B3	B	0	B	08
B4	C	0	C	10
A3R	D	08	D	0

Finally, for each track section, we need a word to tell whether that section is busy or idle. We will let 1 = BUSY and 0 = IDLE. Using the section number that we get from the table in 0210-021D, we can look up a table called BUSY, stored in cells 0310-031C, to see if a section is busy or idle.

RUNNING ONE TRAIN

Before we take on the task of running two trains, let us see what we have to do to get one running. BUSY (i) will contain a zero if the track section i is unoccupied and a one if there is a train in this section. (For only one train, it is rather superfluous but we will need it later.) In ALITE (i) (the ith entry of the vector ALITE), we will store the pattern needed to turn on the light connected to PORTA associatid with block number i, and similar information for PORTB will be stored in BLITE (i). Thus, for section 0 we will have:

$$\text{ALITE }(0) = 0000\ 0001 = 01_h$$

$$\text{BLITE }(0) = 0000\ 0000 = 00_h$$

When we run one train we can execute

```
LDAX ALITE
STA  1700
LDAX BLITE
STA  1702
```

if we use index register X to hold the block number of the train. When we come to run two trains, we can use X for one train and Y for the other. Then

```
LDAX ALITE
ORAY ALITE
STA  1700
```

```
LDAX BLITE
ORAY BLITE
STA  1702
```

will "or" the two lights together, regardless of which port they may lie in.

To move a train between blocks we will have a cell reserved for train 1, called BLOCK 1, which contains the name of the block the train is now in (an index from 0 to D).

Figure 10.3 shows what we need to do when we move from one block to another. When we enter a block, if its successor (the block after the one we just entered) is not free, we will stop the train so that it doesn't run into the rear end of the train ahead. If the train is stopped, we will keep an eye on the block ahead and when it becomes free we will advance again.

Each train will dwell in a block for an amount of time inversely proportional to its speed. Let us use a double loop (one inside the other) to control dwell. If the inner loop takes 0.5 milliseconds, then 100 times around the outer loop will be half a second, and 200 times around will represent 1 second of dwell. Therefore, if we store "speeds" as a number between 100_d and 200_d with 100 being "fast" and 200 being slow, we can control the train handily. When we time out, we will advance the train. If the train is stopped, then at each exit from the inner loop we can check the track ahead to see if it is clear.

TWO TRAINS

When we come to run two trains at the same time, we have a somewhat more interesting problem. If we imagine that the crossover is via a bridge so that no collisions can take place, then we simply give A3L and A3R different numbers (with the same light pattern) and the problem is solved. But let us suppose, to the contrary, that the crossing is at grade level and that only one train can occupy block A3, whether it comes from the upper left or the upper right.

Look at Fig. 10.4.

Suppose train 1 is in section B1 approaching A3R. Suppose train 0 is just crossing from A4 to A0. It tests the block ahead (that is A3L) and finds it empty so it proceeds at full speed. Because train 1 is going slower than train 0, they both arrive at the crossover at the same time and have what the New Zealanders call a "wizard prang"! That seems like "a hell of a way to run a railroad" if you ask me, so we must complicate our scheme a bit to prevent this sort of thing.

Suppose when we test the block ahead we make the block busy (if it is available). Now what happens? When train 1 enters block it examines block A3R and finds it free. It then reserves block A3R by marking it busy. Now train 0 comes along into block A0. It looks at A3L and finds that block busy so it stops and waits until A3L goes idle. Then it can proceed. We really need to do this only for B0, blocks A3L and A3R, but it will be easier if we always do it when we enter a new block, rather than having to test to see if it is a "critical" block.

In the KIM-1 (and most other microprocessors), we are going to

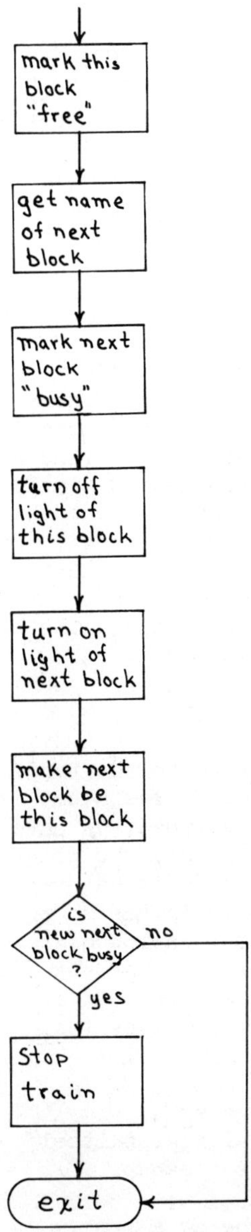

Figure 10.3 Things to do when moving from one block to another.

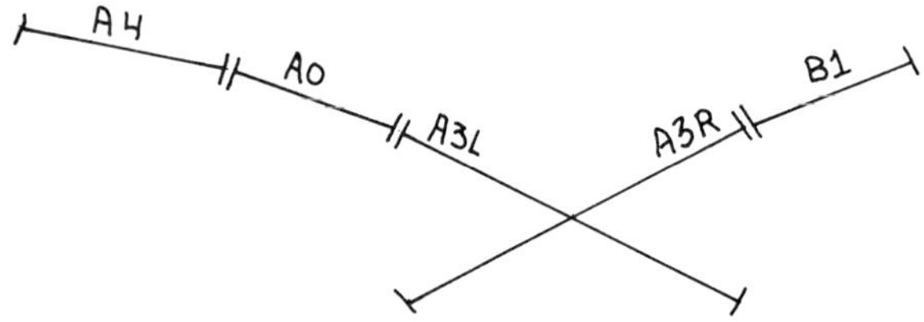

Figure 10.4 The crossover, showing the blocks and their names.

program this "train advance" section of code as a loop that waits N microseconds and then, first, sees if train 0 needs to advance and then, second, sees if train 1 needs to advance. Given this procedure there can be no races and the program as outlined above is sufficient. But suppose we had two processors, one running train 0 and the other running train 1. It could happen (and given Murphy's law probably will happen) that both processors simultaneously test the block A3 and each finds it idle. So each one thinks it is O. K. to reserve the block and continue at full speed. Result? Bang! This is called a "race condition" and occurs frequently enough so that people have worked out a solution for it. This situation can also occur if one train is run as a main program and the other as an interrupt program.

SEMAPHORES

It is appropriate to introduce the topic of semaphores in the context of a railroad because, of course, that is where the ideas originated. In a computer, as in a railroad, we have a section of code (track) which must be occupied by only one program (train) at a time. In a computer this is called a "critical region." In our train example it is the crossover section. In the computer this critical region usually deals with the allocation of resources -- the assignment of a tape unit, or a block of core, or use of some facility (such as A3) which, by its design, precludes multiple occupancy. The standard solution to this problem involves four pieces of code:

The call
The entry gate
The critical region itself
The exit or cleanup.

Let us consider these one at a time.

The call

The main program will call the subroutine with a standard subroutine jump, passing parameters (if necessary) in any of the standard ways.

When the subroutine returns, the first thing the main program must do is check to see if it got what it wanted from the subroutine. By convention we will call the subroutine with the number of the desired track section in the accumulator. On return the accumulator will contain a one if the call was successful (we get what we asked for) and a zero if it was rejected. If we test the accumulator immediately on return, we can go forward in confidence if successful, or repeat the call if we failed.

The entry gate or P

For historical reasons the entry gate is called "P". You may remember this as a "request for Permission to enter." In this section of code, we are going to see if the critical region is already occupied. If not, we will mark it as occupied and then enter the critical region. If it is occupied already, we will execute a return with zero accumulator indicating failure to enter. The following code carries this out reasonably efficiently:

```
P:      INC SEM     - "SEM" is a flag which contains a -1 if the
                      region is idle and a 0 if the region is
                      busy. Incrementing this flag will give a
                      0 if it was idle and +1 if it was busy and
                      simultaneously make it busy if it was idle.

        LDA SEM     - Get the flag so we can look at it.

        BEQ CRIT    - If now zero we win and go ahead.

        DEC Sem     - Subtract one removing our request. This
                      brings the flag back to zero since it had
                      to be busy to get here.

        LDA #00     - Set the accumulator to "fail."

        RTS         - Return to the calling program.
```

The critical region

Beginning with a cell labeled "CRIT", the critical region does the assignment of the resource to the calling program and marks that resource as being "in use" and not available for others to use. This can be done in any convenient fashion because we know that only one program can be executing this code at a time. The critical region ends by executing a clean-up or V-operation.

V-operation

This piece of code is going to unlock the critical region so that somebody else can use it. It will do this by decrementing the flag (SEM) and then loading a one in the accumulator (to indicate successful execution of the critical region), and returning to the calling program. For example:

```
V:  DEC SEM
    LDA #01
    RTS
```

carries out these operations with dispatch.

Now let us go back and examine P again under the assumption that two independent processors are trying to execute it asynchronously (the second one butts in at the most inconvenient possible time). First of all, we should note that the DEC and INC instructions are not susceptible to interference. Once we start to execute an INC instruction, for example, we are going to complete it without letting anybody else get at the variable before we finish. That is built into the hardware. So process 1 does an INC on the flag SEM. We assume it was set to idle, or -1. At the conclusion of this instruction, SEM contains 0. Now, before process 1 can do the LDA SEM, process 2 butts in and does its INC SEM changing the contents of SEM to +1. Whatever happens, process 2 will see the value of SEM as being not zero, so it will go away unsatisfied and try again later. But now process 1 does its LDA SEM and seeing a one there thinks the critical region is locked up. So it goes away in disgust, believing that somebody else owns the critical region. Process 1 then removes its request (does DEC SEM) and returns. We see that, in this particular case, both processes have gone away unsatisfied when the critical region was actually available for use. Tough luck, but better that than a collision. Next time around, one will get in there first and do both its INC and LDA before the other does its INC, and that lucky process will get the critical region for its very own - until it tires of it. Then the other guy will get a chance.

In more complicated situations we don't want to keep knocking on the door if the critical region is busy. In these cases we will put a process "to sleep" if it can't be served. Then the V-operation must be more complex, also. It must check to see if anybody is "sleeping on the doorstep" before it exits, and "wake up" whoever is at the head of the queue waiting for service. We won't try to do that here. Indeed, as was mentioned above, we don't even need P's and V's in our simple problem, but it is good for the soul to know about such things.

THE GENERAL APPROACH

Now we are ready to lay out the general principles of controlling our trains. We will run train 1 at a constant speed but we would like to be able to vary the speed of train 0. We will use an A-to-D converter, as described in the chapter on Tracking, to get a continuously variable speed command. Since none of the timing here is really critical let us arrange things for our convenience.

We will sense the analogue voltage on B7 and use B5 to output to the A-to-D converter. Once every 500 microseconds, we will sample B7 and output B5 accordingly, keeping a count of either the zeros or the ones output (depending on the way the system works out -- we want clockwise rotation to mean faster motion). We will do this 100 times and at that point the count is our estimate of the knob position. This will become the dwell time of train 1. The problem of moving into the next track section we have already discussed in generalities, so you should have no problems drawing the flow diagram. See Fig. 10.5 and 10.6 after you have tried on your own.

At a number of points in the program, we are going to need the current track section number and the next track section number. I wrote a little subroutine called MAP, which dug these things out of the linked lists of the blocks. It is called with the train number (0 or 1) in X and looks like this:

```
MAP:  LDYX   BLOCK        Get the block number for this
                          train in Y
      LDAY   SECTNO       Load the section number of this
                          block and store it in PRESENT
      STAX   PRESENT
      LDAY   NEXTBLOCK    Get the link of this block
      TAY                 Put it in Y
      LDAY   SECTNO       Get the section number of this
                          next block and store it in NEXT
      STAX   NEXT
```

If train 1 is in block A2, this subroutine will set up

PRESENT(1) = 2

NEXT(1) = 8

so that the main program can test the next section to see if it is busy and release (make idle) the present section if it advances the train.

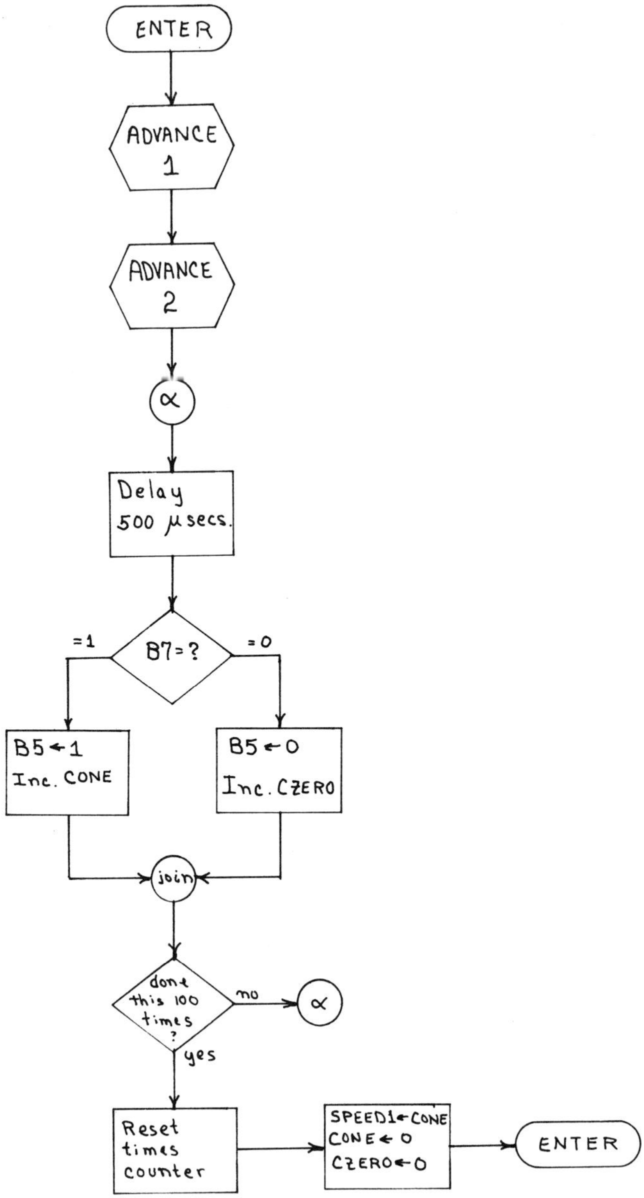

Figure 10.5 Overall flow diagram of the train problem.

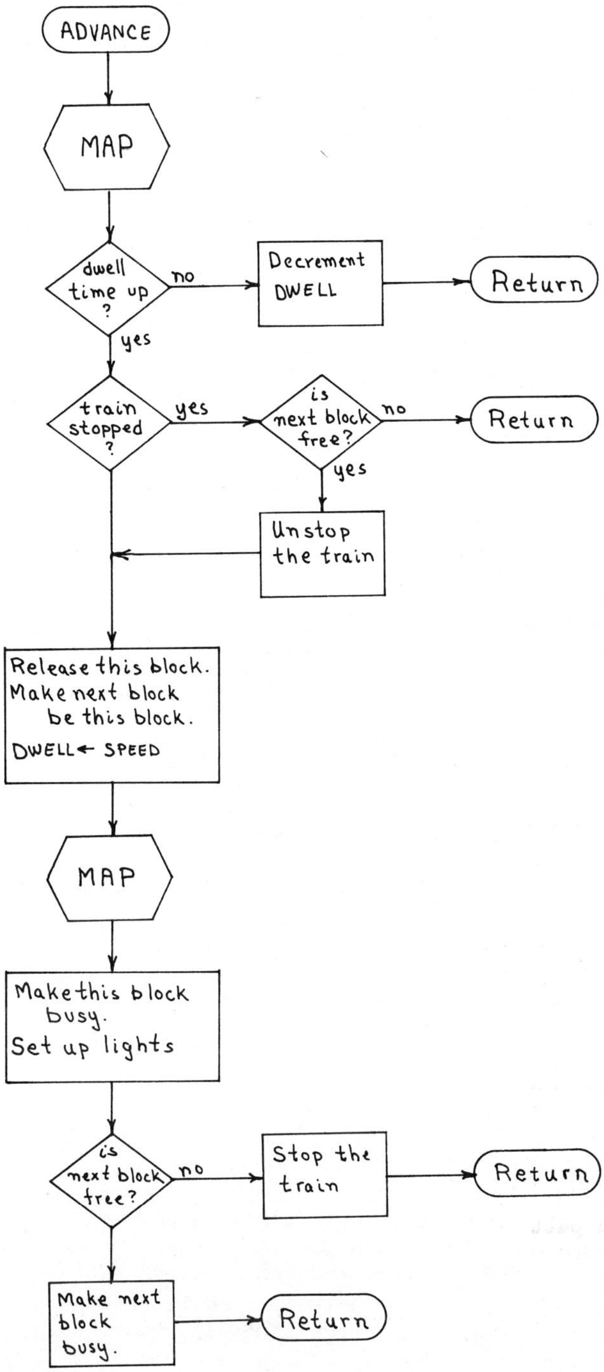

Figure 10.6 The Advance subroutine to move a train from one track section to the next, index register X is used to tell ADVANCE which train to look at.

11 TOP SECRET AND DISCRETE

If you have a typewriter connected to your computer, then this chapter will be of immediate interest to you. If you do not have a keyboard and display or a teletype or such device, then read for general information, against the day when you either acquire one or move to a system which has one. Our experiment this time will consist of building a coding device. During the Second World War (and probably since), there was a great deal of activity in codes and code breaking. Secret and Urgent by Fletcher Pratt, The Codebreakers, by David Kahn, and the Ultra Secret by F. W. Winterbotham.
are good books to read if you are interested in spy stories, or mathematics and cryptography.

What we propose to do is to write a program that will:

1. accept a "secret key word",

2. accept "cleartext" (plain English),

3. on receipt of a dollar sign, the computer will print out the encrypted (coded) version of the message.

If, in step 2 above, the first character is not an E (for ENCODE), then the program will accept ciphered text and output clear text.

As usual, before we can get on to the fun part, we have to find out some nitty-gritty details. In this case those details involve how a Teletype works.

ASCII

The American National Standards Institute has developed a set of bit patterns for representing various letters, numbers, punctuation signs and so forth inside computers. This is called the American Standard Code for Information Interchange (ASCII -- pronounced "Ass-Key-Two"). These patterns are 8 bits long and hence permit up to 256 different characters to be defined. At present only 128 characters are in use. This requires 7 bits and the leftmost bit is used as a "parity" bit. Both even and odd parity versions of ASCII exist. Even parity means that the 8th bit is chosen so that there are always 0,2,4,6, or 8 ones in the pattern. Odd parity means that the 8th bit is chosen (zero or one) so as to give an odd number of ones in the pattern (1,3,5,7). Since both versions exist, we will simply ignore the 8th bit and assume it is always zero. Figure 11.1 shows the 128 defined

← Most significant digit →

LSD	0	1	2	3	4	5	6	7
0	NVL	IDLE	Space	0	@	P		p
1	SOU	DC1	!	1	A	Q	a	q
2	STX	DC2	"	2	B	R	b	r
3	ETX	DC3	#	3	C	S	c	s
4	EOT	DC4	$	4	D	T	d	t
5	ENG	NAK	%	5	E	U	e	u
6	ACK	SYN	&	6	F	V	f	v
7	BEL	ETB	'	7	G	W	g	w
8	BS	CAN	(	8	H	X	h	x
9	HT	EM	)	9	I	Y	i	y
A	LP	SUB	*	:	J	Z	j	z
B	VT	ESC	+	;	K	[	k	
C	FF	FS	'	<	L	\	l	|
D	CR	GS	–	=	M	]	m	
E	SO	RS	.	>	N	↑	n	~
F	S1	VS	/	?	O	←	o	DEL

Nonprinting characters used for various functions to control the typewriter

Figure 11.1 Seven-bit ASCII characters.

characters of ASCII. In ASCII then, the letter A is represented by the bit pattern 0100 0001, or 41_h for short and B is 0100 0010 or 42_h, so if we had a Teletype connected somehow to PORTA of our computer, then, when a person struck the key "A", we would expect to find the number 41_h in PORTA. How it gets there is what we have to look at now.

ASYNCHRONOUS SERIAL INTERFACES

Teletypes consist of two separate devices inside one box. These are the keyboard or "transmitter" and the print box or "receiver." They were made to be used over long distances. Consequently, the designers did not want to have to run 9 wires (8 signals and a ground) between New York and San Francisco. It was thought to be less expensive to connect two teletypes with a single pair of wires (one signal and one ground). Furthermore, this made them compatible with the telephone system and the telegraph system. So what they had to do was to take the 8-bit character at the transmitter and disassemble it into 8 separate bits sent down the wire one after the other, and, at the receiver, reassemble these bits into a character that could be used to control the print mechanism. Because there was no telling when somebody would strike a key, the system had to be made asynchronous, and each character was made to begin with a "start" bit and end with 1, 1½, or 2 "stop" bits, depending on the system.

Presumably because wild Indians still occasionally cut the telegraph lines, it is conventional to have the "line idle" state be represented by a current flowing. Thus, when the line goes down, you know at once and can call out the cavalry. Be that as it may, the idle state is represented by a flow of current and is called a "mark". The start character is always a noncurrent (open circuit) and is called a "space". This is followed by 8 bits (marks or spaces depending on the character) which are called the "information bits". For a model 33 Teletype, the information bits are followed by two stop bits, which are always <u>ones</u> (see Fig. 11.2).

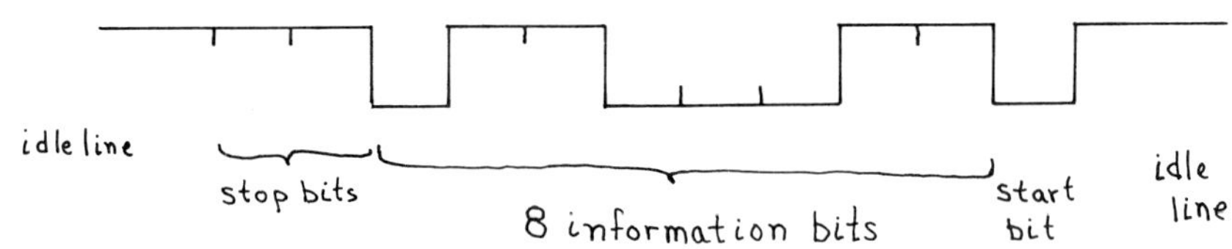

Figure 11.2 The structure of a bit serial character.

Thus, each character comes down the line as a sequence of 11 bits and at 10 characters per second we need to send 110 bits per second or 110 "baud". Faster, more modern typewriters than the model 33 use only one stop bit, so 300 baud, (at 10 bits per character) represents 30 characters per second.

At 110 baud, each bit occupies 9.09 milliseconds. When we are trying to detect and recognize a character, to avoid uncertanties at the "joints" between bits we would be wise to sample each bit near its middle.

Thus, for a TTY (teletype) we should have a program that sits around waiting for a <u>zero</u> to come over the wire. When it sees that <u>zero</u>, it will recognize it as the leading edge of a start pulse. The program should then wait 13.64 milliseconds to get over the start pulse and midway into the first information pulse. At this point it should sample the line to see if it is a <u>zero</u> or a <u>one</u> and enter this information into a register. Now the program waits 9.09 milliseconds and takes another sample. It shifts the first sample left one bit and adds the new sample to the register. It repeats this delay-and-sample procedure until all 8 information bits have been collected in the register. The program now has 2½ bit times, or better than 22.73 milliseconds, to do something clever with the character it just received and get back in time to wait for a new start pulse. Thus, if we were to connect the keyboard of a Teletype to an input bit of our microcomputer and the print box to an output bit, as in Fig. 11.3, we could easily write a program to input characters from the keyboard and print characters out on the paper.

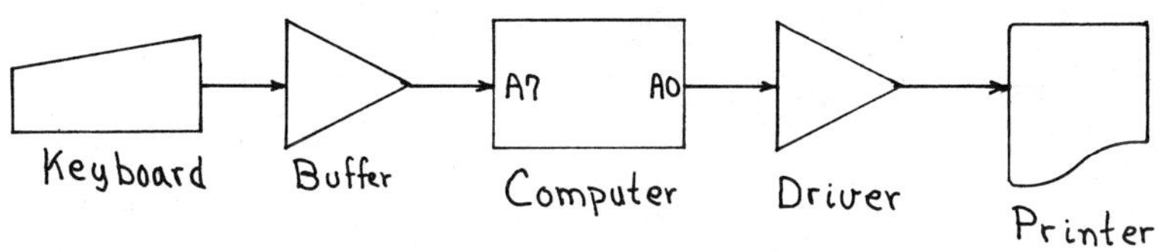

Figure 11.3 Connections for a typewriter. Note that, in real life, you will need buffers and drivers and power supplies, depending on what kind of typewriter you have.

Some terminals have a direct connection between the keyboard and the print box, so that whatever you type appears at once on the paper. The model 33 Teletype does not. In order to make anything appear on the paper you must send out a character. Thus, the computer must be turned on and running an "echo" program in order to be able to see what you are typing.

<u>UARTS AND KIM</u>

We have outlined a program above that will capture characters, and an output program is an obvious modification of this. Given the proper buffer and driver connections, any computer can be connected to any typewriter. Now this problem is so common that the semiconductor houses have designed a chip that will do parallel-to-serial and serial-to-parallel conversions. These are called UARTS (Universal Asynchronous Receiver and Transmitters) and sell for about the same price as a microprocessor.

Even though this appears absurd, it is sometimes very useful to add a UART to your computer system. For under $25 you can take all this programming load off your CPU's back and have it always present, ready to run, without having to load it in.

The manufacturers of KIM-1 have taken another approach and have provided the hardware buffer and driver for a "20-ma loop" standard interface, and in the read-only memory have provided subroutines for reading and writing characters. These subroutines are located at:

GETCH	Begins at 1E 5A and delivers its character in the accumulator. Y is set to FF.
OUTCH	Begins at 1E A0 and prints the character stored in the accumulator. Y is set to FF.

These subroutines can be initialized to accommodate baud rates between 110 and 300 by pressing reset and typing a "rubout" character. This initializing routine measures the time between the beginning of the start pulse and the beginning of the first stop pulse and divides this by 9, to get the time to be used by the GETCH and OUTCH packages.

We will now assume that, by one of these three mechanisms (software, firmware, or hardware) you have gotten into communication with your typewriter and can exchange characters with it.

REMOTE TYPEWRITERS

Terminals are so ubiquitous that it is worth taking a couple more minutes to discuss how they can be hooked up to a computer or another terminal that is far away. There are three standard methods called "simplex", "half-duplex" and "full duplex". The first of these consists of a "send only" station at the originating end and a "receive only" station at the destination (see Fig. 11.4).

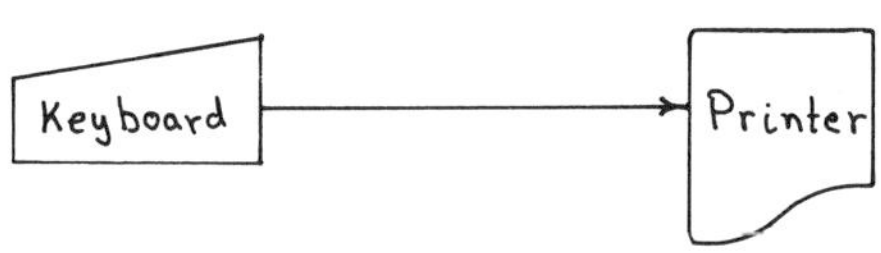

Figure 11.4 Simplex connection.

This scheme is used by the news wire services and has relatively limited applications to computing. In a half-duplex connection, A can talk to B or B can talk to A, but not both at the same time. (see Fig. 11.5).

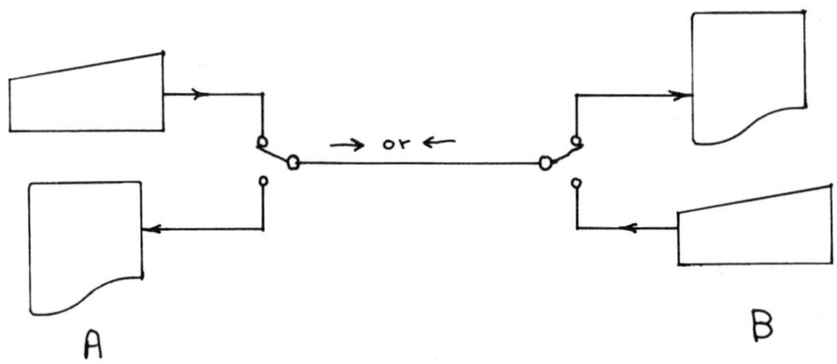

Figure 11.5 Half-duplex connection. Both switches are up or both are down.

This scheme is sometimes used for computing, especially with the old IBM 2731 terminals. Special signals are sent out from the computer end of the conversation to unlock the local keyboard at the remote site and allow the user to enter information. This means that the computer only has to listen for information when <u>it</u> is ready.

The most common connection is the full duplex, in which two pathways exist between the two stations (see Fig. 11.6).

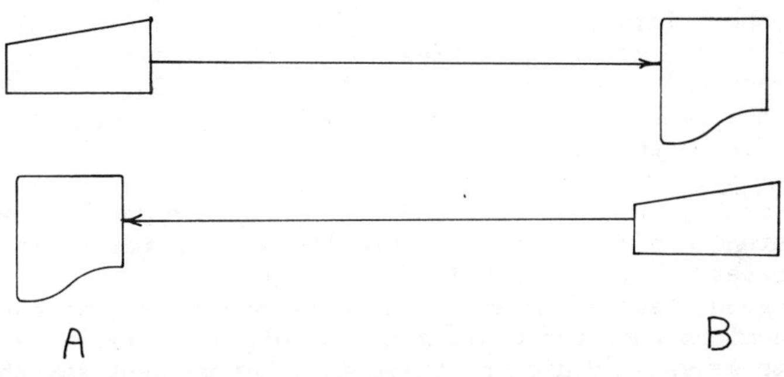

Figure 11.6 Full duplex connection.

Here both parties can be talking at the same time and each can receive the other's transmission without garbling.

A fourth connection scheme called "echoplexing" is often used when one of the parties is a computer (see Fig. 11.7).

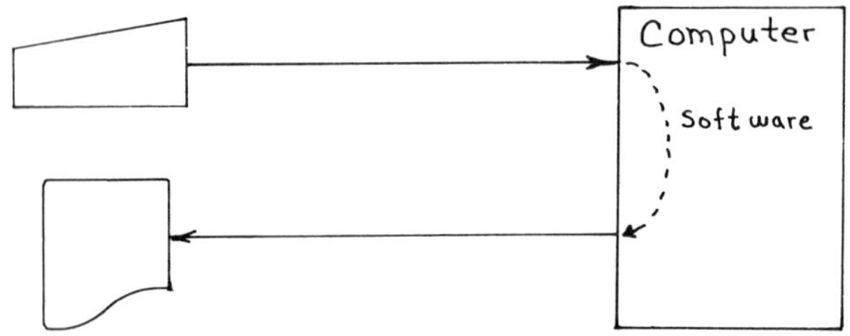

Figure 11.7 Echoplexing.

What the user types goes into the computer. What the computer thinks the user typed gets sent back to the user right away. Thus, any errors that might be caused by noise on the line can be seen and corrected by the user at once.

How can we send signals in both directions over a phone line at the same time without one of them interfering with the other? We do it by something called "frequency division multiplexing". This is a fancy name for the following situation: If a basso profundo (very low) and a counter-tenor (very high) are talking at the same time, by using a high-pass filter, we can listen only to the tenor, and with a low-pass filter we can listen only to the bass. Our ears and brain are so built that we can do this without any auxiliary equipment, but a computer or a terminal needs filters to aid it.

We use four distinct frequencies that I will call A,B,C, and D. The originating station (the one dialing the call -- usually the terminal) uses frequencies A and B while the receiving station (usually the computer) uses C and D.

When the originating modem is presented with a logical zero, it generates frequency A. When presented with a logical one, it generates frequency B -- always one or the other. This is called FSK, or frequency shift keying. When the originating modem hears a frequency C, it outputs a zero, and when it hears D on the phone line it outputs a one. The receiving modem listens for A or B, and generates either C or D. Should either modem fail to hear one of the two tones it is listening for, it assumes that the phone circuit has gone bad and indicates a "loss of carrier".

Having our vast experience with tone generation, we can easily see how a micro computer could generate either of two tones. Without going into details of digital filtering, let me just say that there exist ways of sampling an input signal to determine whether a given frequency is present or not. Briefly, we can arrange to subtract out the signal we generate (which leaves the other guy's signal), and then count the number of zero-to-one transitions we hear in a given time period. We can allow some slop to account for noise on the line, but if the number of transitions isn't close to one or the other of the two magic numbers, we will declare the "carrier to be lost".

I don't believe that you are quite ready to put Ma Bell out of business knowing just what we have discussed above, but it does cover the general ideas.

CIPHERS

There are three schemes of enciphering messages that I would like to discuss. In order of increasing difficulty of breaking them, they are a substitution cipher, the Playfair cipher, and a pseudo one-time pad. We will devote almost no time to how you go about breaking somebody else's cipher. That would require a book of its own, and I'm not quite ready to tackle that yet.

Substitution Cipher

The substitution cipher is the standard one you find in the cryptogram section of many newspapers and which most school boys (and girls?) develop or use at one time or another. As its name implies, we substitute one letter for another. Here is an example:

Clear alphabet: A B C D E F G H I J K L M N O P Q R S T U V W X Y Z

Cipher alphabet: X E I B J Y M A F H N Z K C P L D G O Q R T S V U W

Then when the clear text uses the letter A, we substitute X; for B we substitute E, and so forth. Deciphering is the inverse. When we receive an X, we output A; a received E causes a B to be typed.

This form of code is almost trivial to break, especially with the aid of a computer even when, as is usual in serious cryptography, spaces are suppressed and output is blocked into five letter groups. Breaking such a code relies on the fact that, in any sizable collection of English, letters have certain fixed relative frequencies. E,T,O,A,I,N are all popular whereas X,Z,Q and certain others are infrequent. We can count the number of occurrences of each letter of cipher sent, and in a short time find out what stands for E, and so forth. After that, a little guesswork will bring us home safe and dry. Still and all, it's fun to send "secret messages", as long as we aren't playing for keeps.

Rather than trying to remember a whole random alphabet assignment, I suggest you use the "key word" technique. To set up your secret cipher alphabet you type in a phrase or sentence that you and your agent both know. For example: MISTER SPOCK WEARS FALSE EARS. Carriage return. The first part of your program accepts this phrase up to the carriage return. It throws away all blanks and all repeats of letters after their first appearance. This gives:

MISTER ~~S~~POCK W~~EARS~~ ~~F~~AL~~SE~~ ~~EARS~~

We put these letters in association with the clear text alphabet as shown and tack on the unused letters of the alphabet after them:

Clear: A B C D E F G H I J K L M N O P Q R S T U V W X Y Z

Cipher: M I S T E R P O C K W A F L B D G H J N Q U V X Y Z

And now we are ready to accept clear text and type out the cipher. If we restrict ourselves to the 26 letters of the alphabet, we can use a dollar sign to tell the program to print out the cipher text. At this point, we might rebuild our alphabet with the cipher letters in order, or we can search the table we built above to find the clear text equivalent. Figure 11.8 shows a flow diagram for this method of enciphering.

I had gotten as far as show in Fig. 11.8 when I realized that this situation cries out for the use of a single subroutine to scan and add both lists to the cipher alphabet. So Fig. 11.9 shows a revised version of our flow diagram. We will do the key-word characters as they come in and then do the regular alphabet for i= 1 to 26.

PLAYFAIR

This enciphering scheme was a favorite of British intelligence 75 years ago. The name, however, does not come from the good sports of Eton or Harrow, but from the name of the gentleman who popularized the method. To set up for a Playfair cipher, we input a key word just as before, but this time we arrange the letters in a square, treating I and J as the same letter, so the square is 5 by 5. Taking the same key word as before, we get:

M	IJ	S	T	E
R	P	O	C	K
W	A	F	L	B
D	G	H	N	Q
U	V	X	Y	Z

The same square is used both for enciphering and deciphering. Input letters are taken in pairs and on enciphering we read "across from the first letter to the corner of the square defined by the input pair and then across from the second letter to the remaining corner". Thus the clear text pair RN would generate the cipher text C D. The clear text pair UE would generate ZM. If the two clear text letters lie in the same row (as, for example, WL, we generate the letters immediately to the right of each letter in turn), in this case, AB. LW would generate BA.

If one of the letters is at the right end of the row, we assume that the letter at the left end "follows" it around in a circle so that SE would encipher as TM. Similarly, if the clear text pair lies in a single column, we look down to find the cipher pair, with wraparound from bottom to top (OX gives FS).

To decipher we "read across to the corners" if a square is formed, leftwards if they are in the same row, and upwards if in the same column. The only remaining problem is that of double letters in the clear text. This is usually handled by either deleting one of the repeats or else inserting a noise character (like Z) between them, or both, as the context may call for.

Breaking a Playfair cipher involves collecting enough cipher text so that one can study the letter-pair frequencies (which are known for English), and by matching frequent cipher pairs with known high-frequency clear-text pairs like TH and ST and so forth, we can recon-

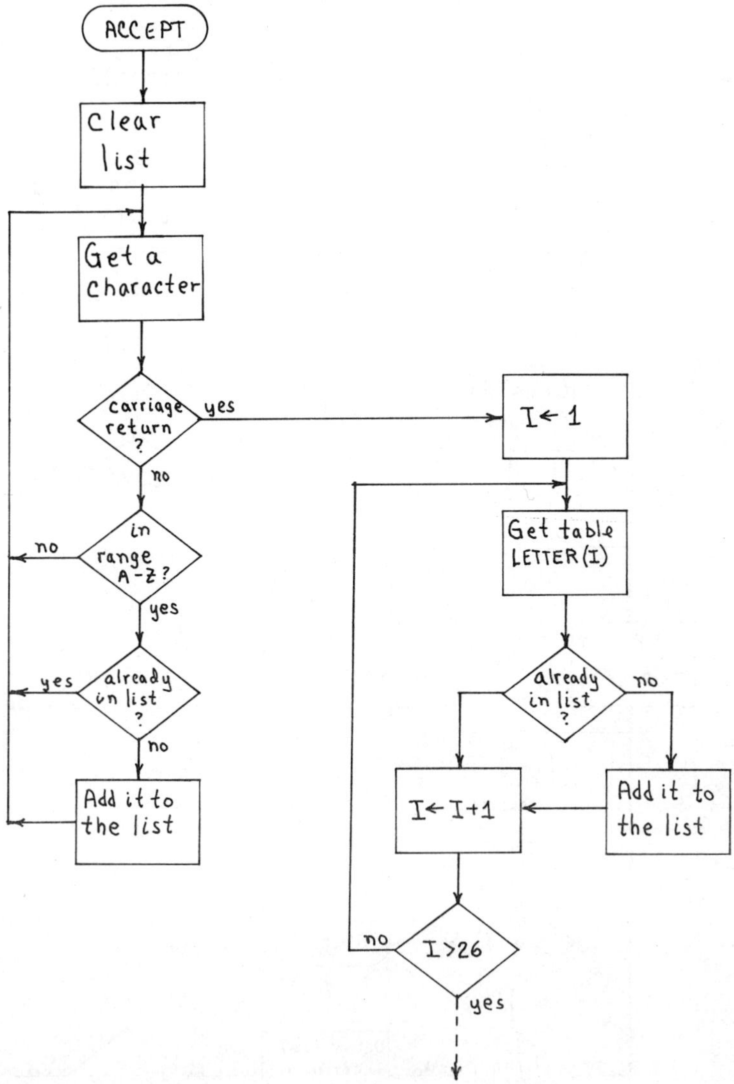

Figure 11.8 A start of a flow diagram.

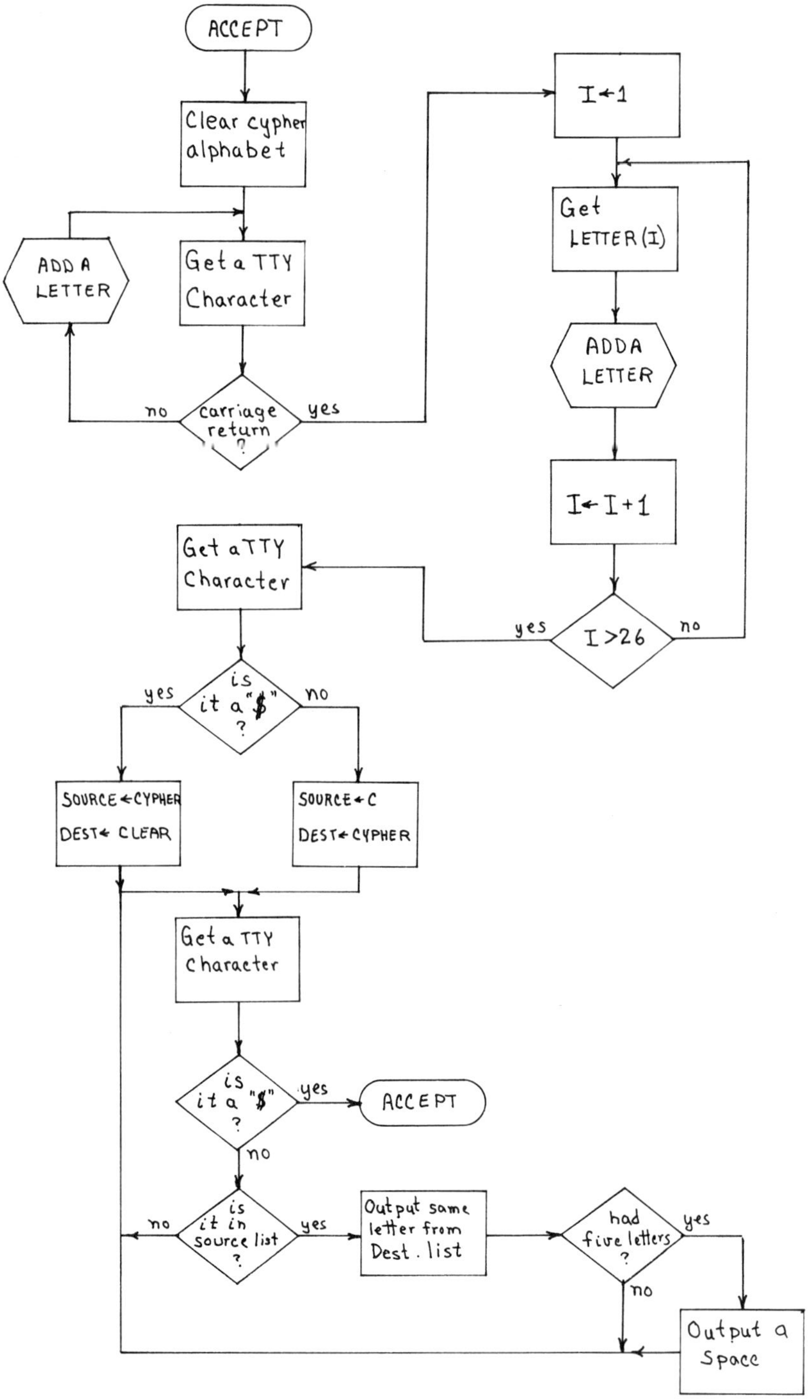

Figure 11.9 A flow diagram for the substitution cipher.

struct the square and hence break any future messages using the same key word.

Now we must face the problem of how we are to store the Playfair square in our computer and perform the required acrobatics of moving around on the grid. One brute-force method would be to store the 25^2 = 625 possible letter pairs plus their translations. Aside from a lack of elegance and the danger of using up most or all of our storage to hold this table, we still have no scheme for generating the translations given only the keyword, and I, for one, am not about to work them out by hand and type them in. So a cleverer scheme is called for.

Let us label the rows and columns with numbers between 0 and 4 each. Then a letter in row a, column b will have an index of (a,b). As we gather letters for the square from the key word, we begin with an index of (0,0), and proceed via (0,1), (0,2) and (0,3) to (0,4). At this point we follow with (1,0). That is, we count the right index modulo 5 and add the carry to the left index. Since each index is guaranteed to be less than 5, we can store both indices in one word. Now when we get a clear text pair, we look up their indices. Let us suppose that they are (a,b) and (c,d). First we compare a with c. If they differ, we compare b with d. If they differ also, then we find the two letters with indices (a,d) and (c,b) and print them out. If a = c, the letters are on the same row so we read out the pair (a,b + 1) and (c, d +1), where the addition is done modulo 5. If b = d, we read out the pair (a + 1,b) and (c + 1, d).

We must make arrangements for weeding out the letter J and equating it to I, but other than that and a lot of details, this program should be relatively straightforward to flow diagram and code.

Pseudo One-Time Pad

The only enciphering scheme that is theoretically unbreakable is the "one-time pad." It works like this:

1. First prepare a large number of pairs of pieces of paper, each pair consisting of two sheets of paper, each with the same string of random numbers on it.

2. By appropriately devious means, get one copy of each sheet to the destination. Perhaps you send a bunch (pad) of them (each different and each with its twin remaining at headquarters) with your correspondent when he first goes abroad.

3. Write down the clear-text message on your copy of the top sheet of the pad. Convert the letters to numbers (A = 0, B = 1.... Z = 25).

4. Add the random number to the letter number you have just written down.

5. Suppose the random numbers range from 0-31 in magnitude. Reduce the sums generated in 4 above to a number between 0 and 25, by subracting 26 from the sum as many times as necessary

(0,1, or 2 times).

6. Convert these numbers back into letters (0 = A, 1 = B, ..., 25 = A). This is your cipher text and is the message you will send to your agent.

On receipt of an enciphered message he will write it down on his copy of the same page you used (unless things get screwed up). He will then convert the letters to numbers, <u>subtract</u> the random number and add in 26 as often as necessary to get the difference between 0 and 25, and finally convert these numbers to letters.

If the sequence of numbers on the pads is truly random and if you use each page only once, this cipher is truly unbreakable, since even having old used sheets from the pad tells the decipherer nothing about the next sheet.

The problem with these one-time pads in the real world is that (1) you are bound to run out of sheets just when you have a priority message to transmit; (2) if counter-intelligence catches you with a big supply of sheets of paper with random numbers they are apt to become a mite suspicious.

How can a computer help the would-be spy? Well, everybody has hand calculators these days. Suppose the special-effects group had some built up that would generate random sequences of numbers when you pushed both plus and minus at the same time? Sounds ideal if we can do it.

We almost can. We can cause a computer to generate a string of digits that is almost random. Now in theory that is not quite good enough, but if the repetition time of the pseudo-random string (the number of numbers it will put out before beginning to repeat itself) is of the order of 100,000, there are going to be more agents dying of old age than of compromised messages.

Let us look at how we can generate a pseudo-random string in a computer and leave the logistics of getting the special calculators to the special-effects group.

Pseudo Random Strings

There is a large body of work dealing with the generation of pseudo (almost) random strings by computer. Many of the methods can be applied to microcomputers, but many others need the full arithmetic facilities of a large-scale machine, or a large set of mathematical subroutines, if they are to work on a machine as limited as one of ours.

Most of these routines share the following features:

1. The routine is initialized with a starting number called the "seed".

2. On each call for a random number, the seed is multiplied (or otherwise compounded) with a constant built into the generator. This product (or result) is taken as a new seed, and the next time the generator is called, it uses the new seed.

3. Part of the new seed is extracted and returned as the generated random number.

Starting with a given seed, we generate a series of apparently random digits, one each time we call the generator. But, starting with a given seed, we will always get the same sequence of numbers, so it is obvious that they are not truly random. But this reproductability is just what we want for our agent so he can use the same set of random numbers of decipher that we used to encipher.

Now, instead of bulky and incriminating one-time pads, our agent in the field need only carry around a handheld calculator and a set of seed numbers, one for each day of his trip.

Multiplicative Algorithm

One standard pseudo-random generator is the "square and extract" routine. What we do is take a 16-bit seed. We multiply this seed by itself, generating a 32-bit product. We throw away the 8 high-order and the 8 low-order bits, keeping the 16 middle bits as a new seed. We may generate our random numbers by taking the low-order 5 bits of the new seed -- giving a number between 0 and 31. In most micro machines, this calls for quadruple-precision multiply subroutines. We begin with the multiplier in the high-order 16 bits of a 32-bit product word. The low-order 16 bits are all zero (see Fig. 11.10).

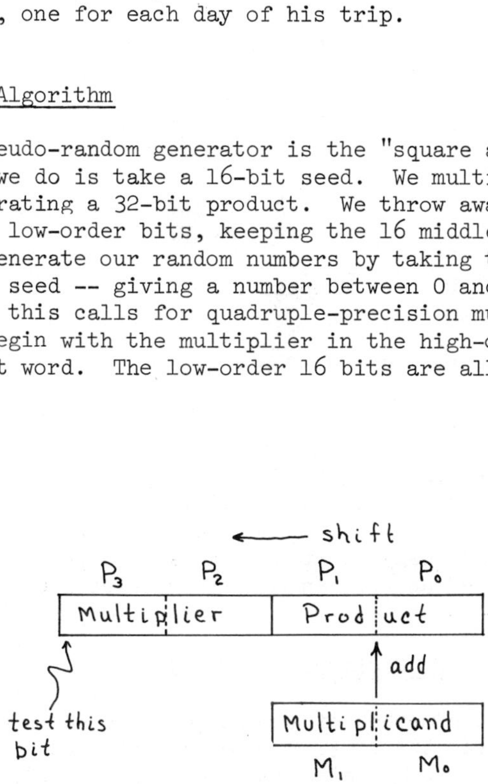

Figure 11.10 Arrangement for multiplication.

We test the leftmost bit of the multiplier. If it is one, we add the multiplicand to the product and shift all 32 bits (multiplier and product) left one position. If the multiplier bit is zero, we just shift left without adding. To perform the add operation, we execute the following steps or their equivalents:

```
CLC              Clear carry
LDA    PO
ADC    MO        Add the low order half of the multiplicand
STA    PO        and set the carry bit if there is an over-
```

```
                        flow.
LDA     P1
ADC     M1              Add carry from low half plus
STA     P1              P1 and M1 for new value of P1

LDA     P2
ADC     #00             Take care of any carry into
STA     P2              P2

LDA     P3
ADC     #00             Take care of any carry into
STA     P3              P3.
```

To shift P3-P2-P1-P0 left one bit, we execute:

```
CLC                     Clear carry
LDA     P0              Shift P07 into carry and
ROL                     rest of P0 left one place
STA     P0
LDA     P1              Shift P17 into carry and
ROL                     carry into P10
STA     P1
LDA     P2              Repeat for P2
ROL
STA     P2
LDA     P3              Repeat for P3
ROL
STA     P3
```

When we have done this shift (and add if $P3_7 = 1$) 16 times, we have formed the product of the multiplier and the multiplicand. Now we move P_2 to M_1, P_1 to M_0, P_2 to P_3, and P_1 to P_2. Then we clear P_1 and P_0 and we are ready for the next call on the generator. We should return M0 bits 4-0 as the random number between 0 and 31.

Maximal-Length Shift Register

Another well known method of generating pseudo-random numbers is a feedback shift register. (This one is better known to coding theorists than to most practicing computer scientists). The method is very simple and fast in any machine that has an _exclusive or_ operation. It works like this:

Set up a 32-bit-long shift register (or longer if you like). Seed it with any pattern of _ones_ and _zeros_ except the "all _zeros_" condition. Observe the leftmost bit. If it is _zero_, just shift the whole register left one place. If it is _one_, take the _exclusive or_ of the contents of the register with a constant that you can discover in almost any book on coding theory (not cryptography, but a study of signals and how to get them from one point to another). For a 32-bit register, one good constant looks like this:

Contents:	00	76	B5	53
Cell names:	C_3	C_2	C_1	C_0

We _exclusive or_ C_3 with P_3, etc.

To generate a 5-bit number, we have to call this generator 5 times and each time it will return one bit. This is still simpler and faster than a 16-bit multiply and for a 32-bit register it is known not to begin repeating for 2^{32} bits or 2^{27} characters. That is the order of 128 million and no agent or control should be that verbose.

The beauty of these methods is that we can make the shift register as long as we like. 64 bits would give a repetition time (and a set of possible seeds) of roughly 0.5×10^{18} characters, which, at 10 characters per second, will require about 2 billion years before repeating. Most secret information will be out of date by then, I imagine.

A flow diagram for this pseudo one-time pad is presented in Fig. 11.11. As you might imagine, it is not very complicated except for the random-number generator.

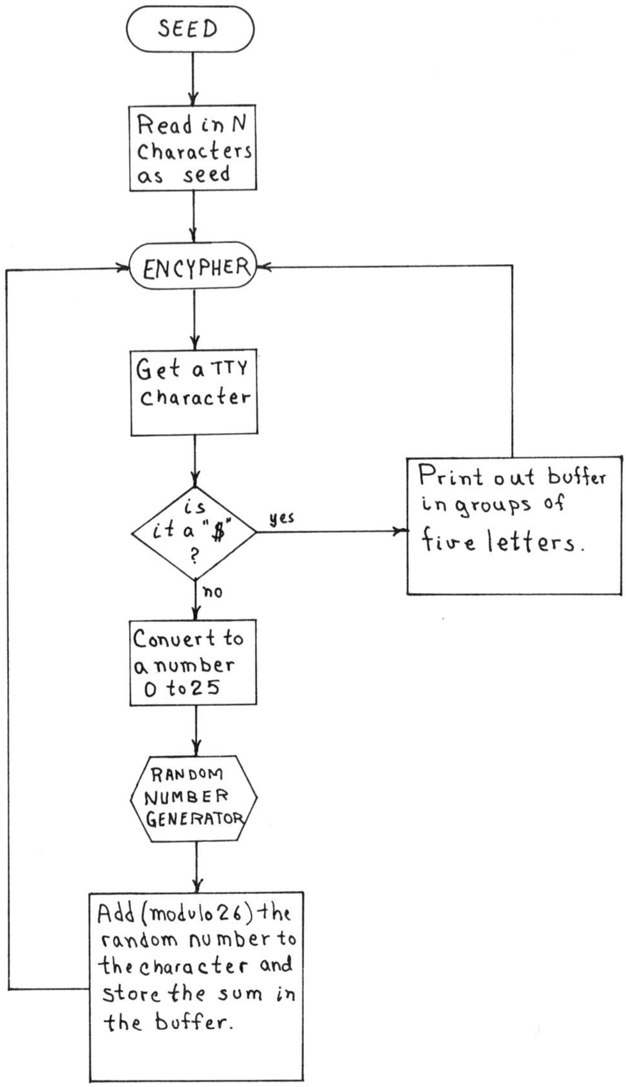

Figure 11.11 Flow diagram for seeding and enciphering. Deciphering is the same except that we subtract the random number from the number input.

12
ELEVATOR CONTROL

You approach the elevator and push the "up" button. Pretty soon the doors open and you get on the car. You push the button for the floor you desire. The doors close. On the way to your floor, the car stops to pick up (or discharge) other passengers. Eventually you get to your floor, the doors open and you walk away and forget about the elevator till you want to use it again.

In this experiment we are going to take a closer look at the control program for a simple unsophisticated elevator serving four floors of a building. Figure 12.1 shows the controls we will need. On the lefthand side of the figure, there is a set of four lights that tell you which floor the elevator is at. There is also a "corridor" request-button pair for each floor allowing potential passengers to call the elevator. (Note that there is no down call for floor 1 and no up call for floor 4.) On the right there are four buttons representing the in-car console at which passengers may request a trip to a floor. At the right top there are three "state of the system" lights that tell whether the door is open, or whether the elevator is on an upward trip or a downward trip.

Suppose the elevator is idle, sitting at the first floor with its door open. You board the car and push the button for the fourth floor. The doors close. You begin to move upward. A person approaches the elevator on the second floor and pushes up. The car stops, waits for him to board and select his floor and then starts up again. (we go up even if he called for an up ride and then pressed button 1.) A person on the third floor requests a down ride. You do not stop for him but continue on to the fourth floor, where you get out. The elevator starts down and stops at the third floor to pick up that passenger.

At all times, your program is going to have to monitor the buttons both on board and in the corridor, but in drawing your first flow diagram, ignore this fact and assume that button pushes get taken care of by magic. There are five recognizable states to our system. They are:

1. Moving up

2. Stopped but upward bound

3. Idle

4. Stopped but downward bound

5. Moving down

Take a first cut at a system "state diagram" by drawing five circles and labeling them with the names of the states just listed. Under what conditions do you go from one state to another? Stay in the same state?

- Draw your diagram before reading further -

(To make the behavior of the elevator more lifelike, assume it takes 6 seconds to go between adjacent floors. Note next to each state what actions, if any, you must take in that state).

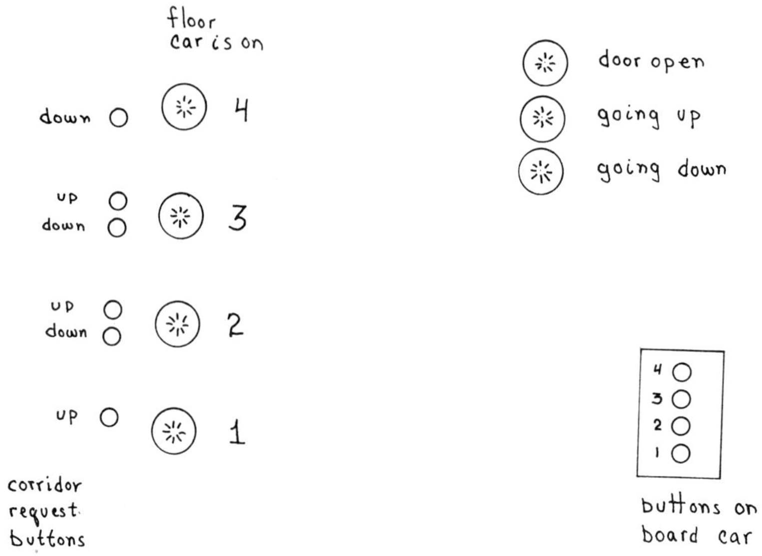

Figure 12.1 Elevator simulator control panel.

Let's look at my system-state diagram, which represents a very simple-minded control program (see Fig. 12.2). K_i represents an on-board request for floor i, U_i a corridor call to go up from floor i, and D_i to go down from floor i. R_i is the logical OR of those three $R_i = K_i \vee U_i \vee D_i$ and indicates that a request of some kind should bring the car to floor i.

Suppose the car is on floor i, sitting idle. We look at all the R's and see whether there exists a request for floor above i ($R_j = 1$ for $j > i$) or a floor below i ($R_j = 1$ for $j < i$). If so, we clear U_i, D_i, and K_i, and go to the "moving up" or "moving down" state. Suppose it is moving up. We close the door, wait 3 seconds, make i = i + 1 and wait 3 more seconds. If $K_i = U_i = 0$ (no on-board requests for this floor and no "up-please" corridor requests for this floor), we stay in the moving-up state. If $K_i = 1$ or $U_i = 1$, we stop at this floor and open the door. After a brief delay, we look to see if there are any outstanding requests for yet a higher floor. If there are, we go back to the moving up state. Otherwise we fall idle. The moving down and stopped down states are similar.

In each of the states there is one (or more) time delay(s) to simulate the transit time of the elevator or the door-operating time. In all, there are 7 time delays required. Here is an obvious application for a delay subroutine.

INPUT/OUTPUT

Let us look at the input and output of our problem. There are seven lights to be lit (or not lit) and there are 10 buttons to be monitored. That makes seventeen lines to worry about and we have only 15 I/O lines on KIM-1. We must therefore "matrix" the input buttons or the output lights. We have chosen to connect the I/O as shown in Fig. 12.3.

This scheme gets all the switches on the PORTA, so we can assign one bit of PORTB to each of the lights. Note that these LED's have a polarity, and if they don't light up when you expect them to, try reversing their leads. There are ways to multiplex the lights as well as the switches, but since we don't need them here, let us postpone that until some other day.

With standard LED's you will need a driver circuit. Figure 12.4 shows a simple driver.

THE TIME-DELAY AND SCANNING ROUTINE

Now at last we are ready to consider the subroutine to do time delays. Since this is a routine in which our program is going to spend a great proportion of its time, this would be an ideal place to look for button-pushes.

Let us reserve three cells of storage (called UP, DOWN, and KAR), and in those cells we will keep track of the as-yet-unanswered requests. Thus, when somebody pushes button U_2 we will set bit 1 of the cell called UP. Since this routine doesn't worry about clearing those bits, we don't need to worry about key bounce. We will input the first bank of buttons ($D_2D_3D_4$) and logical OR what we find into

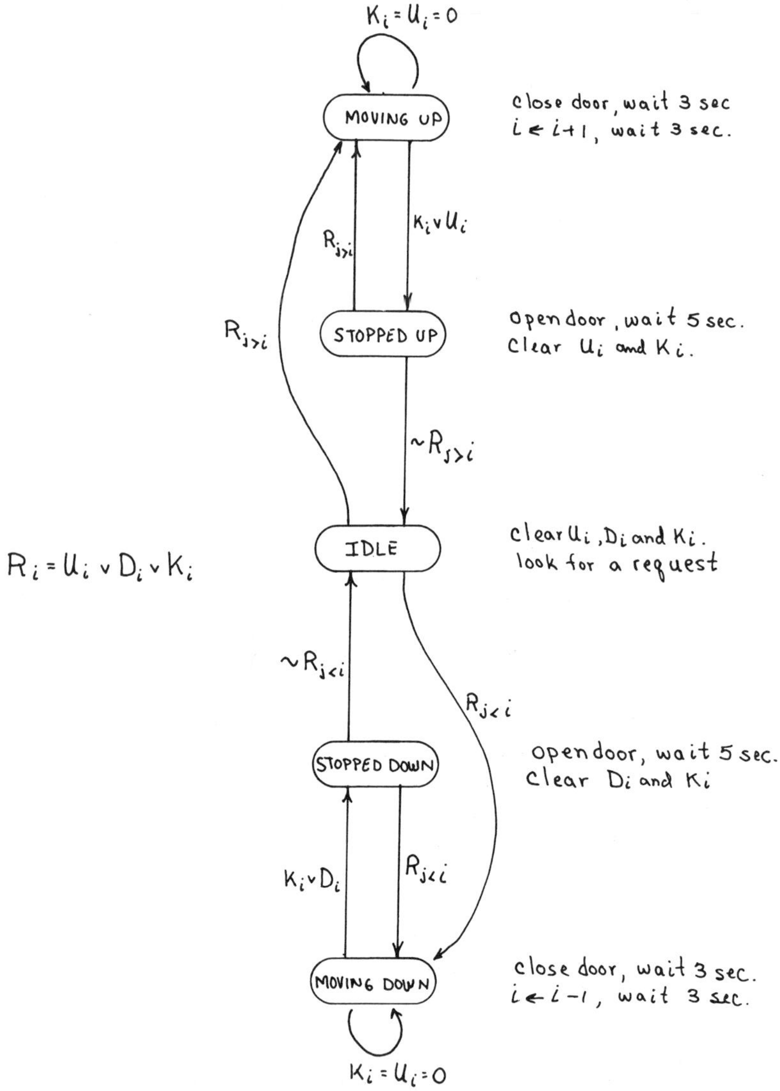

Figure 12.2 A system state diagram for the elevator control program.

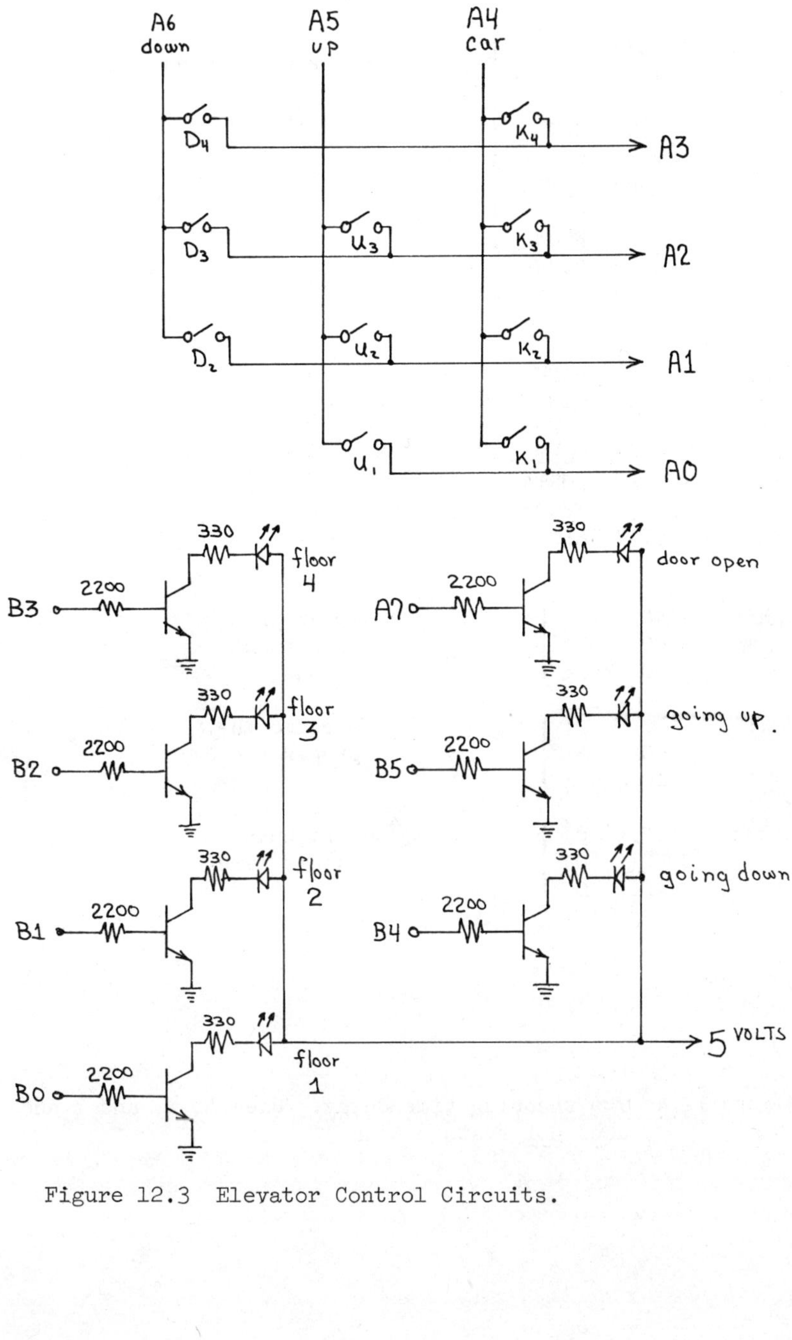

Figure 12.3 Elevator Control Circuits.

```
DELAY:      STA    COUNT            save delay

LOOP:       LDA#   00               set up inner
            STA    L                loop

ROUND:      LDY#   00               check up buttons
            JSR    GET
            INY                     Down buttons
            JSR    GET
            INY                     in car buttons
            JSR    GET
            DEC    L                inner loop end
            BNE    ROUND
            DEC    COUNT            outer loop end
            BNE    LOOP
            RTS

GET:        LDAY   BANK
            STA    DIRA
            LDAY   ROW
            STA    PORTA
            LDA    PORTA
            ORAY   RECORD
            STAY   RECORD
            RTS

BANK:       A0                      select proper
            C0                       bank to be
            90                        input

ROW:        20                      energize the
            40                       proper row
            10

RECORD:     UP:    0                store button
          DOWN:    0                 pushes here
           KAR:    0
```

Figure 12.4 The scanning time delay. Uses A, X, and Y and does not restore them.

the cell DOWN. No need to test. Thus any button-push will appear in one of the cells UP, DOWN, or KAR. We do this as follows:

```
LDA     PORTA
ORA     DOWN    (or UP or KAR)
STA     DOWN
```

If we set up the right direction conditions for DIRA (X111 0000) and put a "100", "010", or "001" in $A_6A_5A_4$, we then look at a bank of buttons. We can repeat this for the other two banks and do this scan as part of the body of the timing loop. We will not only keep close tabs on the inputs but we will have a nice long timing loop.

- Before looking at Figures 12.4, 12.5, and 12.6, write your version of the basic timing loop and see how long you spend in each iteration (pass through the loop) -

Let us now examine the delay subroutine, shown in figure 12.4 and 12.6. We enter the subroutine with the delay count D in the accumulator which we save in a cell named COUNT. We set another cell named L to zero. We count down on L until it is zero again and then subtract one from D. If D is not now zero we go back and do the inner loop on L again 256 times. Thus in total we do the innter loop 256*D times.

The inner loop consists of three calls to a subroutine GET. The first time we get up button pushes then down button pushes and finally on board button pushes.

MAIN PROGRAM

Now that we have the timing subroutine out of the way, let us go back to the system-state diagram of Fig. 12.2. Using this diagram you should be able to draw a flow diagram for the elevator-control program at this point. In the idle state, you will want to stick in a call to the delay routine just to get the keys sampled. Other than that it should be a fairly straightforward translation with the insertion of a good bit of detail.

- Before reading further draw your diagram -

Figure 12.5 shows one approach to the problem. The hexagonal box is used to represent subroutine calls. A word or two about how I propose to scan the requests would be helpful.

First, I am going to compute the "request vector" RV which will have a <u>one</u> in bit i if either U_i or K_i is a one:

```
LDA   UP
ORA   KAR
ORA   DOWN
```

This leaves RV in the accumulator. Now if the floor we are at is i and i is in index register X, then by doing an indexed AND with a mask corresponding to this floor, we will clear out everything except the bits of the floors above us:

```
        ANDX    UPMASK
```

where:

```
        UPMASK    :      Nothing - there is no floor zero
                + 1:     0E     0000 1110 for floors 2,3,4
                + 2:     0C     0000 1100 for floors 3,4
                + 3:     08     0000 1000 for floor 4
                + 4:     00     0000 0000 for no floor
```

A similar set of masks for the downward trip scan must also exist.

```
      DOWNMASK    :      Nothing - there is no floor zero
                + 1:     00     on floor 1 we don't want to
                                go down
                + 2:     01     to go to floor 1
                + 3:     03     to go to floors 1 or 2
                + 4:     07     to go to floors 1,2,3
```

This scanning routine is going to be used a lot, so we have made it a subroutine. That will save some coding and thus eliminate a few possibilities for errors. If we do that, we should let the subroutine set a flag if there are any up requests, and set another flag if there are any down requests.

Let us call these flags UPREQ and DWNREQ. They should be set to zero if there are no up requests (down requests), and to nonzero if there are some. So we might just put the computed word of up requests in UPREQ and the computed word of down requests in DWNREQ. This is an example of a subroutine with one input parameter i: the floor the car is now at.

Note: As drawn there is a flaw in the logic. If floor 3 calls the elevator to go up and then floor 2 calls it to go down the car will shuttle between the two floors forever. Try to correct this flaw before writing your code. What change to the logic does this require? Is that a good way to run an elevator?

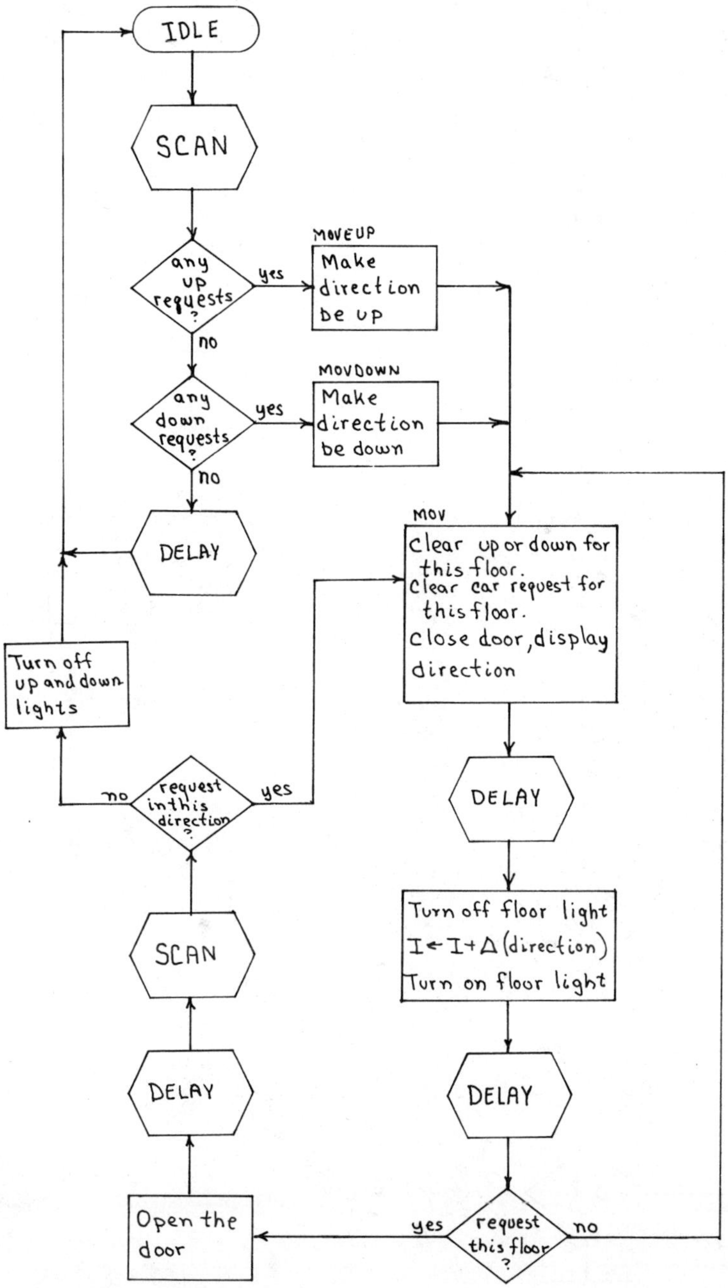

Figure 12.5 Overall flow diagram of elevator problem.

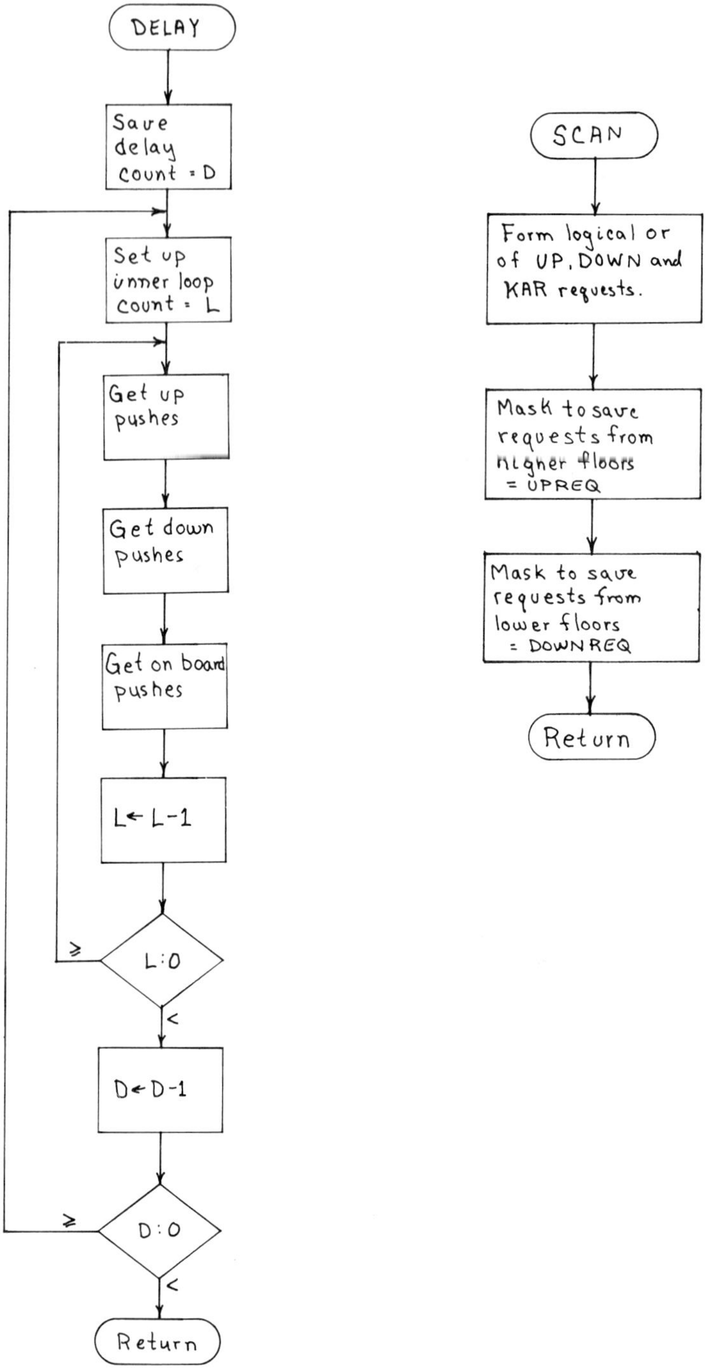

Figure 12.6 DELAY and SCAN subroutines.

13
AN INTERPRETER FOR A "DREAM MACHINE"

You say you're not happy with the machine you bought? You say you saw a shiny new model in the salesroom that simply captured your heart? You say you're tired of the same old op-codes and want to try out something new? Let me tell you what we're going to do. We are going to take that old, that wornout, that weary computer of yours and, through the magic of "interpretation," we are going to turn it into the computer of your dreams. Well, that's assuming you are not a really first-class dreamer. Because your realization of your dreams (or mine) is going to be severely curtailed by the energy, time, and above all, the on-line storage space we have available.

What we propose to do is write a program called an interpreter. This program will live in a certain microcomputer. Mine will, of course, live in a KIM-1 and will run on a KIM-1. What this program will do is accept instructions written in the machine language of the dream computer and execute those instructions one by one just as if the dream computer really existed. We are going to keep the dream computer (properly called the "target machine") very simple for two reasons. The first is the obvious one that it will make our interpreter simpler, and the second reason is that in the next chapter we are going to write an assembler for the dream machine.

GENERAL OUTLINE

What do we need in a computer? The standard answer is:

1. an input device,
2. a control unit,
3. an arithmetic logic unit (ALU),
4. some storage
5. an output device.

Certainly we need input, output, and storage, and we can simulate the control unit and the ALU by program. Probably the best choice for input is a Teletype keyboard and for output a Teletype printer. For storage we will use part of our real machine's on-line storage. If we work very hard we may be able to keep the interpreter down to 500 bytes, which would give us 512 for the dream machine. Should the dream machine have an 8-bit word? Despite the obvious advantages of keeping compatible with our host machine (which is probably an 8-bit micro), I say let's go for 16-bit words. That will give us 256 words of main memory for our target. That requires 8 bits for an address. Sixteen op-codes, which will be plenty to worry about, take up four bits. We will use two bits as a "modifier" field and that will leave two bits unused in each instruction. Provided we are clever enough to label them "for future expansion," no one will complain about the "waste." Our instructions will look more or less like this:

First byte			Second byte
(unused)	op-code	mod	8-bit address
15 14	13 . . 10	9 8	7 0

If we assume that DM has a 16-bit accumulator (A) and an 8-bit index register (B), then the meanings of the modifier field might be:

00	Immediate addressing
01	Direct (absolute) addressing
10	Indirect addressing
11	Indexed addressing.

For immediate addressing we have an 8-bit operand taken from the second byte of the instruction. This will be treated as if it were a 16-bit operand with the high-order 8 bits all zero. When we load the index register B we will take the low-order 8 bits of the effective operand, and similarly, any time we do indirect addressing we will take the low 8 bits of the word we pick up as the address of the real operand.

What sorts of instructions should we have? We need to load and store both A and B. We should be able to add, subtract, and, or, and exclusive or. Clearly we need some conditional jump instructions (at least jump on minus A) and we need an input and an output instruction. Let's list these out with the obvious mnemonics and see what we have left:

0	LDA	8	EOR
1	LDB	9	JMA
2	STA	10	JZA
3	STB	11	JZB
4	ADD	12	INP
5	SUB	13	OUT
6	AND	14	JMP
7	ORA	15	JSR

We have included five jump instructions; jump, jump on minus A, jump on zero A or zero B, and jump to subroutine. Since the index register is only 8 bits long and we have said that 8 bit operands will be considered to be positive, we can't very well "jump on minus B". We have eliminated all flags and the processor status register, so we don't need to jump for them. We have a subroutine jump but no stack and no subroutine return. We do this by storing the return address in the lower half of the target address (a) and transferring control to $a + 1$. When the subroutine ends, we will return by doing a "jump indirect on a". Simple, but no neat way to nest subroutines such as we have with a stack.

In a real machine we would probably miss shifts (left and right) and the carry bit most of all, but we still have plenty to work with.

THE INTERPRETER

First of all, we are going to reserve some cells to act as the DM's registers. We will need AHI, ALO, BLO, PCLO, IRHI and IRLO to store the accumulator (16 bits), index register (8 bits), program counter (8 bits), and instruction register (16 bits). We are going to fetch the word pointed at by the PC and put it in the IR, increment the PC by one, examine the instruction and branch to a routine to carry out the instruction. Before flying away to the 16 separate routines, one for each instruction, we would like to decode the modifier field, but we are in something of a quandary about what a "jump immediate" might mean -- or a "store immediate", for that matter. (Actually, "jump immediate" is just what you might expect; it loads the 8-bit address field into the PC, but the name seems clumsy.)

There is a reasonable way to handle this problem if we have just a mite of patience. Let the input instruction

```
INP  m  add
```

take a character from the typewriter and store it in the effective address discovered by applying the right sort of modification (specified by M) to the address field (add). It is therefore just like a "store" instruction in the way it uses m and add. Let the output instruction

```
OUT m add
```

generate a character (immediate, direct, etc.) and output it to the typewriter. It now looks like a "load" instruction.

Now we can divide the instructions into two groups and renumber them for convenience. We now have:

Group 0		Group 1	
0	INP	8	OUT
1	STA	9	LDA
2	STB	10	LDB
3	JMA	11	ADD
4	JZA	12	SUB
5	JZB	13	AND
6	JMP	14	ORA
7	JSR	15	EOR

and with this numbering scheme we can distinguish group 0 from group 1 on the basis of the high-order bit of the op-code.

Our first fan-out on op-code will be on the basis of whether we have a group 0 or group 1 op-code. For all group 0 op-codes, we will interpret the modifier field the same way: that is, we are going to generate an address (to be put into the PC or to be used as the address of a place to put something). Immediate mode will be illegal. Direct mode will return *a* -- the address field of the instruction.

Indirect will return the contents of a. Indexed will return a + (B). Now the stores (INP, STA, STB) use this as the address to put the operand into and the jumps use it as the value to stuff in the PC if the jump takes place.

For group 1 the mode-decoding section needs to return a value. For immediate mode this will be a. For direct the contents of a, for indirect the contents of the contents of a, and for indexed the contents of a + (B). What we actually do is generate both the address and the contents of that address and let the op-code choose which one it wants.

After we decode the mode, we can fan out on the basis of the remaining three bits of the op-code to the individual routines for each instruction. If our host machine had an indexed jump instruction (as DM does) we could just put the op-code in an index register and jump to one of a table of jump instructions that would take us to the correct routine. But alas, KIM for one does not, so we will have to figure out another way. How about the following:

The op-code has been isolated and three times the value of the op-code is in the X-register.

```
        STX   VAR + 1

VAR:    BEQ   [      ]   VAR + 1 is the address of the second byte

        JMP   INPUT

        JMP   STOREA

                .
                .
                .
```

After we have executed the instruction we go back and fetch another one. And on and on. The flow diagram is given in Fig. 13.1.

And that's the way a real computer works, except that the steps are carried out by hardware rather than software. I think you can go ahead and write up the code now.

There are one or two things it would be nice to have on our DM. First of all is a single-step switch and a GO button. The first can be a two-position switch either shorting A7 to ground (run) or not (single-step). The GO button can be a momentary contact switch shorting A0 to ground to start the DM. Since the input ports tend to drift up to +5 volts on their own, it will be easy enough to detect the difference between 0 (ground) and 5 volts. If the toggle switch is in "run" position, then once the DM is running we won't bother to test GO. We can stop DM at the end of the current DM instruction by putting the toggle switch to the single-step position. In single step we will look for (a) the GO button open (not pushed) and then (b) the GO button pushed. That will take care of double cycling in case we aren't fast enough getting off the GO button.

In a proper interpreter we should take care of displaying DM's registers whenever DM is stopped, but we are going to be too crowded for space to do this and will have to rely on the host machine to do this for us. You should have a pretty good idea how you would go about building a display and displaying A,B, PC, or IR, as desired. You might want to lay it out just for fun.

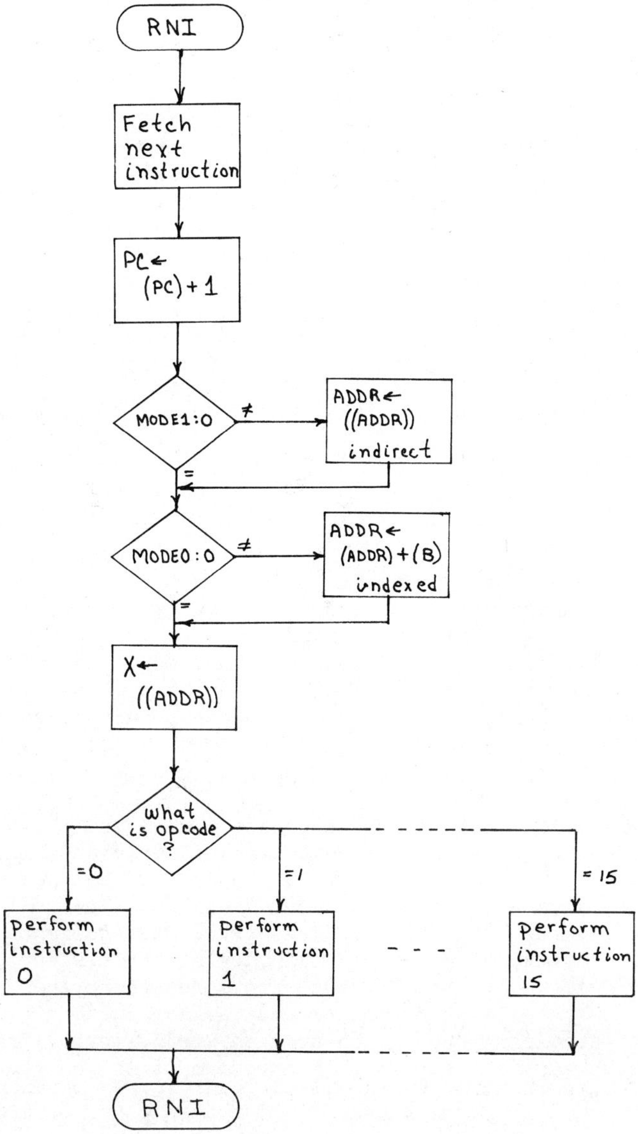

Figure 13.1 Flow diagram for the interpreter.

14
AN ASSEMBLER FOR THE DM

So far we have limped along without an assembler for our host machine. (Or, if you had one, you sneaked it in the side door without telling me.) It is time to move up in the world to wider horizons and so forth, and put away childish things like absolute hexadecimal.

Unfortunately good assemblers for real machines are hard to come by. It takes several hundred hours to write one (even if you know how) and the machine manufacturers are currently asking around $100 a copy for them, or more. So we are going to content ourselves with building a mini-assembler for the so-called Dream Machine of the previous chapter.

As you will recall, we have a 16-bit machine which stores an instruction as four fields:

	Waste	Op-code	Modifier	Address	
of	2	4	2	8	bits.

We have not chosen what the assembly language is supposed to look like, but if we are going to get this assembler and its tables into 500 words (so that we can assemble to storage and avoid having a loader, and all that jazz), it had better be pretty simple.

As a first pass, try a general statement such as this one:

Label: Op-code b̸ modifier b̸ address b̸ CR

Where b̸ stands for one or more blanks (spaces) and CR stands for carriage return. (We have to have alpha-numeric capability to make an assembler possible, so I am going to assume that you have a typewriter-like device connected to your machine.) The <u>modifier</u> might be "#" for immediate, "blank" for direct, "@" for indirect, and X for indexed. I think, to start off with, we had better keep it to 0, 1, 2, and 3 until we see how expansive we dare become and how much space we are going to have to expand around in.

The <u>op-code</u> can probably be held to two letters. They may look a little queer at first but it will cut down by 1/3 on the size of the table required to hold the "valid op-code list." I propose that we use:

0	IN	input	8	OT	input
1	SA	store A	9	LA	load A
2	SB	store B	10	LB	load B
3	MA	jump minus A	11	PL	add to A

4	ZA	Jump Zero A	12	SU	Subtract from A
5	ZB	Jump Zero B	13	ND	And with A
6	JP	jump	14	OR	Or with A
7	JS	jump subroutine	15	XR	exclusive or with A

The address is next. The BASIC language has risen to great popularity with a very restricted set of symbolic names. One letter from the alphabet, followed by nothing, or at most one digit 0-9. Thus A, A0, A1, B5,Z, and so forth are all valid variable names. Let us be a little less restrictive and decide that a symbolic name must consist of two characters: one letter or digit followed by a blank, a letter, or a digit. We will permit everything that BASIC does, plus names of the form: AA, AB, 7C, etc. When the modifier is zero, the assembler will expect a pair of hex characters to define the immediate constant.

Labels, of course, are names of instructions and there is no reason why they should be different from other symbolic names (FORTRAN to the contrary notwithstanding). So a typical line of assembly language might look like:

```
A3: LA 2 BC
```

or, if there is no label, like:

```
LA 2 BC
```

Assembler directives

All assemblers need to be told certain facts of life about a particular assembly and ours is no exception. These facts are generally presented in statements called assembler directives. Our assembler has to be told where to start its assembly, and when to cease assembly.

To set the location counter (equivalent to the address-display register of KIM-1), we will type a star followed by two hex characters (00-FF). Thus:

```
* 23
```

will adjust the assembler so that the next instruction will be stored in cell 23_h of the DM. This directive may be issued at any time. When the assembler starts up and initializes itself, it sets star equal to 00. The letters END will finish an assembly. Large assemblers have many other directives but we will content ourselves with just two.

Constants

In a full-sized assembler, we would be able to enter constants in hex, decimal, ASCII, binary, and possibly some other bases. A leading (or trailing) key character tells the assembler which kind of constant is meant, so that it can take care of all translations.

Once again we are going to pare away a lot of problems and accept only constants in hex -- one to four characters, leading zeros not required. The format will be

```
AX = 1357
```

A sample assembly

Even though we have done the assembly process a number of times by hand, it is a good idea to look at a sample of code and see what is going to happen to it. Since source statements are going to be typed in by the user and since we have no place to store the source statements so that we could re-examine them at a later time, we have to make our assembler of the "one-pass" variety (that means that we look at the source code only once). Second, we are going to need a symbol table to store symbols in. Each symbol-table entry will require two characters for the symbol (that's why we limited symbolic names to two characters) plus an 8-bit field to store the address that has been assigned to this symbol. We will store the value associated with the symbol in the DM's memory. If a symbol has not yet been defined, we will set the leftmost bit of its second character word (7-bit ASCII characters, remember) to 1. Once a valid address has been assigned, we will clear that sign bit to 0. Should a second attempt be made to define that symbol, we will print out a "DD" (meaning doubly defined) before we echo the carriage return of the offending line of code.

If a symbol is mentioned or used before it is defined, this is called a "forward reference." For example

```
LA  3  AA
 ⋮
AA: = 0
```

is a forward reference to AA. Since we don't have a valid address to stick in the address field of the instruction LA when we first see it and assemble it, we will put in a zero. In the symbol-table entry for AA, we will also have no valid address, so we will mark the second letter of the name with a minus, and we will put the address of the instruction LA 3 AA in the address field of the symbol table so that we can find that instruction later on when AA does get defined and we can put in the proper address.

Taking a short sample of nonsense code, we have

```
*  05

A3: LA  1 PQ      Load Acc from PQ

    SA  1 RS      Store it in RS
```

```
        ZA  1 A3      If it was zero, repeat

    M6: JP  1 M6      Dynamic halt
```

Here is what we would build up as machine code and in the symbol table:

SYMBOL TABLE

A	3	05
P	-Q	05
R	-S	06
M	6	08

DM STORAGE

	op-code	mod	address
05:	9	1	0
06:	1	1	0
07:	4	1	05
08:	6	1	08
09:			
0A:			

Now suppose another line of source code comes along referencing RS, i.e.,

```
    LA  1  RS
```

The first thing we can do is translate and store the LA 1 in DM location 09. Now we look up RS and find it undefined but referenced. In the address portion of DM location 09, we will store the address portion of the RS entry in the symbol table. This will give:

```
    09:  9 1 06
```

Then we put the address of the latest reference to RS in the address field of its symbol-table entry:

```
    R ¯S  09
```

One more suppose. Suppose sometime later, say, when star is pointing to DM cell 3A, we find the source-code sentence

```
    RS = 0
```

which means that cell 3A of the DM gets a <u>zero</u> and all previous references to RS get 3A, in place of what they now hold.

We find RS in the symbol table but it is undefined, so we define it (make the ¯S become plain S). We pick up the link (=09) from the RS entry and in its place we put the real address of RS (that is 3A). Now, in DM cell 09, we pick up the link (that is 06) and replace it with the real address of RS (that is 3A). Since this link is not zero, we proceed to where it points (06) and repeat the operation. Now at last the link is 0 and "all forward references to RS have been resolved." Any references to RS that come up in the future can be treated as if RS had been defined since the year one.

We mentioned looking up and translating the op-code above. We can build a permanent table of op-codes and their translations into the assembler. It can be searched any way that seems good at the time we write that part of the assembler.

The user will type in a sentence and end it with a carriage return. At this point we begin to scan the sentence to see what came in. Three routines are used: GET -- returns with the next character in the accumulator; GET2 discards initial blanks and returns with the next two characters. Non-alpha-numeric (0-9,A-Z) characters generate an error. Finally, GETN (i) finds up to 4 numeric characters, converts them to hex, and returns.

We begin right after the assembler has issued a carriage return and line feed indicating that the previous line has been digested and we are ready for a new line. The user types in characters, which we echo, until he again types a carriage return. At this point the scanner will begin to look at the line to see what it has been given. It begins at the left end of the line.

There are five basic sentences that we can have. They are:

(0) * nn
(1) LL: Op n AD
(2) OP n AD
(3) END
(4) LL = nnnn

where n stands for a digit 0-F, LL for a two-character label, and AD for a two-character address. If the modifier field of (1) or (2) is "0", then AD must be a number nn.

Figure 14.1, 14.2, and 14.3 are diagrams of the assembler. In a less rigidly controlled language, each attempt to get characters from an input string will continue to collect characters until it finds a blank or some other field-terminating symbol. Then the assembler will have to interpret what GET has found and act accordingly. Once we have made the four way branch (:, ƀ, D, =), our language is so structured that we know exactly (or almost exactly) what to expect, and we can therefore simplify the program by asking for only what we will find acceptable.

Since we propose to write this assembler in the language native to our own real machine and not in the language of the Dream Machine, this is technically a "cross assembler," generating code for machine A but running on machine B (B ≠ A).

Symbol Table

In the above discussion we have indicated most of what has to be done with the symbol table. Each symbol-table entry consists of three words called FIRSTCHAR, SECONDCHAR, and LOCATION. When we get a label or an address, we look up the first character of the label in FIRSTCHAR. If we find a match there, we check to see whether the second character matches. If not, we look for another first-character match. If we fail to find a matching pair, we will enter this character pair. If this is a label, we will assign the present value of the Address Pointer as the LOCATION. If this is an address field, we also put in the address pointer as the LOCATION but we mark SECONDCHAR negative, so that we know this is as yet undefined.

If we find the character pair in the symbol table and it is

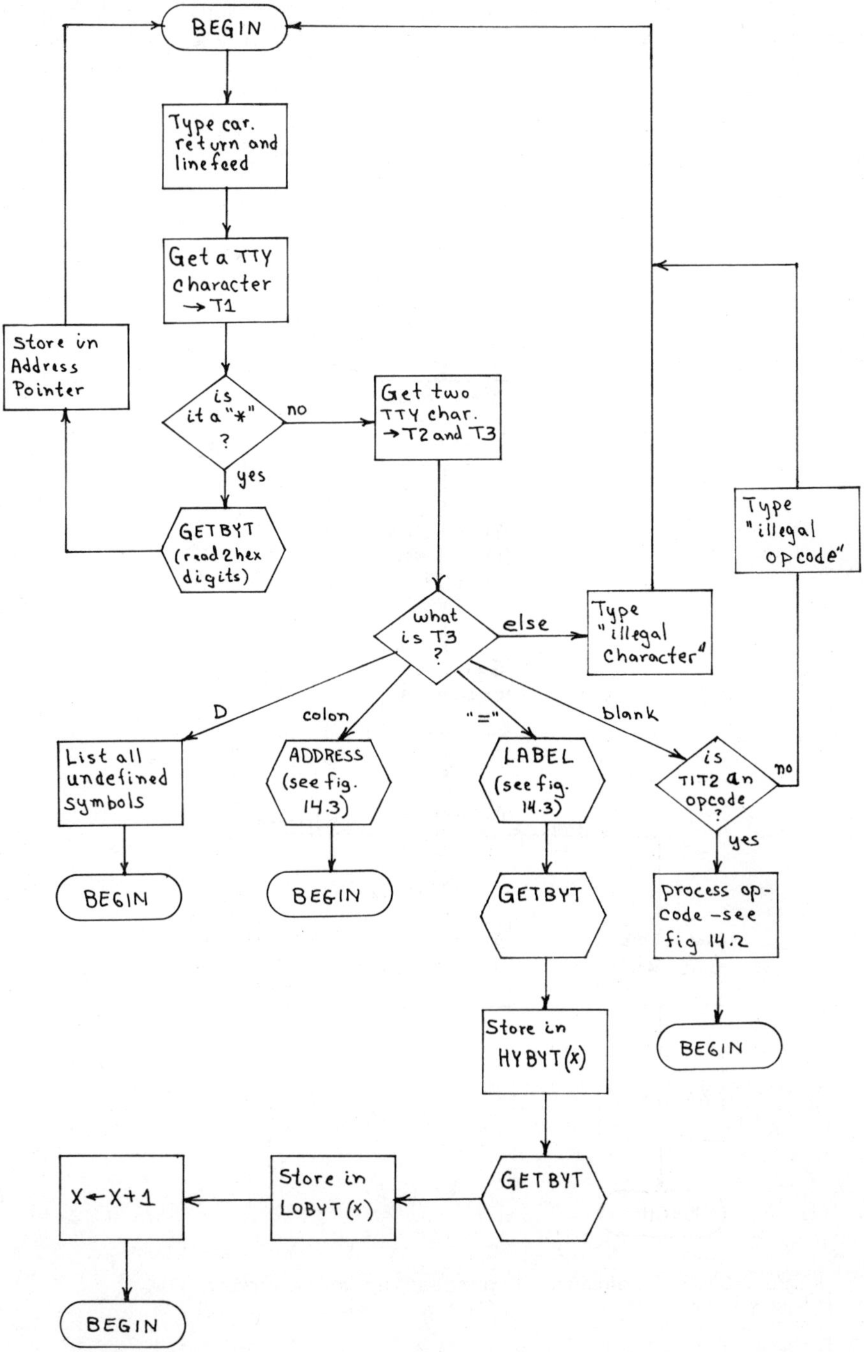

Figure 14.1 Main flow diagram of the assembler for DM.

already defined, we return the address in LOCATION unless this is a label field, in which case we type out a "DD" before the carriage return to indicate that this label is "doubly defined." If the pair matches but the location is "undefined," we either add the present address to the chain (if it is an address reference) or unravel the chain (if it is a label reference -- and hence a definition). Figure 14.3 shows the flow diagrams for these two subroutines.

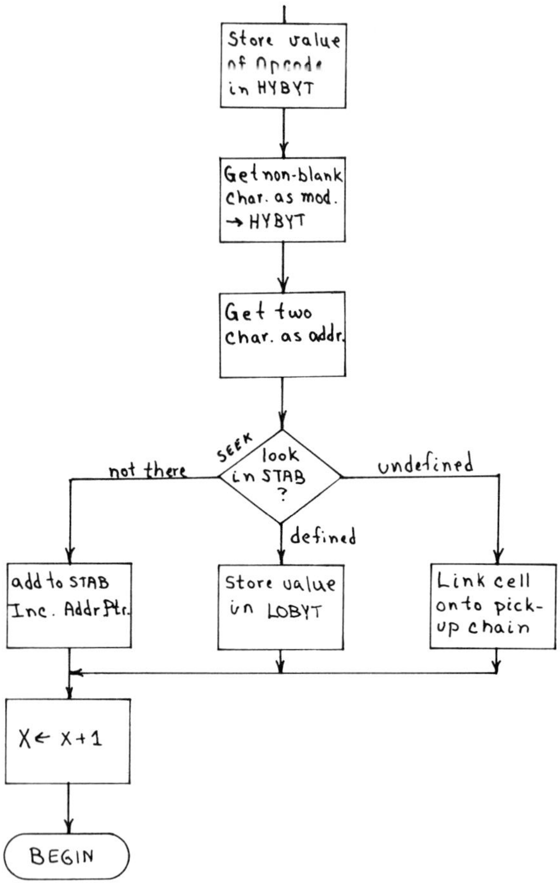

Figure 14.2 Details of processing an op-code.

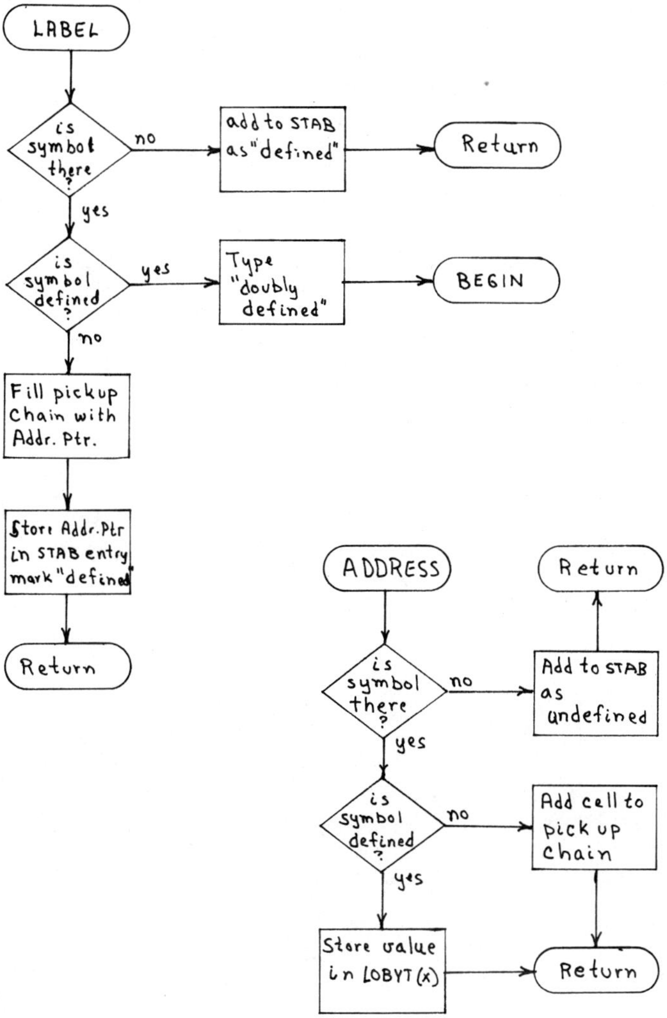

Figure 14.3 The subroutines LABEL and ADDRESS.

APPENDIX A
BINARY ARITHMETIC

We have all grown up using the decimal number system. Many, if not all readers, under 25 will have been exposed to various arithmetic bases in school. For the benefit of those who did not have the "new math" or who might wish to review, this appendix will cover the base-two number system and its application to digital computers.

The basic storage mechanism of a modern microcomputer is called a "flip-flop". Each flip-flop may be in one of two possible conditions: "flipped" or "flopped". Let us agree to call the first condition *zero* and the other *one*.

Because modern computers use flip-flops for storing information, they must perforce use a number system with only two values: *zero* and *one*.

Let's try the following argument and see if we can develop the binary number system out of it. Consider a large group (say 4) of flip-flops arranged in a row:

Suppose they are all storing *zeros*. We will let that pattern 0000 represent the number "0". Now concentrate on the righthand flip-flop. We want to represent the number "1". Let us change the rightmost flip-flop to a *one* and call the new pattern "1". So far we have

0000 = 0
0001 = 1

That is all the changes we can ring on the rightmost flip-flop, so look now at the second from the right. It has always been *zero* so far so let's change it to a *one*, and now we can repeat the previous *two* patterns for the rightmost (0 and 1), and we can say that

0010 = 2
0011 = 3

That's all we get from those two, so we make the next flip-flop be a *one*, and repeat all *four* of our previous patterns:

0100 = 4
0101 = 5
0110 = 6
0111 = 7

We can do the same with the leftmost flip-flop and get eight new patterns:

1000 = 8
1001 = 9
1010 = 10
1011 = 11
1100 = 12
1101 = 13
1110 = 14
1111 = 15

Look at the four patterns

0001 = 1
0010 = 2
0100 = 4
1000 = 8

Suppose we assigned a "weight" to each flip-flop cooresponding to its position. That is, from left to right, they get weights of 8,4,2, and 1. Now let us agree to count the weight of a given flip-flop if it contains a <u>one</u> but not to count it if it contains a <u>zero</u>. Suddenly it all falls together (with only a couple of nudges). To find the number that a particular pattern represents, we add up all the weights where there are <u>ones</u>. For example 1101 = 8 + 4 + (no two) + 1 = 8 + 4 + 1 = 13.

Putting this in more mathematical language will allow us to generalize. Imagine a row of flip-flops numbered 0,1,2,... from <u>right to left</u>. The weight of flip-flop <u>i</u> is then 2^i. Thus,

$2^0 = 1_d$
$2^1 = 2_d$
$2^2 = 4_d$
$2^3 = 8_d$
$2^4 = 16_d$
$2^5 = 32_d$
$2^6 = 64_d$
$2^7 = 128_d$
$2^8 = 256_d$

and on and on, where the "sub-d" stands for "decimal number". Using this scheme we can <u>calculate</u> that

1 0 1 1 0 0 1 = 1 + 8 + 16 + 64 = 89

rather than trying to arrive at it by counting up from 0. By extension, we are obviously able to represent any <u>positive</u> interger whatsoever if we use enough bits. What do we do about negative numbers? To decide how to represent negative numbers we need to know how many bits there are in a computer word. The scheme most microcomputers use is called "two's complement" (for various reasons we won't go into here) and works as follows:

Suppose your computer has N bits per word. Eight, twelve, and sixteen are common values for N for micromachines. The weight of these bits will be:

$$2^{N-1}, 2^{N-2}, \ldots 2^2, 2^1, 2^0$$

If all these bits are <u>one</u>, the sum of their weights will be

$$2^N-1.$$

So to represent the number 2^N we would need one more bit position to the left of the leftmost bit. Suppose N = 8. Then

$$1111\ 1111 = 255_d$$

and

$$1\ 0000\ 0000 = 256_d$$

This number (2^N) is called the modulus (M) of the arithmetic done in your machine. To represent a negative X we express it as

$$M - X.$$

That is to represent -1 we write down 255_d because $256_d - 1 = 255_d$. To represent -13 we write down $256_d - 13 = 243_d$ but, of course, we write these in binary, so we get

$$-1 = 1111\ 1111$$

and $$-13 = 1111\ 0011$$

We don't have to go through the work of actually doing this to get the representation of a negative number because there is a short-hand trick that makes it easier. It consists of 3 steps:

1. Write down the integer X in binary,

2. Replace <u>ones</u> with <u>zeros</u> and <u>zeros</u> with <u>ones</u>,

3. Add one to the result.

Let's try it for -13. First we write down 13, remembering to include leading <u>zeros</u> up to the size of the computer word. Thus

$$13_d = 0000\ 1101$$

Now step 2 replaces <u>ones</u> with <u>zeros</u> and vice versa, so we get

$$1111\ 0010.$$

Step 3 adds one to this and we get:

```
        1111 0010

  +     0000 0001
        ---------
        1111 0011
```

Same as before, right? But the example was chosen with malice aforethought because we don't really know how to do binary addition yet. Better get that squared away before we try another example. The addition table in binary is simple:

```
0 + 0 = 0
0 + 1 = 1
1 + 0 = 1
1 + 1 = 10   (what else?)
```

So let's try -8:

1. 8_d = 0000 1000

2. 1111 0111

3. 1111 0111
0000 0001

= ?

Starting at the righthand end, 1 + 1 gives 0 and carry 1. 1 + 0 + 1 (from the carry) gives 0 and a carry. Third place is the same result, 0 and carry 1. In the fourth place 0 + 0 + 1 (from the carry) gives 1 and no carry. The rest is easy, so the result is

1111 1000.

Check: 1111 1000 = (-8)

0000 1000 add 8 gives:

----

1 0000 0000 = 256_d

Good enough. That seems to work. We can recognize a negative number when we see one because it always starts with a one. Positive numbers always start with a zero. This is why the leftmost bit of a computer word is called the sign bit.

Now if the leftmost bit is zero in an 8-bit word, then there are exactly 128 patterns that can be placed in the remaining 7 bits. These are assigned to the positive integers, 0,1,..., 127. Thus 127 is the largest (most positive) signed integer we can store in an 8-bit word. What happens if we add 64 and 70?

$$
\begin{array}{rrl}
 & 64_d = & 0100\ 0000 \\
+ & 70_d = & 0100\ 0110 \\
\hline
 & & 1000\ 0110
\end{array}
$$

which is a negative number. Going through our 3-step conversion routine (which works equally well in either direction) we have:

1. X = 1000 0110

2. 0111 1001

3. + 0000 0001

$$\overline{0111\ 1010}$$

$$= 2 + 8 + 16 + 32 + 64 = 122_d$$

So $X = -122_d$

So we have 64 + 70 = −122. Not exactly ordinary arithmetic. We have added two positive numbers and gotten a negative result. Obviously an error. In most micros when this happens it sets a bit called the "overflow" bit. It is the programmer's responsibility to test this bit to see if overflow has occurred. The machine couldn't care less and in fact sometimes you want to be allowed to compute this way.

Consider: Suppose I am interested only in positive numbers and would like to store numbers between 0 and 255 in one 8-bit word. Now, when I add 64 and 70 I would expect to get 134. I do. It's just when I try to interpret it as a signed number that I get into trouble. This is why the microcomputers will tell you (via the overflow bit) if you have added two "positives" and gotten a "negative" or added two "negatives" and gotten a "positive" but they won't do anything about it unless you ask.

<u>Carry</u> When I add two unsigned numbers and their sum is too large to fit into a computer word, I am again in danger of getting an erroneous result. Suppose I add 128_d and 128_d. I should get 256_d, but in an 8-bit word the largest unsigned integer I can store is 255_d.

$$
\begin{array}{r}
1000\ 0000 \\
\underline{1000\ 0000} \\
1\ 0000\ 0000
\end{array}
$$

The number on the third line is indeed 256_d as represented in binary, but in an 8-bit word there is no place to store the <u>one</u> in the ninth position. In all microcomputers (and all the minicomputers, also), that leftmost bit is placed in a central register, one bit long, called "the carry bit". If an addition results in a carry out of the leftmost position that can be stored (out of the sign position), the carry bit is set to <u>one</u>. If not, the carry bit is cleared to <u>zero</u>.

Now, aside from telling you about the fact that "unsigned overflow" has occurred, the carry bit is there for another purpose. It is there to facilitate multiple-precision arithmetic.

The carry bit can be set (SEC) or cleared (CLC) and tested for zero (BCC) or one (BCS), and in the KIM-1 (but not in all computers), enters into every arithmetic operation. Most computers have an ADD instruction and an ADC (add with carry). The first of these adds the two operands together and places the resulting sum in the accumulator and the carry in the carry bit. The second not only adds the two operands, but also adds in the initial value of the carry bit to form the sum. The KIM-1 has only the ADC instruction so if you don't want the carry bit added in, you had better clear it before you do the add.

Subtraction In addition to addition, we sometimes need to be able to do subtraction. Very few computers have both adder and subtractor circuits. They make do with just adders. The trick is this:

$$8 - 5 = 8 + (-5).$$

So what they need is a circuit to take the two's complement of a number and an adder. These circuits are called into play automatically when you issue a subtract instruction (SUB) or a subtract-with-carry (SBC). Only the latter is available on KIM-1.

Caution must be employed about the use of the "carry" bit. For a subtraction the "carry" bit becomes a "borrow" bit. For there to be "no borrow," the carry bit must be one. A zero means "somebody has borrowed the one that should be there," and the difference when it is calculated will be one less than you would have expected.

In brief, the SBC operation takes the contents of the accumulator and subtracts the contents of the designated memory location and then subtracts the complement-of-the-carry-bit (the borrow bit) from the difference and puts the answer in the accumulator.

If this result does not generate a borrow, it leaves the carry bit set. If it does generate a borrow, it will clear the carry bit. So, before doing an SBC, you must set the carry (SEC); and before doing an add, you must clear carry (CLC).

Multiple Precision At times you will need numbers larger than 255 (or 127 signed). The carry bit gives you a convenient way of carrying out multiple-precision arithmetic. Suppose we need numbers in the range between 0 and 65,535 (2^{16}-1). We will need 16 bits to store each number of this size, or two computer words for each number. Our procedure is the same as we use to add multiple digit numbers by hand. We add the least significant digits. Then we take the carry from that operation (if any) and add it and the next more significant digits together, and so on. Let us add A and B and put the result in B, and do it in double-precision: A will be stored in cells AHI and ALO and B in BHI and BLO -- the "hi" portion having the more significant half and the "lo" the less significant half. Then:

```
CLC            Clear carry if you don't have a plain
               ADD instruction

LDA BLO  )
ADC ALO  }     Add the lower halves
STA BLO  )
               Don't clear carry.  We need it.

LDA BHI  )
ADC AHI  }     Use the ADC instruction
STA BHI  )     This stores the sum of
               AHI + BHI + C in BHI
```

This can, of course, be generalized to any order of precision required, and works as well for subtraction as for addition (if you remember to set carry before beginning) and to use SBC for all subtracts after the first one -- if you indeed get a choice.

Hexadecimal or Hex For large numbers it becomes very tiring to write out all those ones and zeros in order to express the thing in binary. A shorthand is needed, and by a strange coincidence, one exists. It is called hexadecimal notation, or "hex" for short. To convert binary to hex (this is done for the purpose of writing and reading only; the computer still works in binary), we begin at the righthand, or least significant, end of the binary number and group the digits into groups of four. Thus:

101 1101 0010 1010

If there aren't enough to make four in the leftmost group we add leading zeros as needed. Using the table immediately below, we can convert each group of four bits to a single character:

Binary pattern	Hex character	Decimal equivalent
0000	0	0
0001	1	1
0010	2	2
0011	3	3
0100	4	4
0101	5	5
0110	6	6
0111	7	7
1000	8	8
1001	9	9
1010	A	10
1011	B	11
1100	C	12
1101	D	13
1110	E	14
1111	F	15

This table shows the binary pattern, the hex character that represents that pattern, and the decimal equivalent.

The number we wrote above is then translated as:

```
0101 1101 0010 1010
 5    D    2    A
```

that is, 5D2A.

It is possible to build a complete arithmetic system using hex numbers. All you need to remember is that 9 + 1 = A, not 10, and F + 1 = 10 (that is _zero_ with a carry of _one_). When you subtract and have to borrow _one_ from a column to the left, you convert the _one_ you borrow to 16 to add to the column you are working on. But don't worry too hard about that. If you need it, you'll learn it in due time. If you don't, you don't.

One of the endpapers of this book gives all 256 hex pairs from 00-FF and their decimal equivalents. Another reproduces the table given above for your ready reference.

APPENDIX B
KIM SUBROUTINES

Those readers fortunate enough to own a KIM-1 will be able to use the subroutines stored in the read only memory of the KIM.

We present here a brief description of these subroutines for your information since several of them are used in the code we have written.

Teleprinter

The KIM-1 routines provide more or less complete control of the system (except for the STOP key) via the teleprinter.

Initialization: press the RESET key on the keyboard of the KIM and then the rub out key on the teleprinter. The teleprinter will type KIM and then the address pointed at by the address pointer and the contents of that cell.

Address Selection: Enter four hex keys (leading zeros not required) and then the space bar. The teleprinter will respond by repeating the address typing a space and then the contents of the cell so addressed.

Next Cell: Press carriage return. KIM will type out the next address and its contents.

Previous Cell: Press line feed, KIM will type out the previous address and its contents.

Modify a Cell: After KIM has typed the contents of a cell you may type a new contents followed by a period. This new value will be stored in the cell and then the address and contents of the next cell will be typed out. Leading zeros are not required.

Load Paper Tape: If you have a teleprinter with paper tape you may load a properly prepared (see below) paper tape by placing the tape in the reader, typing L and then activating the paper tape reader.

Punch Paper Tape: Put the low order byte of the ending address in cell 17F7. Put the high order byte of the ending address in cell 17F8. Set the address pointer to the starting address (see address selection). Turn on the paper tape punch. Type Q. Each record (printed line) will begin with:

;18

followed by the records starting address (4 hex characters) followed by 48 hex characters listing the contents of the starting address and the next 23 cells thereafter. Finally there is a two byte (4 character) check sum. The last record has zero data cells (;00) and the "starting address field" indicates the total number of records printed out. This is followed by a 4 character check sum and an X-OFF character.

Running a Program: Set the address pointer to the first instruction to be executed. Type G for GO. If the machine is in single step mode only one instruction will be executed. Otherwise it will run free.

Stopping a Program: Press the STOP key on the keyboard

Recording on Audio Cassette

To record a part of the KIM memory (presumably a program or data) on an audio cassette recorder connect the recorder to the KIM as shown in the KIM manual. Next:

00F1 - gets 00, to clear the decimal mode.

17F5 - gets starting address low order byte.
17F6 - gets starting address high order byte.

17F7 - gets ending address (one greater than the last cell to be written out) low order byte.
17F8 - gets ending address high order byte.

17F9 - gets a two hex digit (01-FE) program name or identifier.

Set the address pointer to 1800. Start the tape recording. Press GO. When the recording is completed the display will light up with 0000 XX. Any other address indicates an error has been made.

Loading Data from an Audio Cassette

To load back in data or programs recorded from a KIM, proceed as follows:

00F1 - gets 00 to clear decimal mode.

17F9 - gets program name or identifier.

Set the address pointer to 1873. Press GO. Start tape recorder replaying the program.

If loading is successful the display will relight with 0000 XX. Any other address indicates that an error has been made. If 17F9 contains a number from 01 to FE inclusive, KIM will search the tape for a record bearing that identifier. If 17F9 contains 00 KIM will load the next valid record from the tape into the addresses specified in the record. If 17F9 contains FF the next valid record will be loaded into memory beginning at the address specified in 17F5 and 17F6 (low order byte first).

Useful Subroutines

The following subroutines in the read only memory of the KIM may be used by any programmer. They are called with a subroutine jump (JSR) and end with a return from subroutine (RTS).

CRLF (1E2F) causes the teleprinter to type a carriage return and line feed. Destroys contents of A, X, and Y.

GETBYT (1FD9) accepts two hex characters from the teleprinter and returns with them packed in the accumulator. For example, 3A will return as 0011 1010. Any character within the range 30_h -46_h (ASCII) will be accepted.

Those greater than or equal to 40_h will be augmented by 9_h before being truncated to their lower four bits. Characters outside the range 30-46 will be ignored and the character or characters entered by the previous invocation of GEYBYT will be returned. Old contents of A are lost. X is preserved. Y is returned equal to 0.

GETCH (1E5A) gets one ASCII character from the teleprinter and returns it in the accumulator. Old contents of A are lost. X is preserved. Y is returned equal to FF. If teleprinter is not selected GETCH returns with A = 01.

GETKEY (1F6A) will examine the keyboard to see if any key is now depressed. Returns with A coded as shown below. Old contents of A, X, and Y are all destroyed.

0, 1, 2, 3, 4, 5, 6, 7, 8, 9, A, B, C, D, E, F } hex key 0-F

10	AD	address mode
11	DA	data mode
12	+	increment address pointer
13	GO	go
14	PC	recall program counter
15	-	no key is now pressed

OUTCH (1EA0) prints one ASCII character held in A on the teleprinter. A and Y are destroyed. X is preserved. Y is returned equal to FF.

OUTSP (1E9E) prints a space on the teleprinter. A, Y are destroyed. X is preserved.

SCANDS (1F1F) outputs on the 7 segment displays the six hex characters stored two to a word in 00FB, 00FA, and 00F9. Destroys A, X, and Y.

APPENDIX C
6502 OP-CODES

We present a brief description of what each instruction does and its effects (if any) on the condition flags (shown in parenthesis). In what follows A means the accumulator, m means the operand (as determined by the addressing mode).

ADC - add with carry. A←(A) + (M) + (C). The operand and the carry are added to the contents of the accumulator (N,Z,C).

AND - logical and A←(A) ∧ (M). The operand and the contents of the accumulator are ANDed together bit by bit and put back into the accumulator (N,Z).

ASL - arithmetic shift left. C←bit 7, bit 7←bit 6,..., bit 0←zero. (N,Z,C).

BCC - branch on carry clear. If C = 0, add m to the contents of the PC (no effect).

BCS - branch on carry set. If C = 1, add m to the contents of the PC (no effect).

BEQ - branch if equal. If Z = 1, add m to the contents of the PC (no effect).

BIT - bit test. The operand and the contents of the accumulator are ANDed together bit by bit and the result is discarded except for its effects on the condition flags (N←M_7, Z, V←M_6).

BMI - branch if minus. If N = 1, add m to the contents of the PC (no effect).

BNE - branch if not equal. If Z = 0, add m to the contents of the PC (no effect).

BPL - branch if plus. If N = 0, add m to the contents of the PC (no effect).

BRK - break. Set break bit in PSW. Save PC plus PSW on stack. Load PC from IRQ vector. (B←1). See 6502 programming manual.

BVC - branch if overflow clear. If V = 0, add m to the contents of the PC (no effect).

BVS - branch if overflow set. If V = 1, add m to the contents of the PC (no effect).

CLC - clear carry (C⟵0).

CLD - clear decimal mode flag (D⟵0).

CLI - clear interrupt inhibit bit (I⟵0).

CLV - clear overflow bit (V⟵0).

CMP - compare. (A)-(m). Subtract the operand from the contents of the accumulator and discard the result except for its effects on the condition flags (N,Z,C).

CPX - compare X. (X)-(m). Subtract the operand from the contents of the X register and discard the result except for its effects on the condition flags (N,Z,C).

CPY - compare Y. (Y)-(m). Subtract the operand from the contents of the Y register and discard the result except for its effects on the condition flags (N,Z,C).

DEC - decrement. m⟵(m)-1. Subtract one from the operand and place the difference in memory (may refer to the accumulator) (N,Z). Does not change carry bit.

DEX - decrement X. X⟵(X)-1. Subtract one from the contents of the X register and place the difference in the X register (N,Z). Does not change the carry bit.

DEY - decrement Y. Y⟵(Y)-1. Subtract one from the contents of the Y register and place the difference in the Y register (N,Z). Does not change the carry bit.

EOR - exclusive or. A⟵(A) $\veebar$ (M). The operand and the contents of the accumulator are exclusive or-ed together and the result is placed in the accumulator (N,Z).

INC - increment. Add one to the operand and replace it. May refer to the accumulator. (N,Z). Does not change the carry bit.

INX - increment X. Add one to the contents of the X register and place the sum back in X. (N,Z). Does not change the carry bit.

INY - increment Y. Add one to the contents of the Y register and place the sum back in Y (N,Z). Does not change the carry bit.

JMP - jump. Place the operand in the program counter (no effect).

JSR - jump to subroutine. Save the present contents of the program counter on the stack. Then place the operand in the program counter (no effect).

LDA - load accumulator. Place the operand in the accumulator (N,Z).

LDX - load X. Place the operand in the X register. (N,Z).

LDY - load Y. Place the operand in the Y register (N,Z).

LSR - logical shift right. Shift the operand one bit right. Bit 7 gets 0. Old value of bit 0 goes to the carry bit. (N⟵0,Z,C⟵bit 0).

NOP - no operation. Do nothing (no effect).

ORA - logical OR to accumulator. A⟵(A) v (M). The operand and the contents of A are or-ed together bit by bit and the result placed in A (N,Z).

PHA - push accumulator. S↙⌒⟵ (A). Copy the contents of the accumulator onto the stack, then decrement the stack pointer (no effect).

PHP - push processor status. S↙⌒⟵ (PSW). Copy the processor status register onto the stack. Then decrement the stack pointer (no effect).

PLA - pull accumulator. A⟵⌒ (S). Copy the top of the stack into the accumulator, then increment the stack pointer (no effect).

PLP - pull processor status. PSR⟵⌒ (S). Copy the top of the stack into the processor status register, then increment the stack pointer (N,Z,C,I,D,V, from stack).

ROL - rotate left. Circular shift the operand and the carry bit one bit to the left. Old carry goes to bit 0 and old bit 7 goes to the carry bit (N⟵bit 6,Z,C⟵bit 7).

ROR - rotate right. Circular shift of the operand and the carry bit one bit to the right. Old carry goes to bit 7 and old bit 0 goes to carry (N⟵C, Z, C⟵bit 0). Note: early 6502's did not have this instruction.

RTI - return from interrupt. PSR⟵⌒ (S), PC⟵⌒ (S). Restore the program status register and the program counter from the top three bytes on the stack. Then add three to the stack pointer. (all condition flags loaded from stack).

RTS - return from subroutine. $PC \leftarrow\frown (S)$. Load the program counter from the stack (two bytes) and add two to the stack pointer (no effect).

SBC - subtract carry. $A \leftarrow A-(M)-(\overline{C})$. Subtract the operand and the complement of the carry from the contents of the accumulator. Place the difference in the accumulator. The complement of the carry bit is the "borrow bit" so it is necessary to set the carry bit before doing a subtraction (N,Z,C,V).

SEC - set carry. $(C \leftarrow 1)$.

SED - set decimal mode $(D \leftarrow 1)$.

SEI - set interrupt inhibit $(I \leftarrow 1)$.

STA - store accumulator. $m \leftarrow (A)$. Copy the contents of the accumulator to the cell designated by m (no effect).

STX - store X. $m \leftarrow (X)$. Copy the contents of the X register to the cell designated by m (no effect).

STY - store Y. $M \leftarrow (Y)$. Copy the contents of the Y register to the cell designated by m (no effect).

TAX - transfer A to X. $X \leftarrow (A)$. Copy the contents of the accumulator to the X register (N,Z).

TAY - transfer A to Y. $Y \leftarrow (A)$. Copy the contents of the accumulator to the Y register (N,Z).

TSX - transfer S to X. $X \leftarrow (S)$. Copy the contents of the stack pointer to the X register (N,Z).

TXA - transfer X to A. $A \leftarrow (X)$. Copy the contents of the X register to the accumulator (N,Z).

TXS - transfer X to S. $S \leftarrow (X)$. Copy the contents of the X register to the stack pointer (no effect).

TYA - transfer Y to A. $A \leftarrow (Y)$. Copy the contents of the Y register to the accumulator (N,Z).

APPENDIX D ADDRESSING MODES OF 6502

There are 13 addressing modes in the 6502. No single instruction permits the use of all the modes. Many instructions have only one mode. Some have as many as eight possible modes. The symbols in parenthesis are the op-code suffixes used in this book.

Immediate (#) The one byte address field serves as the operand. For example, LDA# m puts m in the accumulator. Available for loads, compares and arithmetic and logical operations.

Absolute (no suffix). The two byte address field designates a cell in memory. For store operations this cell is the destination and for loads, compares and arithmetic and logical operations, the contents of the designated cell serve as the operand.

Zero page (Z) The one byte address field designates a cell in page zero (0000 - 00FF). Otherwise just like absolute addressing.

Implied (nothing) No address field at all. The instructions are one byte long and the source and/or destination is specified by the op-code.

Accumulator (A) The shift and rotate instructions may be made to act on the accumulator in this mode.

X Indirect (XI) The one byte address field plus the contents of X designates a cell m in page zero (0000 - 00FF). The contents of m and m + 1 (low order byte first) are used as a 16 bit address. The cell designated by this address then serves as a destination or a source for the operand. This is called indexed indirect or pre-indexing.

Indirect Y (IY) The one byte address field m designates a pair of cells (m and m + 1) in page zero - low order byte first. The contents of the Y register are added to the 16 bit address in these two cells and the resulting sum designates a cell in memory. That cell serves as the source or destination for the operand. This is called "post indexing" or "indirect indexed".

Zero page X (ZX) and Zero page Y (ZY) The one byte address field is added to the contents of the index register. This sum designates a cell in page zero (0000 - 00FF) which serves as the source or destination for the operand.

Absolute X (X) and Absolute Y (Y) The two byte address field (low order byte first) is added to the contents of the index register. This sum designates a cell which serves as the source or destination for the operand.

Relative (no suffix) Used only for branches. The one byte address field is added to the program counter. Bit 8 of the address field is treated as a sign bit and if equal to one the field is considered to be negative. This allows forward branches of 0-127 and backwards branches of 0 to 128 bytes.

Indirect (I) Used only for the jump instruction. Rather than placing the two byte address field in the program counter as is usual with a jump, when indirect mode is specified, the contents of the cell designated by the two byte address field is placed in the program counter.

SAMPLE CODING SHEET

Address	F_1	F_2	F_3	Label	Instruction	Cycle	Comments
0000	AD	20	01	START:	LDA ZERO	4	set stoskey address
03	8D	FA	17		STA 17FA	4	to
06	AD	21	01		LDA ONEC	4	1C00
09	8D	FB	17		STA 17FB	4	
0C	AD	23	01		LDA K2	4	holds FE = 1111 1110
0F	8D	01	17		STA 1701	4	makes A0 be input
12	AD	22	01		LDA ALLONE	4	holds FF = 1111 1111
15	8D	03	17		STA 1703	4	makes B be output
18	AD	20	01		LDA ZERO	4	Clear PORTA
1B	8D	00	17		STA 1700	4	to zeros
1E	AD	00	17	LOOP:	LDA 1700	4	wait for the key
21	F0	FB			BEQ LOOP	2/3	to close
23	EE	02	17		INC 1702	6	toggle the speaker
26	AD	24	01		LDA CONST	4	set counter to 59
29	8D	25	01		STA COUNTER	4	
2C	CE	25	01	WAIT:	DEC COUNTER	6	count down to zero
2F	10	FB			BPL WAIT	2/3	
31	4C	1E	00		JMP LOOP	3	go back and do it again
0120	00			ZERO:	00		
1	1C			ONEC:	1C		
2	FF			ALLONE:	FF		
3	FE			K2:	FE		
4	3B			CONST:	3B		59 decimal
5	00			COUNTER:	00		

Sample Coding Sheet and solution for Morse Code experiment

APPENDIX E SOLUTIONS

We now list all the possible 6502 instructions by mode of address. Following the mnemonic we show the numeric op-code, the number of cycles required to execute the instruction, and the number of bytes it occupies, including the address field.

Immediate	Absolute	Zero Page
ADC# - 69,2,2	ADC - 6D,4,3	ADCZ - 65,3,2
AND# - 29,2,2	AND - 2D,4,3	ANDZ - 25,3,2
CMP# - C9,2,2	ASL - 0E,6,3	ASLZ - 06,5,2
CPX# - E0,2,2	BIT - 2C,4,3	BITZ - 24,3,2
CPY# - C0,2,2	CMP - CD,4,3	CMPZ - C5,3,2
EOR# - 49,2,2	CPX - EC,4,3	CPXZ - E4,3,2
LDA# - A9,2,2	CPY - CC,4,3	CPYZ - C4,3,2
LDX# - A2,2,2	DEC - CE,6,3	DECZ - C6,5,2
LDY# - A0,2,2	EOR - 4D,4,3	EORZ - 45,3,2
ORA# - 09,2,2	INC - EE,6,3	INCZ - E6,5,2
SBC# - E9,2,2	JMP - 4C,3,3	LDAZ - A5,3,2
	JSR - 20,6,3	LDXZ - A6,3,2
	LDA - AD,4,3	LDYZ - A4,3,2
Relative	LDX - AE,4,3	LSRZ - 46,5,2
	LDY - AC,4,3	ORAZ - 05,3,2
BCC - 90,2,2	LSR - 4E,6,3	ROLZ - 26,5,2
BCS - B0,2,2	ORA - 0D,4,3	RORZ - 66,5,2
BEQ - F0,2,2	ROL - 2E,6,3	SBCZ - E5,3,2
BMI - 30,2,2	ROR - 6E,6,3	STAZ - 85,3,2
BNE - D0,2,2	SBC - ED,4,3	STXZ - 86,3,2
BPL - 10,2,2	STA - 8D,4,3	STYZ - 84,3,2
BVC - 50,2,2	STX - 8E,4,3	
BVS - 70,2,2	STY - 8C,4,3	

Indirect

JMPI - 6C,5,3

Implied or Accumulator

ASLA - 0A,2,1
BRK - 00,7,1
CLC - 18,2,1
CLD - D8,2,1
CLI - 58,2,1
CLV - B8,2,1
DEX - CA,2,1
DEY - 88,2,1
INX - E8,2,1
INY - C8,2,1
LSRA - 4A,2,1
NOP - EA,2,1
PHA - 48,3,1
PHP - 08,3,1
PLA - 68,4,1
PLP - 28,4,1
ROLA - 2A,2,1
RORA - 6A,2,1
RTI - 40,6,1
RTS - 60,6,1
SEC - 38,2,1
SED - F8,2,1
SEI - 78,2,1
TAX - AA,2,1
TAY - A8,2,1
TSX - BA,2,1
TXA - 8A,2,1
TXS - 9A,2,1
TYA - 98,2,1

X-Indirect

ADCXI - 61,6,2
ANDXI - 21,6,2
CMPXI - C1,6,2
EORXI - 41,6,2
LDAXI - A1,6,2
ORAXI - 01,6,2
SBCXI - E1,6,2
STAXI - t1,6,2

Indirect Y

ADCIY - 71,5,2
ANDIY - 31,5,2
CMPIY - D1,5,2
EORIY - 51,5,2
LDAIY - B1,5,2
ORAIY - 11,5,2
SBCIY - F1,5,2
STAIY - 91,6,2

Zero Page Indexed

ADCZX - 75,4,2
ANDZX - 35,4,2
ASLZX - 16,6,2
CMPZX - D5,4,2
DECZX - D6,6,2
EORZX - 55,4,2
INCZX - F6,6,2
LDAZX - B5,4,2
LDXZY - B6,4,2
LDYZX - B4,4,2
LSRZX - 56,6,2
ORAZX - 15,4,2
ROLZX - 36,6,2
RORZX - 76,6,2
SBCZX - F5,4,2
STAZX - 95,4,2
STXZY - 96,4,2
STYZX - 94,4,2

Absolute X

ADCX - 7D,4,3
ANDX - 3D,4,3
ASLX - 1E,7,3
CMPX - DD,4,3
DECX - DE,7,3
EORX - 5D,4,3
INCX - FE,7,3
LDAX - BD,4,3
LDYX - BC,4,3
LSRX - 5E,7,3
ORAX - 1D,4,3
ROLX - 3E,7,3
RORX - 7E,7,3
SBCX - FD,4,3
STAX - 9D,5,3

Absolute Y

ADCY - 79,4,3
ANDY - 39,4,3
CMPY - D9,4,3
EORY - 59,4,3
LDAY - B9,4,3
LDXY - BE,4,3
ORAY - 19,4,3
SBCY - F9,4,3
STAY - 99,5,3

Code for Morse Code Oscillator. Chapter 3.

```
*First we must set up the stop key so it will work properly

    START:     LDA ZERO          this cell will contain "00"
               STA 17FA
               LDA ONEC          this one holds "1C"
               STA 17FB

*Now we make A0 be input (and the rest of port A be output) and we
*make B0 be output (and the rest of port B be output also)

               LDA K2            this cell holds "FE"
               STA 1701          direction A
               LDA ALLONES       this cell holds "FF" - all ones
               STA 1703          direction B

*We clear port A to have all zeros in it.  Then we look at A0 to see
*if it has changed to a one indicating that the switch was closed.
*If not we loop back to try again.

               LDA ZERO
               STA 1700          clear port A
    LOOP:      LDA 1700
               BEQ LOOP          was it all zeros?

*At this point we have found the switch closed so we toggle the
*speaker.  Then we set up a value in COUNTER and in the loop called
*WAIT we count down until that counter goes to zero.  Then we go
*back and see if the switch is still closed.

               INC 1702          toggle speaker
               LDA CONST         determines how long between toggles
               STA COUNTER
    WAIT:      DEC COUNTER
               BPL WAIT
               JMP LOOP

*The constants we need for this program can be stored right after
*the JMP LOOP instruction.  They are:

    ZERO:      00
    ONEC:      1C
    ALLONES:   FF
    K2:        FE
    CONST:     3B                that will do for a starting value

*The only variable we use here can go right after the last constant:

    COUNTER:   00                will do for a filler value to begin
                                 the program with
```

Code for Piano Keyboard. Chapter 4.

*To initialize the computer we set up the stop key and make port A
*be output and port B 7-2 be input so we can sense closure of the
*piano keys. Bits B1 will be output "just because" and B0 will be
*output so we can toggle the loudspeaker.

```
START:     LDA# 00
           STA  17FA
           LDA# 1C
           STA  17FB
           LDA# 00                   we'll get a new zero in A
           STA  DIRA                 just in case some time we
                                     want something else
           LDA# 03
           STA  DIRB
```

*We look to see if one of the keys connected to port A is closed. If
*port A is not all zero then we try to find out which key by shifting
*and counting in index register X. We exit to SECOND if no key of
*this group was pressed and to FOUND when we discover and identify a
*key. Numbers in parentheses are the cycles required to execute each
*instruction:

```
FIRST:     LDX# 00       (2)     zero the counter
           LDA  PORTA    (4)     (1700)
           BEQ  SECOND   (2/3)   3 if you do jump
LOOP1:     BMI  FOUND    (2/3)   we are testing the leftmost bit
           INX           (2)     increment X
           ASLA          (2)     shift accum. left
           JMP  LOOP1    (3)
```

*SECOND tests port B and is much like FIRST except that we have to
*clear out B1 and B0 (and B6 for good luck) before testing for a key
*in this group.

```
SECOND:    LDX# 08       (2)     start count at 8
           LDA  PORTB    (4)
           AND# BC       (4)     clear unused bits
           BEQ  FIRST    (2/3)   nothing here go to FIRST
LOOP2:     BMI  FOUND    (2/3)
           INX           (2)
           ASLA          (2)
           JMP  LOOP2    (3)
```

*Now at FOUND we have a number in index register X which identifies
*which key was pushed. We get half period delay value from TABLE,
*put it in Y and count down to zero. Then we toggle the speaker and
*go back to see if any keys are still pressed:

```
FOUND:     LDAX TABLE    (4)
           TAY                     get number from A to Y
WAIT:      JMP  WI       (3)
WI:        DEY           (4)
           BNE  WAIT     (2/3)
           INC  PORTB    (6)       toggle speaker
           JMP  FIRST    (3)

*The TABLE holds delays for each note.  These delays are corrected
*for the time it takes to decide that this note was pressed.

TABLE:     00            C
           F0            C#
           E0            D
           D1            D#
           C4            E
           B6            F
           A9            F#
           9D            G
           9D            G#      by coincidence the same number
           00            phantom key
           90            A
           85            A#
           7B            B
           72            C
```

Note this table will generate tones somewhat flat. If you have perfect pitch and this bothers you, try the table of page 52.

Code for Keybounce. Chapter 5.

```
*Once again we must set up the stop key and make port A bit 0 be an
*input with the other bits being output.  Then we initialize the
*stack pointer to point to line FF of page 01:

    START:     LDA# 00
               STA  17FA
               LDA# 1C
               STA  17FB
               LDA# FE
               STA  DIRA
               LDX# FF                  put FF into stack pointer
               TXS
               LDX# F8                  set X to count 248d

*Now we wait until a key is pushed:

    KEY:       LDA  PORTA
               BEQ  KEY

*Once a key has been pushed we start taking samples of the key state
*and putting them on the stack.  We use X as a counter to see if we
*are out of space yet.

    LOOP:      LDA  PORTA
               PHA                      push Acc onto the stack
               DEX
               BNE  LOOP

*We have the samples all nicely stored in page 01 so we can stop,
*using a "dynamic halt" if the machine doesn't have anything better.

    STOP:      JMP  STOP
```

Code for Combination Lock. Chapter 6.

```
*Usual initialization of stop key and stack pointer. Then we make
*A7-A4 be output, A3-A0 be input. We clear PORTA and make PORTB be
*output.

    START:     LDA# 00
               STA  17FA
               LDA# 1C
               STA  17FB
               LDX# FF
               TXS                   set stack pointer
               LDA# F0
               STA  DIRA             1701 gets set
               LDA# 00
               STA  PORTA            clear port A
               LDA# FF
               STA  DIRB             1703 gets made output

*The main program consists of four calls to a subroutine named SUB
*and then a loop back to the beginning of the program.

               LDY# 00
               JSR  SUB              state A
               LDY# 01
               JSR  SUB              state B
               LDY# 02
               JSR  SUB              state C
               LDY# 03
               JSR  SUB              state D
               JMP  START

*The subroutine SUB gets a light pattern for this state and displays
*it. Then it waits for a zero set of keys and then a non-zero set.
*Once a key has been pressed we give the user about 1/4 of a second
*to close any other keys:

    SUB:       LDAY LIGHT            this is a table of patterns
               STA  PORTB            set the lights
    CLEAR:     LDA  PORTA
               BNE  CLEAR            wait for clear keyboard
    HOLD:      LDA  PORTA
               BEQ  HOLD             wait for some input
               LDX# 64
    OUTER:     LDA# FF
               STA  COUNT
    INNER:     DEC  COUNT            inner
               BNE  INNER                  loop
               DEX
               BNE  OUTER
```

*He has had enough time to close all the keys he is going to close
*so we get PORTA and compare it with the required combination stored
*in the table COMB. If it matches we go to the next state (return
*to the main program). If it doesn't match we reset to state A by
*jumping to START.

```
            LDA  PORTA
            CMPY COMB               indexed
            BNE  START
            RTS                     return from subroutine
```

*The tables we need are:

```
    LIGHT:  08                      light A
            04                            B
            02                            C
            01                            D
    COMB:    3
             6
             8                        368
             0
```

*The only variable is:

```
    COUNT:  00                      clear to start with
```

Tune Player. Chapter 7.

*The usual initialization including making B0 be output and B7 be *input:

```
    START:     LDA# 00
               STA  17FA
               LDA# 1C
               STA  17FB
               LDA# 01
               STA  DIRB
```

*First of all go to the KIM subroutine to read in a key. Then put *the key number in index register X. Using this key number we will *get the starting address of the Xth song from TABLO and TABH1. We *store this address in ADR1 and ADR2 which must be in page zero.

```
    GETKEY:    JSR  1F6A           subroutine to get a key
               CMP# 15h            returns 15h if no key
               BEQ  GETKEY
               CMP# 13h            if we find the GO key pay
               BEQ  GETKEY         no attention
               TAX
               LDAX TABLO
               STA  ADR1
               LDAX TABH1
               STA  ADR2
```

*We clear Y and then get the Yth note of the song by indirect indexed *addressing. This note we pull apart into the name of a half period *and a duration over which to play the note.

```
               LDY#  00
    NEWNOTE:   LDAIY ADR1          get the note of the song
               AND#  0F            keep lower half
               TAX
               LDAX  PERTAB        get the half period for this
                                   note
               STA   PERIOD
               LDAIY ADR1          get note again
               LSRA                logical right shift accumulator
               LSRA                four times to get duration
               LSRA                right justified
               LSRA
               STA   TIME
```

*If the note is FF that's the end of the song.

```
               LDAIY ADR1
               CMP#  FF
               BEQ   START
```

*First we start the timer going with a count of 80_h. Then we count

```
*down the half period and toggle the speaker.  We keep on doing this
*till the timer runs out.

    RUNTIME:    LDA# 80          get timer started in slowest
                STA  170F        mode
    HALFPER:    LDX  PERIOD
    LOOP:       JMP  NEXT        this is a time waster
    NEXT:       DEX
                BNE  LOOP
                INC  PORTB
                LDA  PORTB       is sign bit B7=1?
                BPL  CLKOUT      when the timer runs out

*To balance off the time taken at CLOCKOUT we will put in 3 jump to
*the next instruction and then return to HALFPER:

                JMP  N1
    N1:         JMP  N2
    N2:         JMP  N3
    N3:         JMP  HALFPER

*Finally we see if we have played this note long enough.

    CLKOUT:     DEC  TIME
                BNE  RUNTIME     if we haven't played enough
                INY              bump the pointer Y
                JMP  NEWNOTE

*There are two tables we have to have to store the address of the
*beginnings of the songs.  For the songs shown in the main text we
*have:

    TABLO:      00
                38
                80

    TABHI:      02
                02
                02

*There are four variables:

    TIME:       00               holds the length of the note
                                  in 1/8 notes
    PERIOD:     00               holds the half period or
                                  inverse frequence
    ADR1:       00               must be in page zero.  Used
    ADR2:       00                for holding the start of the
                                  song
```

Digital Clock. Chapter 8.

```
*When we load the program from tape the address register ends up
*pointing at cell zero. We will use the first 6 cells to hold hours,
*minutes, and seconds in decimal.

    TH:          00                     tens of hours
    H:           00                     hours
    TM:          00                     tens of minutes
    M:           00                     minutes
    TS:          00                     tens of seconds
    S:           00                     seconds

*Now we will set up the stop key, clear decimal mode, set the stack
*pointer and make ports C and D both be output. Store the address
*0200 (INTER) in the IRQ interrupt vector address 17FE/F so that a
*time out will take us to INTER:

    SETTIME:     CLD                    clear decimal mode
                 LDX# FF
                 TXS
                 STX  DIRC              these ports control
                 STX  DIRD              the display in KIM
                 LDA# 00
                 STA  17FA
                 LDA# 1C
                 STA  17FB
                 CLI                    enable interrupt
                 LDA# 00                set up
                 STA  17FE              interrupt
                 LDA# 02                address
                 STA  17FF

*We will call the subroutine BINARIZE to convert the raw time to
*binary and start up the timer with B7 as input:

                 LDX# 00                X says which characters to
                 JSR  BINARIZE           pick up
                 STA  HRS
                 LDX# 02
                 JSR  BINARIZE
                 STA  MIN
                 LDX# 04
                 JSR  BINARIZE
                 STA  SEC
                 LDA# 00
                 STA  DIRB
                 LDA# FF
                 STA  170E              start timer counting in 64's

*We now set up to drive the display. We begin with the left most
*display character called 08 by KIM. We look up the first thing to
*be displayed stored in 0000 (the tens of hours) and translate it
```

*to the segment code using the table in the KIM stored at 1FE7. We
*put that translation in PORTC and then delay for about 2 milli-
*seconds:

```
DISPLAY:    LDA# 08
            STA  PORTD
            LDX# 00                point to first character
MOVE:       LDYX 0000              load Y indexed by X
            LDAY 1FE7              get translation
            STA  PORTC
            LDA# 00
            STA  COUNT
DELAY:      DEC  COUNT
            BNE  DELAY
```

*Now we bump the index register X by 1 to get the next character and
*bump the number in port B by 2 so it points out the next display
*character. If we have done less than 6 characters we go back to
*MOVE. Otherwise we go to DISPLAY.

```
            INX
            INC  PORTD
            INC  PORTD
            CPX# 06
            BMI  MOVE
            JMP  DISPLAY
```

*The BINARIZE subroutine is short so we put it in here:

```
BINARIZE:   LDAX 0000              get the first character
            ASLA                   shift left 2 places
            ASLA                    so have 4N
            CLC
            ADCX 0000              add N so have SN
            ASLA                   shift left so have 10N
            CLC
            ADCX 0001              add units in
            RTS                    return
```

*The address of the following routine is stored in the IRQ vector so
*each time the timer times out we will come to this routine. We
*preserve context, restart the timer and see if we have had 61d time
*outs. That makes just about one second. If less than one second
*we return from interrupt. Otherwise we go to COUNTSEC.

```
INTER:      PHA
            TXA                    save A,X and Y on stack
            PHA
            TYA
            PHA
            LDA# FF                restart timer
            STA  170E
            DEC  TIMES
            BEQ  ONESEC            have completed one second
```

```
RESTORE:    PLA
            TAY
            PLA
            TAX
            PLA
            RTI
ONESEC:     LDA# 61d
            STA  TIMES
```

*Now we count up the number of seconds that have gone by. If less
*than 60 we go to convert seconds display.

```
COUNTSEC:   INC  SEC
            LDA  SEC
            CMP# 60d
            BPL  COUNTMINS
            JMP  CONSEC
```

*If the seconds have counted out past 59 to 60 we have to change the
*minutes so we do: first resetting the seconds to 0.

```
COUNTMINS:  LDA# 00
            STA  SEC
            INC  MIN
            LDA  MIN
            CMP# 60d
            BPL  COUNTHRS
            JMP  CONMIN
```

*After 59 minutes (60 really, counting 0) we have to change the hour
*display. After 12 o'clock we say 1 o'clock, not zero.

```
COUNTHRS:   LDA# 00
            STA  MIN
            INC  HRS
            LDA  HRS
            CMP# 13d
            BPL  RSTHRS
            JMP  CONHRS
RSTHRS:     LDA# 01
            STA  HRS
```

*This last instruction falls through to CONHRS. Now every time we
*change the hours display we have certainly got to change the minutes
*(from 59 to 0) and whenever we change minutes we have to change the
*seconds. Each time we get a value in the accumulator and jump off
*to a CVT subroutine that does the work. It returns with tens in X
*and units in A. Then we go back to the interrupted main program
*after restoring registers.

```
CONHRS:     LDA  HRS
            JSR  CVT
            STX  TH
            STA  H
```

```
CONMIN:     LDA  MIN
            JSR  CVT
            STX  TM
            STA  M
CONSEC:     LDA  SEC
            JSR  CVT
            STX  TS
            STA  S
            JMP  RESTORE
```

*The CVT routine needs to change a binary number to a two digit
*decimal number. We do it by brute force subtraction:

```
CVT:        LDX# 00
            SEC                      set carry
CVLP:       SBC# A                   subtract 10d
            BMI  TOOFAR
            INX
            JMP  CVLP
TOOFAR:     ADC# A                   add back in the last decade
            RTS
```

*Stop button. Make A0 and B0 be output and A7 be input.

```
START:     LDA# 00
           STA  17FA
           LDA# 1C
           STA  17FB
           LDA# 01
           STA  DIRA
           LDA# 01
           STA  DIRB
```

*Put an initial value in for DELTA.

```
           LDA# 01
           STA  DELTA
```

*ALFA1 is the beginning of the outermost loop of the program. The
*command signal gets changed whenever the OUTCOUNT goes to zero. We
*start with it equal to 20_h. To slow down the rate of change of the
*command signal use a larger integer.

```
ALFA1:     LDA# 20
           STA  OUTCOUNT
```

*This point of the program sets the sampling time to 127. We compute
*the current value of the error and reset the sample count N to zero.

```
ALFA2:     LDX# 127          decimal
           LDA  N
           LRS               divide N by two
           CLC
           ADC  CMND
           STA  ERROR        ERROR = N/2 + CMND
           LDA# 00
           STA  N
```

*Now we get down to the meat. This is the innermost loop of the
*program. We are going to sample the input voltage to see if it is
*bigger than or smaller than the trigger voltage. Then we will send
*out a correction signal on the A to D feedback line (A0). Finally
*we output a 1 on the meter circuit if we have counted down on X so
*far that it is less than the ERROR we wish to display. Otherwise
*we output a 0. Remember: there are two separate outputs here; A0
*is the feedback to the A to D converter and B0 is the output to
*drive the meter display.

```
ALFA3:     LDA  PORTA
           BPL  ISZERO
           LDA# 01
           STA  PORTA        set A0=1
           JMP  COMBINE
```

```
ISZERO:     LDA# 00
            STA  PORTA          set A0=0
            INC  N              bump zero's counter
COMBINE:    CPX  ERROR
            BMI  MINER          go if X < ERROR
            LDA# 00             X ≥ ERROR
            JMP  DISPLAY
MINER:      LDA# 01             X < ERROR
DISPLAY:    STA  PORTB          set display
            DEX
            BNE  ALFA3          if X ≠ 0 do inner loop again
            DEC  OUTCOUNT
            BNE  ALFA2          we haven't done the outer
                                 loop 20 times yet

*It is time to update the command signal.  We add DELTA to the
*command.  If the result is 0 or 63 we reverse the sign of delta.
*Otherwise we just go back to ALFA1

            LDA  CMND
            CLC
            ADC  DELTA          CMND   CMND + DELTA
            STA  CMND
            BEQ  MAKEPLUS       if CMND = 0
            CMP# 63
            BEQ  MAKEMIN        if CMND = 63
            JMP  ALFA1
MAKEPLUS:   LDA# 01
            STA  DELTA
            JMP  ALFA1
MAKEMIN:    LDA# FF
            STA  DELTA
            JMP  ALFA1

*We need the following variables:

N:          00                  count of the number of zeros
                                put out as feedback
ERROR:      00                  sum of response and command
OUTCOUNT:   00                  times around the outer loop
DELTA:      00                  increment for command
CMND:       00                  the signal the response is
                                supposed to equal
```

```
*Initialize the stop key and set port A to be output and B5-B0 are
*output.  B7 is input and set the stack pointer.

    START:        LDA# 00
                  STA  17FA
                  LDA# 1C
                  STA  17FB
                  LDA# FF
                  STA  DIRA
                  LDA# 3F
                  STA  DIRB
                  LDX# FF
                  TXS

*Next we place the trains on the track.

                  LDA# 0C
                  STA  BLOCK0           train 0 in B4
                  LDA# 08
                  STA  BLOCK1           train 1 in B0

*We clear the busy table:

                  LDX# 0D
    CLEAR:        STAX BUSY
                  DEX
                  BNE  CLEAR

*Neither train is stopped:

                  LDA# 00
                  STA  STOP0
                  STA  STOP1

*We initialize speed and dwell time for both trains but we don't make
*reservations in the busy table.  This will take care of itself since
*they start on opposite sides of the layout.

                  LDA# 01
                  STA  DWELL0
                  STA  DWELL1
                  LDA# 30
                  STA  SPEED0
                  STA  SPEED1

*At Enter we check to see if either train wants to advance to the
*next track block.

    ENTER:        LDX# 00
                  JSR  ADVANCE
                  LDX# 01
```

```
                JRS  ADVANCE
```

*At Alfa we delay 500 microseconds and then read B7 and generate feed-
*back via B5. We keep separate count of the times B7 is zero and is
*one because at this point I wasn't sure which one I'd need.

```
ALFA:           LDA# 55                 decimal
                STA  CTR
DLAY:           DEC  CTR
                BNE  DLAY
                LDA  PORTB              get B7
                BPL  POS
                ORA# 20                 pattern 0010 0000 - set B5
                STA  PORTB
                INC  CTONE              was a one
                JMP  JOIN
POS:            AND# 9F                 1001 1111 clear B5
                STA  PORTB
                INC  CTZERO
```

*We join together again and see if we have been round this loop 100
*times. If not we go to ALFA. If yes we reset the counter.

```
JOIN:           DEC  OUTER
                BNE  ALFA
                LDA# 100                decimal
                STA  OUTER
```

*We get the count of ones (or perhaps of zeros) and store it as speed
*of train 0. Then we clear the counts and jump back to ENTER:

```
                LDA  CTONE
                STA  SPEED0
                LDA# 00
                STA  CTONE
                STA  CTZERO
                JMP  ENTER
```

*That ends the main program. Now we will examine the subroutine
*ADVANCE. On entry X holds 0 or 1 determining which train to con-
*sider. First it calls MAP to get the "present" and "next" section
*addresses. If the dwell time is zero we go see if the train is
*stopped. Otherwise we decrement the dwell and return.

```
ADVANCE:        JRS  MAP
                LDAX DWELL
                BEQ  STOPPED
                DECX DWELL
                RTS
```

*When dwell counts out we check to see if this train is "stopped".
*If the train is stopped we check the status of the next track sec-
*tion. If it is busy we just return. Otherwise we are going to clear
*the block.

```
    STOPPED:        LDAX STOP
                    BEQ  GOAHEAD
                    LDYX NEXT
                    LDAY BUSY
                    BEQ  NOSTOP
                    RTS
```

*Nostop is where we clear the stop flag for a train. Then we release
*the present block, then make the next block become the present block
*and remap.

```
    NOSTOP:         LDA# 00
                    STAX STOP
    GOAHEAD:        LDYX PRESENT
                    LDA# 00
                    STAY BUSY                release block
                    LDYX BLOCK
                    LDAY NXTBLK
                    STAX BLOCK
                    JSR  MAP
```

*Now make this block be busy and reset the dwell time.

```
                    LDYX PRESENT
                    LDA# 01
                    STAY BUSY
                    LDAX SPEED
                    STA  DWELL
```

*Next thing is to set up the lights for ports A and B.

```
                    LDY  BLOCK0
                    LDAY ALITE
                    LDY  BLOCK1
                    ORAY ALITE
                    STA  PORTA
                    LDA  PORTB
                    AND# 20                  0010 0000 save B5
                    LDY  BLOCK0
                    ORAY BLITE
                    LDY  BLOCK1
                    ORAY BLITE
                    STA  PORTB
```

*We check the next block after this one and if it is busy we stop our
*train and return. If it is free we reserve it by making it busy and
*then return:

```
                    LDYX NEXT
                    LDAY BUSY
                    BEQ  RESERVE
                    LDA# 01
                    STAX STOP
                    RTS
```

```
RESERVE:     LDYX NEXT
             LDA# 01
             STAY BUSY
             RTS

*The subroutine MAP gets the name of the present section number to
*PRESENT and of the next section number to NEXT.  X still tells which
*train:

MAP:         LDYX BLOCK
             LDAY SECTNO
             STAX PRESENT
             LDAY NEXTBLOCK
             TAY
             LDAY SECTNO
             STAX NEXT
             RTS

*We need four fixed tables,
* NEXTBLOCK tells the name of the next block around the track.
* SECTIONNO translates a block number to a track section.
* ALITE     has the lights to light in PORTA.
* BLITE     tells the same for PORTB.
*To save paper we will list all four in parallel.

NEXTBLOCK: 03   SECTIONNO: 0   ALITE: 01   BLITE: 00
           08              1          02          00
           09              2          04          00
           0A              3          08          00
           00              4          10          00
           0C              5          20          00
           0B              6          40          00
           02              7          80          00
           07              8          00          01
           0D              9          00          02
           01              A          00          04
           05              B          00          08
           04              C          00          10
           06              3          08          00

*Variables are as follows:

BLOCK0:     00          which block is the train now in?
BLOCK1:     00
SPEED0:     00          how fast is the train going?
SPEED1:     00
DWELL0:     00          how long before we are ready to
DWELL1:     00           advance?
STOP0:      00          is the train stopped (=1) or free (=0)
STOP1:      00
PRESENT0:   00          present section number
PRESENT1:   00
NEXT0:      00          next section number
NEXT1:      00
```

```
CTR:        00          inner loop for delay
OUTER:      00          how many samples remaining
CTONE:      00          how many ones were found
CTZERO:     00          how many zeros were found
BUSY: )     00          13 cells one for each section.
      }                 0 means free, 1 means busy
      )
+D:   )     00
```

Substitution Cypher. Chapter 11.

*This program does the simplest of the coding schemes, namely a sub-
*stitution cypher. We begin by clearing out the cypher alphabet
*(after setting up the stop key of course).

```
START:    LDA# 00
          STA  17FA
          LDA# 1C
          STA  17FB
          LDA# 00
          LDY# 26          decimal
LO:       STAY CYPHER
          DEY
          BPL  LO
```

*Now we are going to accept the key phrase and add each (new, valid)
*letter to the cypher alphabet as it is received.

```
GETKEY:   JSR  GETCH
          STA  CHAR
          CMP# CR          carriage return is the end of the key
          BEQ  REST
          CMP# 41          "A"
          BMI  GETKEY      it was less than A
          CMP  5B          "Z" + 1
          BPL  GETKEY      it was past Z
          JSR  ADDALET
          JMP  GETKEY
```

*Next we take the remaining letters of the alphabet and put them in
*order.

```
REST:     LDA# 00
          STA  PTR
MORELET:  LDY  PTR
          LDAY ALFA
          STA  CHAR
          JSR  ADDALET
          INC  PTR
          LDA  PTR
          CMP# 27          decimal
          BMI  MORELET
```

*Next we ask if the user wants to do encoding or decoding.

```
WHICH:    LDX# 04
THIS:     LDAX EORD        address of the letters
          JSR  OUTCH       "E/D Car. Ret. Linefeed"
          DEX
          BPL  THIS
```

*We get a character and if it is not an E we assume "decode". For

```
*encoding we make the alphabet be the source and the cypher be the
*destination.  For decoding it is the reverse.

             JSR   GETCH
             CMP#  "E"             which is 45 in zero parity ASCII
             BNE   DECODE
             LDA#  ALFA            the address (8 bits in page 0)
                                    of ALFA
             STA   SOURCE
             LDA#  CYPHER          the 8 bit address of cypher
             STA   DEST
             JMP   LOAD
    DECODE:  LDA#  CYPHER          an address
             STA   SOURCE
             LDA#  ALFA            and address
             STA   DEST

*We are going to accept letters A-Z until we get a "$".  Then we will
*print out the translation we have been building up in the buffer.
*We are going to find which letter to use by searching the source
*alphabet until we find the letter and then look it up in the destin-
*ation alphabet.

    LOAD     LDX#  01              X is the index of characters
                                    received
    NEXT:    JSR   GETCH
             CMP   "$"             which is 24
             BEQ   ENDIN
             CMP#  "A"
             BMI   NEXT
             CMP#  "Z + 1"
             BPL   NEXT
             LDY#  26
    FIND:    DEY                   search for
             CMPIY SOURCE           the
             BNE   FIND             letter
             LDAIY DEST            get translation
             STAX  BUFFER          store it in buffer
             INX
             BNE   NEXT            if count round 255 fall thru

*We got a $ or 255 characters so we are ready to type out.  We type
*out in 5 blocks of 5 characters per line until the buffer is empty.

    ENDIN:   LDA#  00
             STAX  BUFFER          end of text is a "00"
             LDX#  01
    NEWLINE: LDA#  05              start a new line
             STA   BLOCKCT
    NEWBLK:  LDA#  05              new block
             STA   CHARCT
    OUTONE:  LDAX  BUFFER          get a character
             BEQ   WHICH           have finished bufferful
             INX
```

```
        JSR  OUTCH
        DEC  CHARCT
        BNE  OUTONE
        LDA# Space              20 in ASCII
        JSR  OUTCH              space between blocks
        DEC  BLOCKCT
        BNE  NEWBLK
        LDA# Carriage return    0D in hex
        JSR  OUTCH
        LDA# linefeed           0A in hex
        JSR  OUTCH
        LDA# rubout             7F in hex
        JSR  OUTCH
        JMP  NEWLINE

*Constants in page zero:

  EORD:   3F                    ?
          44                    D
          2F                    /   printout last first
          45                    E
          0A                    linefeed
  ALPHA:  41,42,43,...,5A       26 cells

*Variables:

  CYPHER:                       save 26 cells in page 0
  CHAR:   00                    the current character
  PTR:    00                    which letter we are about
                                 to move
  BLOCKCT:                      how many blocks left this
                                 line
  CHARCT:                       how many characters left
                                 this block
```

Code for Elevator Control Program. Chapter 12.

*For starters we need to set the stop key, the stack pointer, make
*port B be output and set the car to be idle with an open door on
*floor 0. Also we clear all requests.

```
            LDA# 00
            STA  17FA
            LDA# 1C
            STA  17FB
            LDX# FF
            TXS                     set stack pointer
            STX  DIRB
            LDA# FO                 set Port A to be 4 output
            STA  DIRA               and 4 input bits
            LDX# 00                 set floor to "floor 0"
            LDA# 01
            STA  PORTB
            LDA# 00
            STA  UP
            STA  DOWN
            STA  KAR
```

*Here is the main idle routine where the elevator waits for business.
*Using the SCAN subroutine (which examines the up, down, and car re-
*quests) we see if there are any up-requests or down-requests.

```
   IDLE:    JSR  SCAN
            LDA  UPREQ
            BNE  MOVUP
            LDA  DWNREQ
            BNE  MOVDWN
```

*Now delay .1 sec and do input from the keys. Then go back to IDLE:

```
            LDY# OA
            JSR  DELAY
            JMP  IDLE
```

*MOVUP and MOVDWN are two entry points to the same routine. They set
*a flag in UPDWN to <u>zero</u> for up and <u>one</u> for down. This flag is usu-
*ally kept in Y but sometimes we have to refresh it from UPDWN. When
*we get to MOV we have a request to go somewhere. Assume we are
*going up. We clear upward corridor requests for the current floor
*and on-board (KAR) requests for this floor:

```
    MOV UP:  LDY# 00
             JMP  P1
    MOV DWN: LDY# 01
    P1     : STY  UPDWN
    MOV    : LDY  UPDWN             UPO means Up.  UP1 means
             LDAX CLEARI            down.
             ANDY UP
             STAY UP
             LDAX CLEAR I
             AND  KAR
             STA  KAR
```

*Close the door, set the direction light and turn off the "door open'
*light:

```
LDA#   00
STA    DOOR
LDA    PORTB
AND#   OF
ORAY   GROUP                   Group0=uplight, group1=
                                downlight
STA    PORTB
```

*Wait for 3 seconds, then turn off the current floor light, change
*floors by + or - one. Then turn on new floor light and again wait
*3 seconds.

```
LDY#   20
JSR    DELAY
LDY    UPDWN
LDA    PORB
ANDX   CLEARI                  has 0 this floor, one
                                elsewhere
STA    PORTB
TXA
CLC
ADCY   UNIT                    UNIT(0)=+1  UNIT(1)= -1
TAX
LDA    PORTB
ORAX   YESI                    1 this floor, 0 elsewhere
STA    PORTB
LDY#   20
JSR    DELAY
```

*We are moving up about to pass floor i. We look to see if any up
*requests from the corridor or any on-board requests for floor i. If
*so we will stop. Otherwise we will sail right on past if there are
*any requests above us.

```
LDY    UPDWN
LDAY   UP
ORA    KAR                     combine requests
ANDX   YESI                    clear all except this floor
BNE    STOP                    stop if any calls
JSR    SCAN                    see if higher floors have
                                requests
LDAY   UPREQ                   get upreq or downreq
BNE    MOV                     no calls here but a higher
                                calling
```

*Either by request or because no higher calling was found (that
*shouldn't happen, of course), we come to STOP which marks the door
*open, does a delay, then a scan and finally tests to see if any more
*requests in the current direction. If not we turn off the direction
*light and go back to idle.

```
STOP:       LDA#  80
            STA   DOOR
            LDY#  20
            JSR   DELAY
            JSR   SCAN
            LDY   UPDWN
            LDAY  UPREQ
            BNE   MOV               have more requests
            LDA   PORTB
            AND#  OF                turn off direction lights
            STA   PORTB
            JMP   IDLE              go back to idle
```

*Here follows the three subroutines we need to make this program
*work. DELAY is a double loop timer including some calls to GET to
*find out which keys are pushed:

```
DELAY:      STY   COUNT
LOOP:       LDA#  00                set up inner loop
            STA   INNER
ROUND:      LDY# 00
            JSR   GET               up buttons
            INY
            JSR   GET               down buttons
            INY
            JSR   GET               on-board buttons
            DEC   INNER
            BNE   ROUND             -inner loop-
            DEC   COUNT
            BNE   LOOP              -outer loop-
            RTS
```

*GET looks at the buttons to see who, if anybody, is calling. We
*enter with Y containing 0, 1, or 2 meaning UP, DOWN, and ONBOARD.
*We get BANK which contains a one to select the proper bank of but-
*tons and then sample the lower four bits and put it in UP, DOWN, or
*KAR:

```
GET:        LDAY  BANK
            ORA   DOOR
            STA   PORTA
            LDA   PORTA
            ORAY  UP
            STAY  UP
            RTS
BANK:       20
            40
            10
```

*Scan is the third subroutine. What it does is combine KAR requests
*with uprequests and then select only those at a higher floor than
*we are currently at. Then it does the same for down requests:

```
SCAN:       PHA
            LDA   UP
            ORA   DOWN
            ORA   KAR
            ANDX  UPMASK
            STA   UPREQ
            LDA   UP
            ORA   DOWN
            ORA   KAR
            ANDX  DWNMASK
            STA   DWNREQ
            PLA
            RTS

UPMASK:     0E
            0C
            08
            00
DWMASK:     00
            01
            03
            07
```

*Other constants not associated with subroutines are:

```
CLEARI:     0E                    0000 1110
            0C                    0000 1101
            0B                    0000 1011
            07                    0000 0111

YESI:       01
            02
            04
            08

GOUP:       20
GODWN:      10
UNIT:       01
            FF
```

*Variables are:

```
UP:         00                    record of unanswered button
DOWN:       00                     pushes
KAR:        00
UPDWD:      00                    tell the system which way
                                   the car is moving
UPREQ:      00                    is non-zero if somebody
                                   upstairs wants me or I want
                                   to go up
DWNREQ:     00                    same the other way
INNER:      00                    counts for
COUNT:      00                            the delay
DOOR:       00                    is the door open or closed?
```

Code for Dream Machine. Chapter 13.

*We begin with the stop key and then set up A0 and A1 as input bits.

```
START:      LDA#  00
            STA   17FA
            LDA#  1C
            STA   17FB
            LDA#  FC
            STA   DIRA
            LDA#  00
            STA   PORTA
```

*We drop right into the RNI (read next instruction) sequence which
*is going to reset the stack pointer so it doesn't creep down in
*page 1 by any chance. Then we will look at port A to see if A0 is
*one or zero. If it is 0 that means run full speed so we branch to
*RUN. If it is 1 that means at best a single step. We check A1.
*If it is also 1 we go back to the beginning of RNI. If it is zero
*we wait 2 milliseconds for bounce to wear off and then wait for a
*one so we know the switch has been pushed and released. BIT is a
*logical AND of memory with the accumulator. It sets the condition
*flags but does not change the accumulator.

```
RNI:        LDX#  FF
            TXS
            LDA   PORTA
            BITZ  KONE          (KONE) = 01
            BEQ   RUN
            BITZ  KTWO          (KTWO) = 02
            BNE   RNI
DELAY:      DEX
            BNE   DELAY
LOOP:       LDA   PORTA
            BITZ  KTWO
            BEQ   LOOP
```

*Next we get the program counter (and increment it by one) and then
*load the instruction register (OPCODE - ADDR) from memory. Then we
*begin to decode the mode. Bit 1 says indirect addressing if equal
*to one. The contents of the cell pointed at by what's in ADDR goes
*into ADDR as the new address. Then we do indexing. If Bit 0 is a
*one, the contents of register B are added to the contents of ADDR.

```
RUN:        LDXZ  PC
            INCZ  PC
            LDAX  LOBYT         (page 3)
            STAZ  ADDR
            LDAX  HYBIT         (page 2)
            STAZ  OPCODE
            BITZ  KTWO          (KTWO) = 02
            BEQ   DIRECT
            LDYZ  ADDR
```

```
            LDAY  LOBYT
            STAZ  ADDR
DIRECT:     LDAZ  OPCODE
            BITZ  KONE          (KONE) = 01
            BEQ   NOIND
            LDAZ  ADDR
            CLC
            ADCZ  BREG
            STAZ  ADDR
NOIND:      LDXZ  ADDR
```

We get the opcode back and compute 3 op-code. We use this number
*as the offset in a branch instruction to do an indexed jump into
*the table of addresses - one for each op code. We enter each op-
*code section with a zero in the accumulator and the effective
*address in the X register.

```
            LDAZ  OPCODE
            AND#  3C            save the instruction 00111100
            CLC
            LSR
            STAZ  OPCODE
            LSR
            ADCZ  OPCODE
            STAZ  VAR+1
            LDA#  00
VAR:        BEQ   [    ]        VAR+1 is the address of the
                                 second byte
            JMP   INPUT
            JMP   STOREA
            JMP   STOREB
            JMP   JUMPMINA
            JMP   JUMPZEROA
            JMP   JUMPZEROB
            JMP   JUMP
            JMP   JUMPSUBR
            JMP   OUTPUT
            JMP   LOADA
            JMP   LOADB
            JMP   ADD
            JMP   SUBTRACT
            JMP   AND
            JMP   ORA
            JMP   EOR
```

*The input instruction uses the KIM subroutine GETCH and stores the
*character in the low order byte of the effective address. High
*order byte is cleared to zero:

```
INPUT:      STAX  HYBYT
            JSR   GETCH
            STAX  LOBYT
            JMP   RNI
```

*Store A and B are quite similar except that the second one puts
*zeros in the higher order byte of the effective address:

```
STOREA:     LDAX   ACCUP
            STAX   HYBYT
            LDAZ   ACCLO
            STAX   LOBYT
            JMP    RNI
STOREB:     STAX   HYBYT
            LDAZ   BREG
            STAX   LOBYT
            JMP    RNI
```

*Jump on minus A just tests the sign bit:

```
JUMPMINA:   LDAX   ACCUP
            BPL    E3
            STXZ   PC
E3:         JMP    RNI
```

*Jump on zero A has to test both halves but B has only one half.

```
JUMPZEROA:  LDAZ   ACCUP
            BNE    E4
            LDA    ACCLO
            BNE    E4
            STXZ   PC
E4:         JMP    RNI
JUMPZEROB:  LDAZ   BREG
            BNE    E5
            STXZ   PC
E5:         JMP    RNI
```

*Plain unconditional jump could be tucked in as a new name for the
*last two instructions of any one of the jump instruction but it is
*clearer if we have it separate:

```
JUMP:       STXZ   PC
            JMP    RNI
```

*Subroutine jump saves the PC at the effective address (Y) and then
*transfers control to location Y + 1.

```
JUMPSUB:    LDAZ   PC
            STAX   LOBYT
            INX
            STXZ   PC
            JMP    RNI
```

*Output uses the OUTCH subroutine of KIM:

```
OUTPUT:     LDAX   LOBYT
            JSR    OUTCH
            JMP    RNI
```

*Load A and B are straightforward:

```
    LOADA:      LDAX    HYBYT
                STAZ    ACCUP
                LDAX    LOBYT
                STAZ    ACCLO
                JMP     RNI
    LOADB:      LDAX    LOBYT
                STAZ    BREG
                JMP     RNI
```

*If you haven't done a double precision add or subtract this is your
*chance to see one in action. We add the two lower halves and then
*add the carry from that sum to the two upper halves. Subtract is
*just the same except we do a borrow instead of a carry:

```
    AD:         CLC
                LDAX    LOBYT
                ADCZ    ACCLO
                STAZ    ACCLO
                LDAX    HYBYT
                ADC     ACCUP         note we do not clear carry
                STA     ACCUP
                JMP     RNI

    SUBTRACT:   SEC
                LDAZ    ACCLO
                SBCX    LOBYT
                STAZ    ACCLO
                LDAZ    ACCUP
                SBCX    HYBYT         we do not set carry
                STAZ    ACCUP
                JMP     RNI
```

*The three logical instructions are identical except for the substi-
*tution of a different machine code in two crucial places. In order
*to save God knows how many trees, indeed perhaps whole forests, we
*will include the AND and merely indicate the changes for ORA and
*exclusive or.

```
    AND:        LDAX    LOBYT
                ANDZ    ACCLO         (ORA)  (EOR)
                STAZ    ACCLO
                LDAX    HYBYT
                ANDZ    ACCUP         (ORA)  (EOR)
                STAZ    ACCUP
                JMP     RNI
```

*For constants we have only two:

```
    KONE:       01
    KTWO:       02
```

*For variables we have:

ACCLO:	the two halves of the accumulator
ACCUP:	
BREG:	the index register B
OPCODE:	the two halves of the instruction register
ADDR:	
PC:	the program counter

OPCODE:	the two halves of the instruction register
ADDR:	

Code for Assembler. Chapter 14.

```
*This is the code for the assembler. I want to emphasize once again
*that this is a lousy assembler. There are no limits checks or type
*checks; there are almost no diagnostics; input format is very rigid
*in the sense that if n characters are permitted in a given field
*then exactly n are required. Obviously to make this an easy assem-
*bler for a human to use we would probably start over from scratch.
*But we would have very little expectation of fitting into 512 bytes.
*
*We begin with usual setting up of the stop key. We issue a carriage
*return and a line feed. Then we discard blanks, carriage returns,
*line feeds, and deletes (rubouts):

    START:      LDA#    00
                STA     17FA
                LDA#    1C
                STA     17FB
    RESET:      LDX#    FF          set stack pointer to FF
                TXS
                LDX#    00
    READY:      STXZ    T1          save x because CRLF doesn't
                JSR     CRLF        1E2F prints carriage return
    BEGIN:      LDXZ    T1
                JSR     GETCH       get a character
                CMP#    20h            space

                BEQ     BEGIN
                CMP#    0Dh         carriage return

                BEQ     BEGIN
                CMP#    0Ah         line feed

                BEQ     BEGIN
                CMP#    7Fh         rub-out

                BEQ     BEGIN

*Anything else we will accept. If it was an asterisk that means
*that we should set the address pointer. If not an asterisk we will
*save that first character in T1, get another and save it in T2 and
*then get a third character.

                CMP#    2Ah         star

                BEQ     STAR
                STAZ    T1          it wasn't * so we get
                JSR     GETCH        two more characters
                STAZ    T2           because the next decision
                JSR     GETCH        is on character # three

*Now we do a four way branch depending on what the 3rd character is.
```

```
                CMP#   20h          blank "   "
                BEQ    BLANK
                CMP#   3Ah          colon":"
                BEQ    COLON
                CMP#   44h          letter "D"
                BEQ    LETRD
                CMP#   3Dh          "=" equals
                BEQ    EQUALS
                LDY#   31           message saying error "E1" -
                                     unknown type.
                JMP    MES          output message
                                    then look for a new line
```

```
*The first portion to examine is what to do when you see stars.  What
*you do is read in exactly two characters and assume that they are
*either digits or letters and store them as 4 bit patterns in X.  If
*you type 1 then 2,X will hold 0001 0010.  Most of this work is done
*in a subroutine called GETBYT.

    STAR:       JSR    GETBYT       (1F9D)
                TAX
                JMP    READY

*A full colon means it was a label for an instruction.  We use the
*subroutine LABEL to make an entry in the symbol table:

    COLON:      JSR    LABEL
                JMP    BEGIN        do not give new line.

*An equal sign means that we are defining a hex constant.  First
*enter the label in the symbol table and then get four characters
*for the memory cell:

    EQUALS:     JSR    LABEL
                JSR    GETBYT
                STAX   HYBYT
                JSR    GETBYT
                STAX   LOBYT
                INX
                JMP    READY

*A letter D implies that the user typed END.  Save the address point-
*er and check to see if any unresolved forward references are left:

    LETRD:      STXZ   T1
                LDXZ   SIZE
    L1:         LDAX   STABZ        2nd letter is minus if
                BMI    GOTONE        unresolved
```

```
MORE:           DEX
                BNE     L1
                LDXZ    T1
                JMP     READ

GOTONE:         LDAX    STAB
                JSR     OUTCH        print 1st character
                LDAX    STABZ
                JSR     OUTCH        and second character
                LDA     25h          % symbol

                JSR     OUTCH          print it
                JMP     MORE

*When we find a blank or space as the "third" character we have to
*see if the two proceding ones make up an opcode.  Because of the way
*the op-code mnemonics were chosen the sum of the two letters is
*unique.  Further we arrange them so that the index within the table
*of an op-code corresponds to the translation of that op-code:

BLANK:          LDY#    OFh

                LDAZ    T1
                CLC
                ADCZ    T2
LX:             CMPY    OPCODTAB
                BEQ     FNDOP
                DEY
                BPL     LX
                LDA#    32           E2 - unknown op-code
                JMP     MES
FNDOP:          TYA
                ASL                  shift left two places
                ASL
                STAX    HYBYT
MORE:           JSR     GETCH        get modifier
                CMP#    20
                BEQ     MORE
                AND#    03           save two low bits
                ORAX    HYBYT
                STAX    HYBYT
L2:             JSR     GETCH        get 1st character
                CMP#    20             of the
                BEQ     L2             address
                STAZ    T1
                JSR     GETCH
                ORA#    80           set sign = minus
                STAZ    T2
                JSR     SEEK
                BEQ     ADDED        was added to symbol table
                BMI     PUTON        forward reference
                LDAY    STAB3        set address field
                STAX    LOBYT        to what symbol table has
```

```
ADDED:      INX
            JMP    READY
PUTON:      LDAY   STAB3          put on the chain of forward
                                   references get S.T. value
            STAX   LOBYT          store in address field
            TXA                   address pointer stores in
            STAY   STAB 3          the symbol table as value
            INX
            JMP    READY
```

*The message routine is very simple and only prints out "EM" where
*M is passed in the accumulator:

```
MES:        STAZ   T1
            LDA#   45             letter E
            JSR    OUTCH
            LDAZ   T1
            JSR    OUTCH
            JMP    RESET          reset stack pointer to FF
```

*The "label" subroutine is entered when we have the definition of a
*symbol to take care of. It uses the SEEK subroutine to see if the
*symbol has already been mentioned. If not the symbol is entered in
*the symbol table and we return. If the symbol has been mentioned
*and is already defined we issue an "E3" to indicate "doubly defined".
*If mentioned as an as yet undefined forward reference we have to un-
*chain the forward reference list. This routine will <u>not</u> unchain a
*chain which ends in cell 0.

```
LABEL:      JSR    SEEK
            BEQ    ENTERED
            BMI    UNCHAIN
            LDY#   33h
            JMP    MES            issue "E3"
ENTERED:    RTS
UNCHAIN:    LDAY   STAB 2         clear off the minus
            AND#   7F             sign from the second
            STAY   STAB2           letter of the symbol
            LDAY   STAB3          store link
            STAZ   T1              in T1
            TXA
            STAY   STAB3          put (x) in value in symbol table
            LDYZ   T1             get link
LP:         LDAY   LOBYT          get next link
            STAZ   T1              to T1
            TXA
            STAY   LOBYT          put (x) in address field
            LDYZ   T1             get new link
            BNE    LP
            RTS
```

*The "seek" subroutine looks up the symbol in T1 -T2 in the symbol
*table. If it is not there at all we bump SIZE by one and enter it.

```
*If T2 is plus this is a "definition".  If T2 is minus this is a
*"use".  (the subroutine doesn't care).
*We return with (A) = 0 if it was entered, positive > 0 if the sym-
*bol had been previously defined and minus if undefined:

    SEEK:       LDYZ   SIZE
    SL1:        LDAZ   T1
                CMPY   STAB
                BEQ    HALF            if first letter matches, check
                                        other
    S2:         DEY
                BPL    SL1             go back to look some more
                INCZ   SIZE
                LDYZ   SIZE
                CPY#   10              symbol table bigger than 15?
                BPL    TOOBIG
                LDAZ   T1              enter symbol
                STAY   STAB
                LDAZ   T2
                STAY   STAB2
                TXA
                STAY   STAB3
                LDA#   00              set address field to 0
                STAX   LOBYT

    HALF:       LDAZ   T2
                EORY   STAB2           compare if equal gives 0
                AND#   7F              throw away sign bit
                BNE    S2
                LDAY   STAB2           has right sign + or -
                RTS

    TOOBIG:     LDY#   34              give "E4"
                JMP    MES

*The op-code table is stored in memory as a 16 word vector:

     OPCODTAB:   97        -IN         input
           +1    94        -SA         store accumulator
           +2    95        -SB         store index register
           +3    8F        -NA         jump on negative accum.
           +4    9B        -ZA         jump on zero accum.
           +5    9C        -ZB         jump on zero index
           +6    9A        -JP         jump
           +7    9D        -JS         jump subroutine
           +8    A3        -OT         output
           +9    8D        -LA         load accumulator
           +A    8E        -LB         load index
           +B    85        -AD         add to accumulator
           +C    A8        -SU         subtract from accumulator
           +D    92        -ND         logical and with accumulator
           +E    A1        -OR         inclusive or
           +F    AA        -XR         exclusive or
```

*The symbol table has three bytes per cell. There are 16 cells but
*it turns out that cell zero can't be used. The two letters of the
*symbol go in STAB and STAB1 and the value goes into STAB3.

*Three constants are used:

```
SIZE:        0            number of symbols
T1  :                     temporary storage
T2  :                     temporary storage

HYBYT = 0200

LOBYT = 0300
```

INDEX

Powers of two
$2^0 = 1$
$2^1 = 2$
$2^2 = 4$
$2^3 = 8$
$2^4 = 16$
$2^5 = 32$
$2^6 = 64$
$2^7 = 128$
$2^8 = 256$
$2^9 = 512$
$2^{10} = 1,024$
$2^{11} = 2,048$
$2^{12} = 4,096$
$2^{13} = 8,192$
$2^{14} = 16,384$
$2^{15} = 32,768$
$2^{16} = 65,536$
$2^{17} = 131,072$
$2^{18} = 262,144$
$2^{19} = 524,288$
$2^{20} = 1,048,586$
$2^{21} = 2,097,152$
$2^{22} = 4,194,304$
$2^{23} = 8,388,608$
$2^{24} = 16,777,216$

Decimal	Binary	Hex	Display
0	0000	0	0
1	0001	1	1
2	0010	2	2
3	0011	3	3
4	0100	4	4
5	0101	5	5
6	0110	6	6
7	0111	7	7
8	1000	8	8
9	1001	9	9
10	1010	A	A
11	1011	B	b
12	1100	C	C
13	1101	D	d
14	1110	E	E
15	1111	F	F

Decimal to Hexadecimal Conversion

Second Hex Digit

	0	1	2	3	4	5	6	7	8	9	A	B	C	D	E	F	
0	0	1	2	3	4	5	6	7	8	9	10	11	12	13	14	15	0
1	16	17	18	19	20	21	22	23	24	25	26	27	28	29	30	31	1
2	32	33	34	35	36	37	38	39	40	41	42	43	44	45	46	47	2
3	48	49	50	51	52	53	54	55	56	57	58	59	60	61	62	63	3
4	64	65	66	67	68	69	70	71	72	73	74	75	76	77	78	79	4
5	80	81	82	83	84	85	86	87	88	89	90	91	92	93	94	95	5
6	96	97	98	99	100	101	102	103	104	105	106	107	108	109	110	111	6
7	112	113	114	115	116	117	118	119	120	121	122	123	124	125	126	127	7
8	128	129	130	131	132	133	134	135	136	137	138	139	140	141	142	143	8
9	144	145	146	147	148	149	150	151	152	153	154	155	156	157	158	159	9
A	160	161	162	163	164	165	166	167	168	169	170	171	172	173	174	175	A
B	176	177	178	179	180	181	182	183	184	185	186	187	188	189	190	191	B
C	192	193	194	195	196	197	198	199	200	201	202	203	204	205	206	207	C
D	208	209	210	211	212	213	214	215	216	217	218	219	220	221	222	223	D
E	224	225	226	227	228	229	230	231	232	233	234	235	236	237	238	239	D
F	240	241	242	243	244	245	246	247	248	249	250	251	252	253	254	255	F

Some ASCll Character Codes (7 bits)
The eighth, or parity bit, is assumed to be zero

C7-Bell	OA-line feed	OD-carriage return	7 F delete or rubout
20 - blank space	30-0	40-@	50-P
21 - !	31-1	41-A	51-Q
22 - "	32-2	42-B	52-R
23 - #	33-3	43-C	53-S
24 - $	43-4	44-D	54-T
25 - %	35-5	45-D	55-U
26 - &	36-6	46-F	56-V
27 - '	37-7	47-G	57-W
28 - (	38-8	48 H	58-X
29 -)	39-9	49-I	59-Y
2A - *	3A-:	4A-J	5A-Z
2B - +	3B-;	4B-K	5B-[
2C - ,	3C- <	4C-L	5C- \
2D - -	3D-=	4D-M	5D-]
2E - .	3E- >	4E-N	5E- ↑
2F - /	3F-?	4F-O	5F- ←

Lower-case letters may be obtained, on those devices provided with both, by adding 20_h to the upper-case representation.